WHAT PEOPLE ARE SAYING ABOUT

FROM STRESS TO PEACE

Jones is a compassionate and skillful doctor of the heart, showing us how forgiveness of oneself and others births authentic inner peace. This wise and practical book has the power to radically change lives.

Michael Bernard Beckwith, author of *Life Visioning*

The outer layers of people's lives often mask what is going on inside. No matter how deep the inner pain, many individuals go to great lengths to put on the happy face as they go out in the world. *From Stress to Peace* takes us on a journey through one woman's courage to take off the mask and reveal her true self. Jones so generously shares her process of overcoming depression and anxiety, and is open about the struggles she faced along the way to finding peace. I believe many lives will be touched by this book!

Terrie M. Williams, author of *Black Pain: It Just Looks Like We're Not Hurting*

With her excellent book, *From Stress to Peace*, Kandace Jones gives all seekers of the truth a way to practice a kind of forgiveness that will enable them to release the anxiety of the world we seem to live in, and progress to the sanctuary of a tranquil mind. And as *A Course in Miracles* says, 'A tranquil mind is not a little gift.' I highly recommend this book to anyone who is ready to move into the realm of inner peace.

Gary Renard, the best selling author of *The Disappearance of the Universe trilogy*

We are all on a deeply intimate an
darkness to Light. Kandace shares he

and honesty that is both powerful and refreshing. While *From Stress to Peace*, chronicles her unique pathway of awakening as Christ Consciousness it contains within it the universal map that we all walk. Her mastery of the willingness to learn and apply authentic forgiveness is inspiring. Kandace opens her heart and mind to Love in a way that invites us to do the same within ourself.

John Mark Stroud, OneWhoWakes.org

From Stress to Peace is a brilliant and candid book that relates to the wisdom of *A Course in Miracles*, the *Bible* and other valuable wisdom teachings. Kandace has mapped out her own path of Self-discovery, one that will help to illuminate the Light of God within us all.

Nouk Sanchez, author of *The End of Death*,
www.EndOfDeath.com

From Stress to Peace

An Intimate Journal on the Journey from
Living in Darkness to Living in the Light

From Stress to Peace

An Intimate Journal on the Journey from
Living in Darkness to Living in the Light

Kandace Jones

BOOKS

Winchester, UK
Washington, USA

JOHN HUNT PUBLISHING

First published by O-Books, 2014
O-Books is an imprint of John Hunt Publishing Ltd., 3 East St., Alresford,
Hampshire SO24 9EE, UK
office@jhpbooks.com
www.johnhuntpublishing.com

For distributor details and how to order please visit the 'Ordering' section on our website.

Text copyright: Kandace Jones 2013
coach@kandacejones.com
www.kandacejones.com
www.facebook.com/livinginthelight

ISBN: 978 1 78279 604 6
978 1 78279 603 9 (ebook)

A CIP catalogue record for this book is available from the British Library.

A Course in Miracles® is a registered service mark and trademark of the Foundation for
A Course in Miracles.
Unless otherwise indicated, Bible quotations are taken from the New International Version (NIV)
Aspire: Women of Color Study Bible, Copyright © 2006 by Zondervan.

Note: The information contained in this publication is not intended to substitute for seeking the
advice of health care professionals.

Design: Lee Nash

UK: Printed and bound by CPI Group (UK) Ltd, Croydon, CR0 4YY
US: Printed and bound by Thomson-Shore, 7300 West Joy Road, Dexter, MI 48130

We operate a distinctive and ethical publishing philosophy in all
areas of our business, from our global network of authors to
production and worldwide distribution.

CONTENTS

For all who seek to find peace within.

When you get, give. When you learn, teach.
~Maya Angelou

Part I

From Darkness to Light

Chapter 1

Living in Darkness

I was like a child playing hide-and-go-seek: crouched on the floor by the bed, knees tucked into my chest and tears streaming down my face. There was one exception: I didn't ever want to be found. "Please don't let them see me like this," I pleaded internally. My efforts to avoid making that hyperventilating sound while the tears flowed were futile. My husband and our two boys, 11 months and two at the time, were in the next room. I was caught completely off guard when my husband, Kevin, peered around the bed to see me on the floor closest to the wall. My heart raced as I squinted up at him with my puffy eyes and drenched face.

"Honey, are you okay?"

"No, not at all."

"What's wrong?"

"I have no idea, Kev. I just can't stop crying."

I pulled myself together enough to go outside to the car because I didn't want the boys to see me like this. "How did I get here?" I wondered as I walked out to the car. I called one of my dearest friends – with whom I shared most of my deepest secrets – and the waterworks began again. She waited patiently as I blew my nose and took deep breaths to compose myself.

"Melissa, I'm breaking down. I don't know what's wrong, but I feel completely helpless."

"Did something happen since we last spoke, Kan?" she asked. "You don't sound like yourself."

Melissa was a friend that could typically cut through all of my words and get right to the heart of what was *really* going on. This time, my words even left her stumped. She hadn't heard me like this before. I really didn't know what to say. I hadn't processed my emotions; I just called her out of habit. I knew she would listen without judgment. In her typical loving manner, she prayed with me and let me go back to sitting with myself.

"I'll be praying for you," she said. "Let me know if there's anything I can do, and feel free to call me anytime."

"Thanks, Mel. Love you!"

I put my head down on the steering wheel and broke down again. I don't know how long I was out in the car. For once, I wasn't rushing. As I sat there, I had flashbacks to various low points throughout my life. I couldn't think of one that was worse than what I was feeling in that moment; and I had been through some *stuff*.

It was January 2012. Kevin, the boys, and I had been living with my cousin for two months. We had a contract on a new home, but the place we were renting was put up for sale, leaving us without a place to live. My cousin graciously opened up his home to our family. It was such a blessing. He made dinner for us every night, and made us feel completely welcomed and loved during our time there. Even still, it was a challenge for me to be there. Internally, I was experiencing a severe emotional low, and I didn't want my extended family to know that there was anything wrong with me. I put on a happy face while at home, and avoided serious personal conversations with my husband for fear we would be overheard.

Three months earlier, just before moving in with my cousin, I came down with a severe case of pneumonia. The night before I went to the hospital, I had extreme chest pain. The morning I was admitted, I woke up with flu-like symptoms. My temperature was 104 degrees, I was sweating profusely, and the pain in my chest was unbearable. I didn't get sick very often and, when I did, my tendency was to push through it without a doctor's visit. This time was different. I spent four days in the hospital, as the doctors worked to stabilize my blood pressure. They said they hadn't seen a case this bad in someone my age, and were baffled by it. I was antsy, and could not wait to get out of there. I had just started a new job two weeks prior. I was responsible for directing a team of approximately 150 people who operated after-school programs in 102 schools. I felt an obligation to make a good first impression. I pushed myself to work from my hospital bed but my boss and team conspired against my actions, forcing me to rest. Thank God for them.

Now, here I was, three months later, head faced down on the steering wheel, and having yet another health crisis. Albeit, a mental health crisis.

I wasn't feeling like myself after the pneumonia. While I was doing well in my new job and maintaining my home life, internally I was unraveling. I was overly stressed, self-conscious, unmotivated, snappy, and just plain tired. I was overwhelmed with my day-to-day responsibilities, and made little time for myself. I found myself getting annoyed by others more frequently, and could not stop the barrage of negative thoughts swirling around in my head. By the end of the workday, I got into bed completely exhausted and dreading the day ahead.

Up until this point, I blamed these symptoms on a number of things. My family of four was living in one room. The commute from my cousin's house to my new job was over an hour each way. We were in the process of buying a home and dealing with all the back and forth with the mortgage company. (As Kevin said at the time, "They've asked us for everything except our left toe!") I was working with a contractor on designing the remodel of the home we had a contract on. And, my son was going through an extreme case of 'the terrible twos.'

I chose to ignore the warning signs I recognized along the way (and there were numerous signs). I would often say, "I'm just stressed because we have so much going on," and leave it at that. Yet, to this day, one of those signs particularly stands out in my mind, and brings tears to my eyes whenever I think about it.

It was about a week after I got pneumonia. I had just finished doing the final walk-through of our rental so that we could get our deposit back. I left the meeting with the property management company and went to grab some lunch at a nearby restaurant. When I went inside, I felt disoriented. Something told me to go back to the car, but I didn't listen initially. I was moving slowly and felt disconnected from my body – like I was observing myself. I got my food and sat down at a table but quickly decided it was best to leave. I had begun sweating and felt like I was going to pass out. I grabbed my things as quickly as I could and went to the car – just in time.

Pain was piercing my chest, and my heart felt like it was in flames. "Am I having a heart attack?" I thought to myself. I had read many articles about pneumonia being potentially fatal, and my mind started racing. I started thinking about Heavy D, one of my favorite childhood artists, who came down with a case of pneumonia and had recently made his transition. I started replaying the tapes in my mind of other people who had passed of pneumonia and other complications.

Suddenly, it was like I was paralyzed. I couldn't move any of my limbs. It felt like the car was getting smaller, and I was suffocating. I sincerely thought I was dying.

"This can't be it! What about Kevin and the boys? I'm not ready to leave them. I haven't finished my work here. I'm not ready to go yet, Lord!"

Clearly, my inner cry was heard. I began to feel my limbs again. The first thing I did was call Kevin.

"Honey, I can barely move! My chest is in severe pain, and my heart is burning!"

"Slow down, honey. Where are you? Is there anyone around you?"

"I'm in the car. No, no one is around. I can barely move! I feel like I'm dying!"

"Kan, don't be silly. Call 911 and get an ambulance."

I was angry that he was so calm and nonchalant about the whole thing. He really wasn't buying into how serious I thought this was. I got over my frustration quickly when I realized that he was at home with our two boys who were likely driving him crazy. I ended up spending a few hours in the hospital then stayed the night with a friend who lived nearby. I was so grateful to have a husband that could hold it down while I was away, and a friend willing to open her home to me on such short notice. I just didn't have the energy to make the drive back to my cousin's place.

For the next few months, it felt like there was a black cloud over me. I just felt so 'Blah.' I didn't want to meet up with friends. I didn't want to talk on the phone. I didn't want to play with my kids. I didn't want to make love to my husband. I didn't feel like sitting in meetings and putting on the happy face at work. I had no drive or ambition. I just wanted to crawl in bed and stay there.

In spite of what was going on internally, it wasn't enough to stop me from pushing myself. I didn't want to let down my husband. I didn't want to let down my boss. I didn't want to let down my team. Plus, we were about to move into our new place in a couple weeks, which I thought would make me feel better. Again and again, I believed my happiness was tied to some future outcome.

One day, just before walking in to conduct a meeting with my team, I started sweating and feeling the same way I felt that day in the car. I had to get out of there. I walked in and told my team I wasn't feeling well, and that I needed to go home. They were understanding and wished me well. I went into my boss' office and told him I was heading home. He, too, was understanding and encouraged me to take all the time I needed to get better. Little did I know, I would never return to that position.

∞

"I think you're depressed, honey," Kevin said.

"What? Depressed?"

"Yes, and I think you should think about getting some medication."

"You know how I feel about that depression medication." We had discussed it many times given his research as a neuro-scientist and passion for reversing mental health disorders.

"I know, honey, but it works. Just to stabilize your mood while you go to counseling and do some other things to get back to yourself. Then you can get off of it."

His words pierced through my heart, as if I had just lost a battle. Me? Depressed? No way. "I'm not about to be stuck on that medication for years and years." All the excuses about what we had going on crossed my mind, and I quickly convinced myself that *they* were the cause of my upset. Counseling did seem like a good idea though.

"Here we go again," I thought to myself as I walked into the counselor's office. I had been in therapy before, but with a different counselor and for a totally different reason. I was going to have to start from the beginning with her. I let out a sigh loud enough to be heard down the block and walked in.

The office was incredibly soothing. It was full of warm colors and vibrant cultural prints: I liked the counselor's style already. The receptionist was cheerful, but not in an annoying way. After handling the typical first visit business, she handed me a survey to fill out. I had to evaluate my emotional state. The question-naire included things like, "Rate your stress level on a scale of 1 to 10." I rated myself the highest on almost every item. *Man, I'm really messed up. This sista better be good.*

The receptionist escorted me back to the room where we would meet. It looked like a meditation room. There were floor pillows, a beautiful native print rug, a running water fountain, a Zen rock garden, and multiple seating options to choose from; including the comfortable couch I landed on. I couldn't pinpoint the scent, but there was definitely some aromatherapy going on. There were two large bookshelves full of a range of books on mental health. Based on her collection, Dr. Clay was interested in mental health in the black community.

My study of the office was shortly interrupted when Dr. Clay walked in. She had short, natural hair that was dyed light brown; she seemed to be in her 60s. She had a calm and warm demeanor, but also looked like she meant business. I had taken my time in researching therapists in the area and was already pleased with my choice. Something about her gave me a good vibe from the moment she walked in.

"So, what brings you in today?"

"I don't even know where to begin. I feel like I'm falling apart."

For the next 15 minutes or so, I recapped the past few months, beginning with the pneumonia and ending with the breakdown. She listened intently, and even raised her brows a few times. I could sense that she genuinely cared, and that she was already making some connections as I was sharing my story.

She probed a little more, and asked if there was anything else she should know about the past year or so leading up to the pneumonia. I was hoping to leave that part out; at least for this first session. I could already see that there would be no half-stepping with Dr. Clay. I let down my guard some more, and began to give her some of the highlights from the past few years.

In the summer of 2009, I landed what I viewed as a dream job. I moved to Washington DC to serve as a political appointee in the administration of the first black President of the United States, Barack Obama. I was working on an issue that was near and dear to me, education reform. I truly believe that *all* children can learn, and was grateful for the opportunity to work on proving what was possible.

"Sounds like it was great," Dr. Clay said. "So, why did you leave?"

Man, she's good, I thought. *She is going to make me talk about it.*

"After two years of working long hours and weekends, giving presentations across the country, building a solid reputation within the administration, as well as with our external partners, and being known as the 'go-to' person for all things related to my topic area, someone from another office was promoted to take the lead on my area of work. There wasn't even a position open; they just created a position to move him into."

"How did that make you feel?" she asked.

This is where some of my old wounds really started to come up. I wanted to say, "Like shit," but my family taught me not to speak like that in front of an elder. I scrambled for replacement words like pissed, bitter, frustrated, disrespected, and unappreciated. Just speaking those words stirred up the emotions in me, and I started speaking louder.

"They said we would *work together as a team*, but I didn't believe it one bit. Did they really think I was going to stay there and report to *him*?" She had gotten me started. My blood was boiling and I was on a roll.

I was completely unforgiving and full of resentment. I felt overlooked, and took the decision personally. *Was my work good enough? Is there something more I should have done to share my ideas and vision? I knew I should have spoken up more in meetings. What makes this guy better than me? Did they even consider me for this role? How dare they not even tell me this was happening!*

I was the most angry I had been in quite some time, and I have always been a relatively even-keeled person. I would talk about him behind his back with coworkers. And when any of them would co-sign, it would only fuel the fire in me. I was so furious that I could have burned him with one look. No matter how many times my coworkers reassured me and affirmed the quality work I had done over the years, it was not enough to overcome the deep feeling of inadequacy that settled in the moment it was announced.

Staying in that environment was not something I was in the state of mind to consider, although the opportunity to transfer to another role was offered. I took the first external job that I could find that would allow me to bow out respectfully. I was devastated, but pretended I was excited about moving on. I'm not proud to say that on my way out, I let many people know how I *really* felt about the gentleman who had been placed in the new role. I seemed to be unable to curb the desire for vengeance that was adding fuel to the raging fire within me. Three weeks later, I was in the hospital with pneumonia. Three months later, I was at my wit's end.

"That was helpful. Thank you for sharing so openly. Why don't we spend the remainder of our time discussing your childhood and family history? Can you describe your life growing up and your family relationships?"

"Sure." I sat quietly for a moment as I pondered where to begin. After some consideration, I figured it was best to start from the very beginning. The overview I gave her went something like this:

The Early Days

I spent my early years in a mixed-income neighborhood in Queens, New York. My parents grew up in the midst of the Civil Rights Movement and transcended former barriers by being among the first black students to attend an all-white, prestigious university. Their academic achievements, career milestones, and the 'racial divide' were extremely influential in the way I was raised. My family actively encouraged me to strive to achieve much more than they did in life. I was proud of them and, in turn, wanted to make them proud.

We lived around the corner from my grandmother, who was an instrumental figure in my life. She had a master's degree from Howard University, which was an outstanding achievement for her time. She started a homework program at the local Langston Hughes library, where she took me after school on many occasions. The program is still running to this day. Everyone in the neighborhood knew her. She was one of the kindest and most loving people I've ever met.

Grandma always told me not to let others define me. She said, "If you don't love yourself, no one else will." I thought I knew what she meant at the time, but I would not understand the potency of that truism until much later. I spent almost every day at her house. Our favorite pastimes were playing Pokeno, eating fried bologna sandwiches, drinking Tang, and squeezing into a one-person seat together to watch TV. And giggling; lots of giggling.

When I was 8 years old, a job opportunity for my dad moved us from New York to the suburbs of Philadelphia, Pennsylvania. This change in my surroundings considerably shaped the development of my personality. I went from a multicultural, urban environment where I felt accepted, to a suburban, predominantly white environment where I felt rejected. I was in a class in which I was the only black student, and in a school in which there weren't many of us. Although I frequently overheard my parents talking about their struggles being "one of few" in the corporate world, I never really understood it until I was put in a similar situation. My hair was pulled. I was called several racial slurs. I was whispered about. I was made to feel inferior. And, my intelligence was consistently challenged (despite the fact that I was ahead of most of the students in my class).

I developed a shield to protect myself from the judgment of others – a strong, but silent personality. I had some bad experiences when speaking up or sharing my true thoughts in class, so I chose to keep fairly quiet. I worked diligently on doing well and achieving what I viewed as success. I did not want anyone to have a reason to speak negatively of me, so I was constantly trying to exceed the expectations of others. I never felt like I was good enough, so I was always pushing myself to do better.

Another struggle for me at this time was my identity. Of the 20 or so black students in my school, only two of them lived in an upper, middle-class neighborhood like my family. On one hand, the white children were calling me racial slurs, and on the other hand the black children were calling me "white girl." I began to resent our family's move to the suburbs. I strove to connect with the other black students in the school while also trying to blend into this new environment. I was confused, and never felt like I could balance the two worlds quite right.

Once I grew old enough to start working, I spent almost all of my money on clothes. I thought this would help me feel better about myself. I even placed as runner-up for "best dressed" in high school. I looked good on the outside, but that did nothing to pacify the insecurity I felt inside. I became a true master at disguising my inner pain.

"Can you tell me a bit more about your parents? What were they like? And what was your relationship like with them?"

My parents were very career driven and traveled frequently on business. For years at a time, my dad lived in other states pursuing career opportunities, while my mom kept me and my younger sister in Pennsylvania so that we wouldn't have to change schools. Their relationship was OK, but wasn't what I pictured as the ideal relationship.

For years, my mom traveled abroad for one to two weeks out of every month for work. My grandmother on my dad's side came to live with us during those years so that my sister and I could have loving care (and amazing meals!) at home while they were away. Despite the travel, my mom and I remained close. She was fun-loving, enjoyed dancing around the house, could out-cheer any parent at my sporting events, and relentlessly motivated me to do my best in school. She spent a lot of time with me and my sister, and worked just as hard at making sure we were well-rounded as she did at her day job (if not harder). If she was tired, she never showed it. When she came home from work, she would greet us like she hadn't seen us in years.

My dad was always an introspective man. He loves music, and owns a record collection larger than I've ever seen. When I was a little girl, we were inseparable. I spent many hours down in the "basement lounge" where he kept all of his records. He even helped me start my own record collection. By age five, I could sing all the words to my favorite Whitney Houston, Michael Jackson, Grandmaster Flash & the Furious Five, New Edition, Teena Marie, and Prince songs. We spent many summers lying on a blanket at the Saratoga Jazz Festival in upstate New York, where we watched many jazz legends perform (although I was much too young to fully appreciate their greatness). I followed him to sporting events with his friends, to every horror movie that came out, and even opted for a wallet in my back pocket over the pretty purses my mom bought me. I was a daddy's girl, and proud of it.

During my adolescent years, I noticed a significant shift in our relationship. It was likely just the long distance and my less-than-desirable teenage attitude but, in my head, it was much more than that. While my dad was quiet most of the time, he would not tolerate foolishness. He had a serious temper that I managed to set off more times than I would have cared to with my teenage know-it-all ways. I became afraid of him. We went from being peas-in-a-pod to oil and water. I said "I hate you" many times during those years, and was always elated when he left town on business.

The long distance became a strain on my parents' relationship. They argued frequently, and didn't seem to enjoy each other's company. Sometimes, the arguments got so heated that I would go in my room and turn up the music to tune them out. When we were around other people, they acted like everything was fine, which always stuck in my mind.

I used to think, *So, is that what we do in life? We just pretend everything is cool when it's not?*

"So, why do you think your relationship was so hostile with your dad? Can you tell me a little more about that?" Dr. Clay probed.

I envied the close relationships I saw between other fathers and daughters. I also envied the husband and wife relationships that seemed so much more loving and intimate than the interactions I witnessed between my parents. Growing up, *The Cosby Show* was my absolute favorite show. I was always comparing our family to "The Huxtables," and secretly wished mine was like them. The love and affection displayed between Claire and Heathcliff (Cliff), and between Cliff and his daughters Sandra, Vanessa and Rudy, was admirable to me. The women around the father figure in the show always knew they were loved. I didn't feel loved by my dad. I couldn't remember him ever saying he loved me. He never told me I was beautiful. And he rarely said "Yes" to anything I wanted to do.

I would say something like, "Dad, can I go to the party? I got an 'A' on my Algebra test!" and he would say, "Absolutely not. End of discussion." I would try to work my way around him by asking my mom, but he quickly caught on, and stopped that in its tracks. "The answer is no, Kandace. If you ask us again, I'm taking your phone."

> "You respond to what you perceive, and as you perceive
> so shall you behave."
> ~A Course in Miracles

In my mind, he was my enemy. I paid little attention to the ways he *did* spend time with me and how he did show interest in what was going on in my life. I pushed him away, and had no intention of welcoming him back.

For a long time I blamed my dad for what played out next in my life. Through much of my teenage years, I used intimate relationships with young men as a way to feel loved and appreciated. I lost my virginity at age 14. I wanted *so* badly to feel loved and accepted, and I thought that it had to come from a man. By the time I was 18, I had allowed more young men access to me than I'd care to remember. The funny thing is, I didn't even like the sex. I didn't enjoy it in the moment because my thoughts were running wild. *Am I doing it right? Does he think I'm sexy? Is he thinking about someone else? Would he just hurry up?* What I *did* enjoy was spending time together, listening to music together, laughing, joking, and, especially, hearing them say nice things about me.

> "The 'little I' seeks to enhance itself by external approval, external possessions and external 'love.'"
> ~A Course in Miracles

After the sex was over, I could always feel the weight of the guilt on my shoulders. I was a 'slut' in my mind. I hated the thought of that label, but I didn't know another way to describe my escapades. I didn't know how to end this cycle of feeding my desires through the opposite sex.

I gave myself away easily because I thought that would make me more likeable, more popular and, ultimately, make me feel more loved. I was hoping to find 'true love,' but was left heartbroken many times. The young men I was attracting into my life were, for the most part, not looking for serious relationships.

They solely wanted me for my body, and that's all I knew to offer.

Despite the pain that ensued after these encounters, like an addict I continued to go right back for another fix. I never found it hard to meet the next guy who was willing to help me forget about my troubles for the moment. I was attractive, tall, slim, and could recite the lyrics of all the old-school, Hip-Hop songs. I was like a verse out of a song by The Commodores: *easy like Sunday morning*. What was there for a young man *not* to like?

"You've given me a lot to process. That's all the time we have for today, but I'll give you some homework to complete for our next session."

My first counseling session with Dr. Clay left my head spinning. I could barely keep track of my thoughts. *Instead of men, had I become addicted to a successful career to pacify my need to feel good about myself? Had I followed the pattern I witnessed growing up and become overly conscious of how I looked in the eyes of others? Had I viewed someone getting promoted over me as a depletion of my self-worth?*

I knew this was only the beginning. I hadn't even touched on the most painful of my life's experiences, so I knew I shouldn't be too quick to draw any conclusions on the source of my anguish. We had a lot more work to do.

Chapter 2

Break of Dawn

T he week seemed to fly by. I waited until the last possible minute to do the homework Dr. Clay had assigned, and rushed to complete it the night before our appointment. One of the readings was titled, "Negative Thoughts Trigger Negative Feelings."[1] I started with that one, and underlined the following sentence in the opening paragraph: *We used to believe that it was depression or anxiety that made people think negatively but psychologists and psychiatrists have discovered that most people who struggle with anxious or depressed feelings **first** had negative, pessimistic, distorted thoughts that produced those feelings.*

I was intrigued. I had not spent much time paying attention to the thoughts I was thinking. I didn't think I had much control over them. The document went on to highlight the distorted thinking patterns that are common to people who struggle with depression or anxiety. There were 12 categories on the list, six of which were perfect descriptions of my thought patterns:

- **Exaggerating:** Making self-directed critical statements that include terms like never, nothing, everything, or always.
- **Judging/Shoulds and Musts:** Being critical of self or others with a heavy emphasis on the use of should have, ought to, must, have to, and should not have. For example: Feeling you should do something or things must be a certain way; feeling that you absolutely must behave in a particular way or thinking that you should have a level of control of the world around you.
- **Mind reading:** Making negative assumptions regarding other people's thoughts and motives. Feeling that others should have known how you felt or what you wanted even

though you didn't tell them.

- **Feelings are facts:** Because you feel a certain way, reality is seen as fitting that feeling.
- **Self-blaming:** Holding one's self responsible for an outcome that was not completely under one's control.
- **Projection:** Making negative assumptions about the thoughts, intentions, or motives of another person, which are often 'projections' of your own thoughts and feelings about the situation.

> "Depression is reinforced every time a negative thought
> goes unchallenged and is accepted as truth."
> ~Arthur E. Jongsma, Jr.

As I looked over the list, I was amazed by how normal I viewed these ways of thinking. I had no idea there *was* another way to look at things. *Didn't everyone view life this way?*

The next assignment was titled, "Identifying Mistaken Beliefs and Countering them with Assertive Rights."[2] There was a list of mistaken beliefs on the left column and a list of assertive rights on the right column. I was to check off the mistaken beliefs that I still held and the assertive rights that I had difficulty accepting. Three of the assertive rights were jumping off the page at me:

You have a right to ask for help or emotional support
You have a right to feel and express pain
You have a right to be alone, even if others request your company

I really struggled with these three rights. I was looking forward to discussing my struggles with Dr. Clay; I needed help accepting them.

∞

"Welcome back, Kandace. How was your week?"

"It was okay. I'm still staying home from work, but I feel bad about it. I find myself logging in to make sure I'm staying up to date."

"Is your boss asking you to do that?"

"No. I guess I just feel like I should." As it came out of my mouth, I wished I could pull it back. I just caught myself saying I *should* do something. I knew Dr. Clay was going to pick up on it.

"Why is that? As I recall, you mentioned in our last meeting that your boss said to take as much time as you need, right?"

"Yes, I am on medical leave but I still feel an obligation to support my new team. They were just getting used to me and beginning to rely on me and I feel like I left them stranded."

"I see. Did you have a chance to do your homework?" I knew where she was headed. She didn't miss a beat.

"Yes, I wanted to talk to you about the assertive rights I'm having a hard time accepting. They are mostly centered on asking for help and taking time for me. I have always considered myself a strong woman, and never want to appear weak to anyone else. It always felt like a loss of power, or a sign of weakness for me to ask anyone for help. So, I rarely did. I was more likely to suffer through difficult times in order to maintain my positive image."

"Why do you think that is?"

"Well, I think part of it may come from what I witnessed in my parents in my early years, but there's a lot more that has happened throughout my life that I think it could stem from."

"I'm all ears."

I began sharing about my college and young adult years with her in hopes that she could help me make some connections.

College and Young Adult Years

I was excited to get out of the house and finally head to college. After my difficult experience in the suburbs, I was adamant about going to a Historically Black College. I decided on Florida A&M University (FAMU) in Tallahassee. The school was *TIME Magazine's College of the Year* at that time, and its five-year MBA program had a stellar reputation. The high-achiever in me loved the idea of obtaining my bachelor's and master's degrees in five years and graduating with a MBA-level salary.

I got off to a good start academically and socially, but my addiction to sex was still on overdrive. It wasn't long before I found myself on a path that I was hoping to avoid. Toward the end of my first semester, I got pregnant. The young man I was dating didn't want anything to do with a baby, and quickly found another woman to spend time with. I was left on my own to figure out what to do next. I could not face the shame and disappointment that I believed would be inevitable if I told my parents, "I'm having a baby." I did one of the only things I viewed as a viable option for me: I had an abortion.

I was 19 years old, terrified, ashamed, hurt, and felt incredibly guilty. I could barely look people in the eye for a while because I was afraid they would notice something was wrong. I decided to open up to a couple of my closest friends and was so glad I did. They shared stories of other young women they knew who made the same decision and were still able to have children later (something I was worried about). I found some comfort in knowing that I was not alone, and that I had not ruined my child-bearing possibility. It was still tough. I constantly thought about what would have been different had I kept the baby. I felt horrible when I would see young mothers on campus who managed to still hold down their academic responsibilities.

By January of my freshman year (start of second semester), rumors about me being 'easy' had spread all around campus. I had a deep desire to change my behavior and shift the perception of me. I no longer had the urge to sleep with just anyone. I had suffered the consequences of my actions and did not want to repeat them. I was eventually able to rise above the rumors by doing well in school and getting involved on campus. During this period of 're-branding,' I pushed myself to be great in all areas. (I will not say that I *was* great in all areas, but it was indeed my desire to be.)

During the spring semester of my freshman year, I entered into a steady relationship with a young man who liked me for *me* and not just my body. He was popular, smart, and well respected by both students and professors. He was also a DJ, and our mutual affinity for music is what opened the door to our friendship. I can remember the first time he came by my campus apartment. He was flipping through my massive CD collection, and started putting on various songs to see if I actually knew them. We spent hours rapping our hearts out to all of my late 80s and early 90s Hip-Hop music. He couldn't find one song that I couldn't keep up with. That was the beginning of a relationship that lasted for almost my entire college experience.

After attending church together weekly for a couple months, I felt called one day to 'wash away my sins' and start anew via baptism. Each week, the music from the choir would overtake me and move me to tears, and the message seemed to be directed at me. It was a powerful time of renewal and purification for me after all those years of misusing my body.

I had grown up Christian, and went to Sunday school almost every week. At the time, I didn't feel deeply connected to it, and many days even resented having to go. My mom never forced me to get baptized, as I had witnessed many other parents do. She believed it was something I should do on my own when, and if, I decided it was for me. I didn't think I would ever do it but, at that point in my life, I knew no other way to wipe the slate clean when I felt so filthy.

> "You've been searching over here and over there, but only God can take the pain away."
> ~Kirk Franklin

I was grateful for my boyfriend coming into my life when he did, and vowed to never mess up what we had. I naively thought that the baptism would take away all the pain associated with my past. One of the songs the choir used to sing frequently was *He'll Take Away the Pain*,[3] by Kirk Franklin. That's what I was praying for.

The next couple of years were great. After sporting long, straight hair for years, I cut all of the chemical relaxer out of my hair and 'went natural.' It was incredibly liberating – I felt like a new woman. I was making my parents proud with my good grades. I ran for student senate and won. I joined a sorority. I volunteered with youth in the community. I was president of a support group on campus for students from the tri-state area in the northeast. I started interning for a record label and promoting neo-soul and underground Hip-Hop artists on campus. I also started doing marketing and promotions for a popular, local neo-soul and jazz band. I hosted open-mic nights. I wrote and performed poetry. I had settled into a bohemian style that suited me. I picked up a new nickname from friends, Queen, which stuck with me throughout my time in college. And, if there was a contest for "best dressed" on campus, you would have thought that my boyfriend and I were competing to win it every day. We just *knew* we were fly!

Things were going smoothly in our relationship, until I started getting *extremely* jealous. I really thought I loved him and he thought he loved me – the problem was I didn't know how to love *myself*. When I say I was jealous, I don't mean a little bit. I checked e-mails, phone messages, would dig through papers, interrupted his conversations with other women to ensure they knew he was taken, and constantly questioned his love for only me – I was a mess! I was so paranoid and afraid of losing the wonderful feeling of love I was experiencing that I ended up sabotaging it myself.

My behavior started to make him question my actions and, in his own digging, he ended up finding out about my past. From my journals he found out about the promiscuity I displayed in the first semester of my freshman year. I lied about the campus rumors at the beginning of our relationship, when some of his friends warned him about me. He tried to make it work for a few months after uncovering this and even sought counseling from our pastor. Ultimately, he decided he did not want to continue the relationship.

I realized later that I never felt *worthy* of the love I was receiving from him because of the guilt and shame I carried with me from the way I had used my body in the past. It was completely devastating to lose who I thought was 'The One' and, even more so, to accept that it was my doing.

What made this period even more rough for me was that I had pushed myself to finish my bachelor's and master's degrees in 4½ years so that I could be with the man I thought I was going to marry. But now the relationship was over. So much of my identity was wrapped in being his woman. I had already accepted a job with the same company he worked with, and was planning to move to the same city the year after he graduated. Needless to say, I had some serious healing work to do. With us no longer together I needed to figure out who I was – apart from that relationship.

> "Here comes the sun, little darling, and I say, 'It's all right... It's all right.'"
> ~Nina Simone

I was grateful for my dad planting the jazz seed in me because Nina Simone, Cassandra Wilson, and Billie Holiday were helping me cry out my tears. I did manage to have some fun during my final year of college. I made a great set of friends that helped me create new memories, and began to rebuild my self-esteem. At the end of that year, I hesitantly walked across the graduation stage, wishing I hadn't rushed my time in college. I absolutely loved FAMU and was no longer looking forward to being in the same city as my ex. I felt like I still needed time to regroup before walking into that situation. Thankfully, the company with whom I accepted a position offered new employees a grace period of up to 12 months to start. They also gave a hefty signing bonus at that time; part of which I used for a down payment on the house I was having built, and the other part I used to get as far away as possible.

> "Rather than focusing on what you want to have... or get... or do, focus on how you are – NOW – because how you are now is all you'll ever experience."
> ~Cheri Huber,
> The Depression Book

"That's a lot for a young woman to handle," Dr. Clay said. "You mentioned you had been to counseling before; was it during this time period?"

"No. I wish I had, but I didn't attend counseling until many years later when I was dealing with another life crisis."

"I see. Well, that's all the time we have for today. Let's save that story for the next visit. I do have another homework assignment for you. Are you up for reading a book?"

"Definitely. I'm up for anything that can help me get out of this funk I'm in."

Dr. Clay went to her bookshelf and retrieved a small book, *The Depression Book: Depression as an Opportunity for Spiritual Growth*,[4] by Cheri Huber. I didn't know if I liked the idea of walking around with a book with that title, but it did sound like something I needed to read.

Once again, I found my head spinning upon leaving Dr. Clay's office. *Given the way I rushed through college, had I fully healed from all that took place during that time? Were there still open wounds that I was unaware of? Was there still some guilt and shame that I was holding onto that was contributing to my emotional state?* I needed to recall the period immediately after college in order to continue putting the pieces together. I vowed to do so during our next session. In the interim, I had some reading to do.

Since I had free time on my hands while on medical leave, I decided to head to the library to have some quiet time. By this time, my family and I had moved into our new home. There were contractors in and out of the house, so it wasn't an ideal place to read and reflect.

I assumed I would be there for just a couple of hours, but I could not put the book down. I read it from beginning to end in one sitting. I was happy there weren't too many people around me because I could not stop the tears from flowing. What hit me so deeply was that I had not allowed myself to *feel* the pain during the lowest moments of my life. I either suppressed it or I expressed it as resentment toward someone, but I never allowed it to just *be*. I wrote down my favorite passages so that I could share my insights with Dr. Clay. This was a major 'Aha' moment for me. I had a smile on my face as I walked in to my next counseling session.

"You look happy today," Dr. Clay said. "And, from your ratings, I can see that you're feeling a bit better. I'm glad to see that."

"Yes, I do feel a bit better. The book really helped me see how I push away my feelings, and don't allow myself to just let them be what they are. If I'm feeling sad, I just want to feel happy quickly so I never pause to think about the thoughts, emotions, or beliefs that may be causing it."

"I'm glad you liked it. What were your favorite parts?"

"Well, one of my favorite lines was, 'If you cannot be kind to the one person whose suffering you can actually feel, you will never be able to be kind to anyone.' That was an eye-opener for me. For so many years, I have put myself down and viewed myself in such a negative light. I wasn't at all focused on being kind to myself. She also included some questions in the book that were powerful and thought-provoking for me. One of them was, *How do you feel about having pleasure?* That one drove me to tears."

"How *do* you feel about having pleasure and being kind to yourself?"

"I don't feel like I deserve to have time to myself. Whenever I do take time away by meeting up with friends, I feel guilty and am always thinking about getting back home as quickly as possible. I think I know what that comes from. I actually wanted to pick up where we left off last time and talk about the time period after college if you don't mind."

"Of course. Go for it."

After rushing through college, I decided to go to Madrid, Spain, for what I thought would be a one-month journey of 'finding myself' (whatever that meant). I chose Madrid because a colleague from business school, Danisha, was there on internship. We didn't know each other all that well, but whenever we saw each other on campus we would give each other hugs like we were long-lost friends. She had a warm, friendly, and joyful spirit. I remember when I cut my hair natural. Many people would say that I shouldn't have cut off "all that pretty hair," but she was one of a few who affirmed my look. "I LOVE it!" I recall her saying, "You look stunning! Go 'head girl!" It was just the encouragement I needed that day to hold my head high, and settle in to my natural style. She was 'good people.'

While journaling and reflecting on the plane, I made a decision to speak my truth in all relationships going forward. I acknowledged that I would not have had so many issues in my last relationship if I had just been honest about my past, fears, and insecurities. I was a 22-year-old woman with a MBA who had raced through school for a man who no longer wanted me. The last thing I thought I was going to Spain for was to find another one. I needed a break.

I was ready to explore new cultures and subjects that intrigued me. I didn't have time to study anything outside of my business curriculum given my intensive class schedule and extracurricular activities while in school. On the plane, I read a book on world religions, a topic that had always been of great interest to me. I was curious about the similarities and common themes across religions. After finishing the book, *The World's Religions*,[5] by Huston Smith, I started to question my beliefs. *How could only one religion be right? Would God really allow people to go to 'hell' just because they weren't exposed to the so-called 'right' religion?* I didn't have any answers at that point, but knew I wanted to study some more. I also added one more thing to the list of things I must be authentic about in my next relationship – my spiritual confusion.

The next night, Danisha invited me to dinner with some friends she had met throughout her time in Madrid. We went to one of the best paella restaurants in Madrid, *La Barraca*. The first person I saw when I walked in was Kevin. His perfect smile drew me in, and it held me the entire evening. We ended up sitting at opposite ends of the table, but that didn't keep us from talking to one another. I also had a chance to meet Melissa, a FAMU graduate who had been living in Madrid for a couple years. After dinner, we all decided to go over to *Ducados*, a place known for having great music and the best mojitos.

On the walk over, I initiated small talk with Kevin so that we could walk behind the others.

"So, I hear you're a Kappa."

"That's right, I'm a Nupe!" he said.

"I'm a Delta. Crimson and cream love!"

After it came out, I was embarrassed by my corniness. (To clarify, crimson and cream are the colors of both of the Pan-Hellenic organizations we belong to.) I could hear my new friend, Melissa, chuckling at me in the background. Corny as it was, it sparked a conversation that would continue throughout my time in Spain. The music playing at *Ducados* was right up my alley – acid jazz, old school R&B, house music, and funk. My interest in Kevin piqued when he could hold his own with me on music knowledge. Music was clearly the language of my soul.

There were so many old songs that we both knew the words to. We kept joking back and forth with each other on almost every song.

"What you know about Brand New Heavies?"

"Girl, what you know about Incognito?"

"This is my jam! Patrice Rushen is my girl!"

"No, this is *my* jam! This is before your time!"

He had all the credentials a mother would love – PhD, handsome, worldly, loved his family, played an instrument, etc. There was only one hesitation that crossed my mind at the time: our age difference. I was 22 and he was 32. I was fresh out of college, and he had had the time to live on his own and experience a lot more of life than I had. All of that doubt faded the more time we spent together.

From the very beginning, I shared everything with him: my fears, insecurities, life struggles, hopes, dreams, failures, my questions about God and spirituality – *everything*. I wasn't worried about trying to impress him, and I didn't care if it scared him off. I didn't want him to fall in love with a lie. He accepted me for all that I was, and believed in what was possible for us in the future. He found my authenticity refreshing and, in turn, opened up to me in ways he hadn't with other women.

I decided to push my start date back with my new job and stayed in Madrid for three months. We hung out, laughed, traveled to other countries, poured out our hearts, and just enjoyed our time together. It was the most free I had felt in my life. Ever since getting embarrassed and belittled for expressing myself in elementary school, I hadn't given myself permission to be my authentic self because of fear of judgment. I gave everyone what I thought they wanted. With Kevin, I was being my authentic self *and being accepted for it* – something I had never experienced nor imagined.

Six months after I left Madrid, Kevin moved back to the States to be with me. We continued to travel the world and enjoy life together. Being in the same city as my ex-boyfriend ended up not being a problem; they even liked each other. I remember one night we were all out at a party, and they were talking at the bar. When they finished, Kevin came back over to me and said, "You know, if you two didn't have a history, we probably would have been cool." Awkward as it was for me, I was grateful for their camaraderie.

The vulnerability this relationship with Kevin fostered created a deep connection between us that only improved the more time we spent together. Kevin and I got married in July 2005, two and a half years after we met. I sincerely believed we were a match made in Heaven.

Although I thought I was healed from my past at this point, one year after we got married we were introduced to a seminar that proved the wounds were still open. *The Landmark Forum*[6] is a three-day experiential seminar that is designed to bring about positive and permanent shifts in the daily lives of participants. It helped me uncover, and begin to shed, layers of guilt, shame, blame, and resentment that had unconsciously piled up in me. I was able to recognize what they referred to as my "strong suit," the protection I developed to navigate the world and protect myself from getting hurt: my façade of having it all together. I was able to acknowledge the way I had created 'stories' about what really happened in my life and how they have hindered me – like the story I created about my dad not loving me. And, I was able to begin the process of taking responsibility for intentionally creating what's possible in each moment thereafter.

A big part of the seminar was forgiveness of the past. During this session, I was able to forgive people from my elementary and secondary school who thought less of me because of the color of my skin – resentment that I had been holding onto for much of my life. In addition to thinking or writing about situations that needed to be forgiven, participants were encouraged to call someone with whom we were holding onto resentment with and forgive them. I knew exactly who I needed to call.

The forgiveness call to my dad was intimidating. I remember breaking out into a full body sweat just before dialing the number. I rarely called him just to talk. I talked to my mother more openly about what was going on in my life, but the conversations between me and my dad were more surface. I wrote out what I was going to say, but when he answered the phone, I clammed up.

"Hey, Dad!"

"Hey, Kans, what's going on?"

I broke out into tears, and could barely get my words out. After taking a few deep breaths, I began sharing.

"I'm in a workshop this weekend, and it has been so helpful in healing some issues I had from the past. I wanted to call you to let you know I love you and I forgive you. I hope you can forgive me for the way I have pushed you away."

I went on to tell him about the ways I had misused my body, and the bad habits I had developed. I shared that I had been blaming him for all of those negative aspects of my life. I told him that I now realized that no one else is responsible for the way my life has turned out. I let him know I released him from blame, and that I would like to build a closer relationship with him again. I missed how close we were when I was a little girl. I wasn't sure if it would get back to that, but I was willing to try.

He apologized for anything he had done to hurt my feelings in the past, and told me he loved me. He also mentioned he was glad I was in this workshop so that I could move on from the past. A couple days later, he sent me this letter. My dad, the quiet man who rarely expresses deep emotion, touched me at my core with this one. I read it out loud to my classmates.

Dear Kans,

I must say your call this weekend caught me by surprise, but re-affirmed what a special daughter and person you have grown to be. In professional terms, and also speaking for Mom, you are exceeding our expectations!!!

Life has many turns, twists, ups, downs, and bumps in the road. Our experiences as a family were no different. You can't change things said and done, but you can learn, grow, and move on to better things.

I have nothing to forgive you for! That would be hard considering all the wonderful memories I have of times together; remember the bumpy van ride from Syracuse to Buffalo while helping me move? How about at a young age our Saturdays at the movies, and laughing at horror films that Mom will not watch today? Or going to your first baseball game, I can still hear you saying, "Dad you told me we would catch a baseball!"

I am a firm believer that the most important thing in life is to know yourself, a huge enabler to getting the most of your time in this world today. You are well on your way, keep learning and keep growing!!

Love,
Dad

The seminar was worth every penny for that letter alone. It was the most vulnerable I had ever seen my dad. In addition, through hearing other people's stories of their life challenges during the seminar, I had a new awareness that *everyone* has struggles. I don't know why I thought everyone else's life was perfect, but I had it fixed in my mind that I was the only person that had these inner struggles. I realized in that moment the ways in which we free each other when we are our authentic selves; not just in our most intimate relationships, but with *everyone*. I was motivated to begin to be more real with myself and everyone around me. It was life changing, and I was on a high for a while, but reality ultimately set in again; I hadn't done anything to continue the work. I didn't have any type of daily personal growth or spiritual practice in my life. I attended church on some Sundays, but then would go right back to worrying, doubting, and complaining on Mondays. It was only a matter of time before the sweetness turned sour.

"It sounds like that was a powerful growth period for you," Dr. Clay acknowledged.

"It really was. It was eye opening to me. But, I'm getting frustrated as I talk about it. Frustrated with myself because I wasn't able to put all the knowledge I gained in that seminar into practice in my daily life."

"It sounds like you *did* put it into practice. For example, the forgiveness call to your dad."

"Yes, but after the seminar was over I let myself slip right back into my old ways of thinking. I still cared about what others thought of me, so I wasn't fully authentic about what was going on internally."

"And, what *was* going on with you at that time?"

"Well, that brings us to one of the lowest times of my life. After the honeymoon period."

After the Honeymoon Period

After a blissful first three years together, Kevin and I moved to California – far away from my friends and family who were mostly on the East Coast. He was extremely busy with his new job and, from my perspective, wasn't doing the same things he did in the beginning that made me feel loved and appreciated. I interpreted this to mean that he actually *didn't* love me the same anymore and, unfortunately, I believed it. I was not fully healed of my need for attention and appreciation from a man, and hadn't quite learned how to love myself. When the attention I believed I was missing from Kevin came from another man, I allowed myself to get sucked right back into my old pattern.

I was at a work conference and doing my usual networking. I had two reasons for attending that conference. I was on a listening tour for my day job to learn about high school reform efforts, and I was in search of potential school partners for the nonprofit I had recently started. Melissa and I had co-founded a nonprofit dedicated to preparing the next generation of youth social entrepreneurs throughout the African Diaspora. I was super passionate about it, and it felt like it may have been my calling.

There was a gentleman from a school that showed great interest in the nonprofit, and wanted to partner with us to bring a group of students to Tanzania. I was thrilled about the possibilities. We decided to continue the conversation at lunch after the conference was over. I thought nothing of it. I even called Kevin and Melissa on my way to lunch to share my excitement.

> "You cannot behave appropriately unless you perceive correctly."
> ~A Course in Miracles

But the lunch conversation increasingly grew more personal. We had many similar interests, and a similar sense of humor. He began to discuss challenges in his marriage, including his wife's long hours and lack of time for him. Like a magnet, his comment drew out all of the pain that was inside of me. For what seemed like hours, we talked about our disappointments and frustrations with the way our spouses had 'changed.' What I thought was going to be a great business partnership had taken a turn for the worst.

I had an affair – something I *never* thought I would do. I allowed another man to feed my desires for attention and affection. We e-mailed and sent text messages throughout the day. We lied and said we were going to conferences so we could meet up in different cities. We snuck and called each other in the crevices of our day when no one could hear us. He held my hand. He told me I was beautiful. He told me he thought we were soul mates. He even told me he would leave his wife for me. We actually thought we were in love. While I did feel like I was falling in love, I never lost my love for my husband. What I really wanted was for things to be back to the way they were before we moved to California. I didn't know if there was a chance it would ever get back to that given my actions.

The affair went on for months and probably would have gone on longer if I had not experienced something that shook me completely. One night while traveling on business, I had the most unusual visitor. At 3 am I was abruptly awakened by a bitter cold that swept into the hotel room. I was shivering uncontrollably and my teeth were chattering. As I looked up, I saw a black spirit floating by the bed. It had no shape or form; just a moving cloud of blackness. It physically shook my body for what felt like five minutes (it probably was much less than that). It finally left, and the room returned to its normal temperature.

I was scared and couldn't believe what had just happened. *Doesn't this only happen in the movies?* I thought. Later that morning, I heard a Voice say, "It's time to tell him." I was nervous and had no idea what the outcome would be, but I told Kevin *everything* when I returned home the next day. I can't explain why, but I just knew to listen to that Voice.

At the time, Kevin and I were simultaneously taking another class offered by Landmark Education called the *Self-Expression and Leadership Program*.[7] I know it was no coincidence that we were in that class at the time that I shared this devastating news. We were both introduced to *A Course in Miracles*[8] by classmates and were encouraged to forgive and work on healing our relationship. *A Course in Miracles* ("The Course") is a non-denominational, self-study spiritual teaching that includes a text, a 365-lesson workbook, and a manual for teachers designed to move individuals from living a life driven by fear to one driven by love. Centered in forgiveness, it is a handbook and guide to inner peace that is designed to take the individual from feeling separate from God, and desiring external things to make them happy, to returning to the oneness with God from which they came. The book was scribed by a woman who heard the voice of Jesus over a period of seven years. Talk about Divine timing – this was *exactly* what I needed.

> "The Course does not aim at teaching the meaning of love, for that is beyond what can be taught. It does aim, however, at removing the blocks to the awareness of love's presence, which is your natural inheritance."
> ~A Course in Miracles

After I told Kevin about the affair, he asked that I move out for a while. I considered staying in a hotel close to my job so that I could distract myself from my emotions by working more. However, one of my Landmark classmates (I think of him as an angel) encouraged me *not* to do that and to stay in a hotel close to my home instead. This way, I could make frequent visits and be closer to putting the time into healing my marriage. We were also lifted up by my husband's close friends from grad school, a couple who welcomed us with open arms and prayed with us. I felt the unconditional Love of God through their embrace.

Kevin shared the news with his dad, who he is very close with, and I was terrified of what he might say. I was pleasantly surprised, and immensely grateful, when he, too, encouraged us to forgive and work on rebuilding our marriage. Given the way Kevin valued his dad's opinion, I knew that if he didn't say we should work it out, Kevin would have definitely considered leaving.

There was no one around us that said we should *not* work on it. We intentionally didn't share it widely because we knew not everyone was ready to offer support through total non-judgment and forgiveness. There was no one around us speaking negatively about me for what I had done, although I still *felt* judged and had tremendous guilt. There was so much love.

I felt horrible about what I had done. Not only had I messed up my marriage, but I also lost my nonprofit. We were planning a trip to Tanzania for a group of students from the school we had formed a partnership with, but I had to halt the fundraising process and sever my ties to that school in order to focus on healing my marriage. Understandably, Kevin did not want me to have anything to do with that school. My number one goal was healing my marriage. I left Melissa to handle the business of breaking the news to parents, students, and our other partners. I was so ashamed of myself. *How could I have done this?*

I wanted so badly to reverse the thinking that got me to that low place; the thinking that caused me to tarnish my marriage and the entrepreneurial dream I was building with my dear friend, Melissa. I poured myself into the healing process. Kevin and I went to both individual and couple's counseling, which helped bring up and heal some of our old patterns of thinking and behavior. We began reading the text and workbook of the Course individually and together (via phone).

> "Creation is eternal and unalterable. Your sinlessness is guaranteed by God."
> ~A Course in Miracles

The Course reignited my spiritual flame, which had grown dim. It used the Christian terminology I grew up on, but included the practical application to daily living which I so desperately needed. It helped me begin the process of releasing guilt, forgiving myself, and seeing my 'sin' as a mistake instead of something to be punished. This was a major shift in thinking for me because, up until that point, I felt like I had failed God. In the Bible, adultery is said to be a reason to get a divorce, and I had really taken that to heart. I felt like God was angry with me, and I was angry with Him for being so unforgiving of adultery. I thought to myself, *What kind of God doesn't love unconditionally and only forgives certain sins?* The Course explained that God was *not* angry with me, and that all God knows of me is the perfection He created. That allayed my fears, and began to pull away the chip I had on my shoulder.

We also began to attend *Agape International Spiritual Center*. Founded twenty-seven years ago by Dr. Michael Bernard Beckwith, Agape is a trans-denominational spiritual community rooted in the New Thought-Ageless Wisdom tradition of spirituality. His sermons drew from the wisdom of the saints, sages, mystics, and other masters who transcended the boundaries and limitations of the world. There were beautiful paintings of Jesus, Buddha, Martin Luther King, Jr., Gandhi, Krishna, and many other great spiritual leaders around the sanctuary. Seeing those paintings reconnected me to that moment on the plane to Spain when I was contemplating the beauty in all religions.

During this period, I also read every spiritual book I could get my hands on. Some of the most influential to me at that time were Marianne Williamson's *A Return to Love: Reflections on the Principles of "A Course in Miracles"*[9] and *Enchanted Love*,[10] and the visual edition of Philip Yancey's *What's So Amazing About Grace?*[11] I read a lot more books and each one gave me just the right 'nugget' of Truth. My identification with being a 'sinner' who was going to hell was beginning to dissolve. I was starting to feel forgiven.

Oprah introduced her first Web course at that time on the book *A New Earth: Awakening to Your Life's Purpose*[12] by Eckhart Tolle. I logged in faithfully each week with my notebook in hand. It hit on so many of my tendencies and insecurities, especially my inclination to seek happiness outside of myself. I was glad we were going through the content slowly because it was a lot to process at once. I was being broken open.

> "Fulfill me, make me happy, make me feel safe, tell me who I am. The world cannot give you those things, and when you no longer have such expectations, all self-created suffering comes to an end."
> ~Eckhart Tolle

Through all of my reading, the one line that kept replaying in my mind was: *The only thing missing in any relationship is what you are not giving*. It was Marianne Williamson's interpretation on a statement in the Course that said, "The only thing missing in any given situation is what you are not giving," that she shared in her book *Enchanted Love*. I realized that I had spent so much time thinking about what I was *not* receiving in my relationship that I had forgotten about giving. I pulled back my expression of love for Kevin because he wasn't giving it to me, which left the relationship stale. I realized I had the power to transform any situation with what *I'm* bringing to it. It didn't matter what anyone else was doing – I could love regardless. Talk about a breakthrough.

During the healing process, Kevin and I took a meditation and stress-relief course, *The Art of Living*,[13] together that got us off to a good start of meditating and practicing yoga together. After about six weeks of living apart, and working through the Course together, we had an amazing turning point in the healing process. I wrote about it in my journal to document the moment.

May 28, 2007
At the end of the day, I went by our place to watch TV and eat leftovers while Kevin was at his Landmark class. I figured I could eat, relax, and be out of there by 10 pm when he would be home. Well, about 8:15 the door opens and it was him! I immediately apologized for being there, but he said it was fine and that he wanted to talk to me when I was done.

I yelled upstairs when the show was over, and told him I was getting ready to leave. By his tone, it sounded like he was sad that I would be leaving so soon which surprised me. When he came downstairs he said, "Stand up... come here." He gave me a big hug... eventually pulled back, looked me in the eyes, held my face, and said, "I forgive you, Kandace... I forgive you for being human." He went on to further explain and then said, "So, go get your things – I want you to move back in." I was so excited I could hardly contain myself.

We sat down and he read me the "What is forgiveness?" section of the A Course in Miracles' workbook... truly powerful. We cuddled on the couch for a while, just enjoying the indescribable peace that was so present to us in that moment. "God is so good" is all I kept saying in my head at that moment. "God is so good."

There were many highs and lows in the healing process. It took over a year for us to get to a good place, but we did it. We rebuilt our relationship into something stronger than ever before. I thanked God, and Kevin, on a regular basis for this lesson in unconditional love and forgiveness.

In 2008, we decided to grow our family. I got pregnant shortly after setting that intention – we had our first son in March 2009. We had our second son in December 2010. I could not have been happier. Or so I thought.

"Dr. Clay, I had two healthy boys, a loving husband, and a great six-figure job that made a difference in the world. What more could a woman ask for, right? I was so confused about why I was depressed because I appeared to have all the things I wanted. But now, I'm starting to see the negative thought patterns that continued throughout my life that likely got me back to this low place. And I see the importance of continuing some type of daily spiritual practice, no matter how good I feel. Thank you so much for listening."

"You're welcome. You're doing great. I'll see you next week."

I was sincerely grateful for Dr. Clay. Having someone help me wade through the trials and tribulations of my life and identify the patterns that I could not pick up on myself was invaluable. After a few more weeks of counseling, and all of that reflecting on all of my major life experiences, the true problem started to reveal itself to me. It was not at all what I thought.

I realized I was pushing myself incredibly hard to be what I thought was 'perfect' in all areas of my life, but I wasn't allowing any time to take care of myself. Because of the guilt I harbored from my past mistake in my marriage, I pushed myself to be a 'perfect' mom and 'perfect' wife. I rarely took a break to do something just for me. Actually, I would feel guilty if I did do something so I opted to set that desire aside to avoid the pain I envisioned would be the inevitable result. At work, I pushed myself to give my all, which meant working after I got home and on weekends to stay 'ahead of the game.' I had also stopped meditation and any other daily spiritual practices because I was 'too busy.' *Too busy to spend time with God?*

> "A sense of separation from God is the only lack you really need correct."
> ~A Course in Miracles

I overestimated how well I was doing. I had not yet transformed my habitual thinking patterns that caused me to feel guilty and stressed about life. I had many 'shoulds' and 'shouldn'ts' that were running my life – *you should be a better mother, you should do more with your husband, you shouldn't ask for time off, you should be making more money,* and the list goes on. Through the continued counseling, I was able to begin the process of shifting those negative thought patterns, and create affirmations in their place that were empowering for me. Despite that progress, I still had a lot more work to do.

This time I was adamant about developing *and maintaining* my spiritual practice. I was also ready to clear anything from my life, and my mind, that was not in alignment with God. I was willing to let go of everything that was not contributing to my peace of mind. Once I set the intention to get serious about my spiritual practice, everything started unfolding at an unbelievably rapid pace.

Chapter 3

Seeing the Light

I was at home on medical leave, lying in bed wondering what to do next. I had an intense desire to grow spiritually, and continue to learn how to reverse my old thought patterns. I did not want to find myself in this depressed state again. The counseling was a good start, but there was more work I needed to do to release the years of resentments, blame, shame, fear, doubt, worry, and more that were built up within me.

I wasn't sure where to start. All of the sudden, I experienced a ringing in my ear, like an inner bullhorn. I heard a call from deep within beckoning, "Go on a retreat." The first things to come to mind were all the excuses why I couldn't possibly go on a retreat. *I have too much to do... I don't want to leave Kevin with the boys by himself... I don't know where to go... I need to save money.* As my thoughts settled, the inner call rumbled again – this time much louder: GO ON A RETREAT, KANDACE!

I began to search online for a retreat center nearby. It did not take long for me to stumble upon the Yogaville[1] ashram. I read the description on the Web site about personal retreats, and it sounded *exactly* like what I needed.

Customize your Personal Yoga Retreat. Reduce stress. Take time to relax. Create an oasis from the hustle and bustle of your daily life and wrap yourself in the timeless teachings of Yoga, the peaceful atmosphere of the Ashram and the daily schedule of Yoga practices to help you recharge. Perhaps you would like time to honor yourself, to ask and contemplate "What is really important to me? What steps can I take in order to gain inner peace, balance and harmony? How can I lead a joyful and useful life?"

At Yogaville we offer a quiet place in a rural setting to personalize your retreat experience. Immerse yourself in daily Yoga and meditation and meet with a mentor to help you make the best use of this time. Or you can practice silence, rest and take walks in the peaceful countryside.

Join us for a profound opportunity to deepen your spiritual journey with an individually designed retreat. Take time to go within. Be nurtured by the beauty of nature. Meditate at our sacred spaces. A personal retreat offers: Private accommodations in our guest houses, three vegetarian meals daily, three group meditation sessions daily, two Hatha Yoga classes daily, scripture study, and personal spiritual mentoring by a monastic or minister.

The prices were reasonable and the accommodations looked lovely. To top it off, it was only a three-hour bus ride from DC. I was sold! I just had to convince Kevin. I thought about all the years we had been together (eight at this point), and how I had *never once* taken a vacation by myself. I had done 'girls' night' and gone away with girlfriends for a weekend, but had not even taken a day trip alone to sit in quiet contemplation. I wasn't sure how he was going to respond to me being away for a few days and being with the boys by himself.

The inner debate didn't last too long. The earlier inner call sparked something in me; something that knew this retreat was exactly what I was supposed to do, exactly when and where I was supposed to do it. Deep within, I *knew* something was about to happen, and I was certainly ready for it. I was tired of the stress, depression, and anxiety. I wanted relief! I wanted to smile genuinely, laugh wholeheartedly, and love fully again. So, while I had the courage, I went ahead and called Kevin at work.

"Hey, hon!"

"Hey, sweetie! How are you feeling today? Have you been getting some rest?" He was always so empathetic. I appreciated his genuine concern for my well-being.

"I'm doing okay. Taking it one day at a time, you know? I'm excited though because I found a retreat center that looks like *exactly* what I need right now. It's right in Virginia."

"Oh yeah?" he replied with his signature inquisitive, but reserved tone.

"Yes, honey! It has been hard for me to admit for a long time, but I really need a break. I have been going at too fast of a pace for too long... trying to be superwoman or something. I am exhausted, and need some time to regroup. I won't be gone for too long, and I'll go mid-week so that all you have to worry about is the morning and evening routines versus taking care of the boys all day on the weekend by yourself."

"Whatever you need, sweetie. I just want you to get better." He sounded so concerned. I could feel his love embracing me through the phone.

"Thank you so much! I'll take the bus down early on Tuesday morning and come back late Thursday night."

I let out an enormous sigh of relief while putting the phone down, and then burst into tears. Tears of gratitude. Tears of relief. Tears of joy. Finally, after too many years of going at warp speed, I was giving myself the chance to slow down. No checking work e-mails, no conference calls, no chores to do, no conversations to have, no children to take care of... just me focusing on healing. I was beside myself.

I had my appointment with Dr. Clay that day and let her know that I would miss our next session because of the retreat. She was pleased to hear I was taking a break and thought it would be beneficial for the healing process. I was looking forward to it and couldn't wait to share good news upon my return: News of a renewed mind, body, and spirit, and a new sense of freedom and purpose. That's what I was praying for.

It was a cold January morning. I was bundled up in a comfortable sweat suit, scarf, sneakers, and a thick, winter coat.

I was on the bus heading to Yogaville with the latest issue of *Yoga Journal*[2] magazine in one hand and my journal in the other. The retreat had officially begun.

What better way to start my retreat than by clearing the mind? I thought to myself. I started with making lists. Thoughts were swirling around my head so fast; I thought it would be useful to spend some time getting them out on paper in some kind of organized fashion. The first list I made was one of ideas I had for education consulting. The thought of transitioning to consulting and working from home had crossed my mind multiple times over the prior year. The brainstorming session felt good, but I wasn't excited about any of the ideas that emerged so I quickly moved on to the next thing that crossed my mind.

A list of all the symptoms I was experiencing began flowing from my pen as steadily and freely as a waterfall. *Lack of focus, generally in a bad mood/irritable, don't feel like dealing with people, disorganization, memory loss/forgetfulness, dizziness, headaches, exhaustion, pressure, lack of sex drive, hopelessness in dealing with my 2 year old, overly concerned with others' opinions of me, can't think clearly, indecisive, want to be alone, at my breaking point, emotional, lack of ability to rest, negative thoughts, always rushing, pacing, anxiety, trying to control everything, drained, and my body feels heavy.*

Then, I made a list of the stresses in each area of my life where I felt pressure:

- **Job:** Back-to-back meetings, responding to constant needs of team, open workspace, lack of ability to focus and get work accomplished, missed deadlines/excuses, being fake (knowing that a large layoff is coming, but putting on a happy face for my team), quick transition from one job to the next with inadequate time to relax in between.
- **Home:** Living out of boxes/bags, home closing process, taking care of two little ones while feeling completely stressed, 'Terrible twos,' little to no alone time, always

rushing, no quality time with Kevin, and lack of energy to engage fully.

- **Finances:** Feel pressured/trapped by my large salary (like I can't transition or do something different because the family depends on it), daycare expenses, making good money and still being near broke at the end of each month, and the responsibility for paying the bills each month (although we split the bills, the physical act of paying each of the individual bills was stressing me out, as not all of them were on 'auto-pay').
- **Health:** Changes in my body post-pregnancy, lack of exercise, dependency on caffeine, no time to take care of personal health (making the time for doctor visits, etc.), constant snacking, post-pneumonia lung/breathing challenges, panic attacks.

Looking over that list made me feel even more depressed, but it was helpful to see it all written out. I knew it would help me speak about what was going on with the spiritual teachers at the ashram.

When obstructive thoughts arise, practice opposite thought. This was the first quote I saw when I opened up the issue of *Yoga Journal* I had brought on the journey. The article went on to say, "Adopt an attitude of loving kindness to yourself." I felt this issue had been handcrafted for me to read at that very moment. I settled deeper into my chair, making myself more comfortable and receptive to what I was about to read.

I paused when I came to a question posed by one of the columnists: *What will your life look like in 10 years?* This question helped me reconnect with the idea that I can *create* my future, which I hadn't thought much about lately. *What happened to that part of me? That part that used to create vision boards, develop five-year action plans for my life, and be proactive in managing all that came my way.* I was so wrapped up in motherhood, and what I viewed as my present career success, that I didn't make the time to continue visioning about the future. I immediately got back into what I call "ideation mode" and started dreaming about what I desired my life to look like. I made yet another list, one that I made a mental note to turn into pictures before I returned home. I wanted to return with a visual representation of my desired state.

I started with our ages: In 10 years, Kevin would be 52, I would be 42, my oldest son would be 13, and my youngest would be 11. I began thinking about what an ideal state would be. *Daily morning meditation as a family, yoga practice as a family, debt free, entrepreneur, own a cabin retreat, maintaining connections with family and friends, four weeks of vacation/year (absolute minimum, but likely more due to entrepreneurial flexibility), regular retreats (3 times/year), new year meditation tradition, family service projects, prison ministry, and teach yoga/meditation to youth.*

I kept reading the magazine and came across an article that discussed the idea of attachment. The article pointed out that attachment to things of the world will always bring about some form of pain because nothing in the world is constant. The only constant is the Infinite Power – God. It reminded me of the Bible verse I had heard over and over in church throughout my life, "Do not conform to the pattern of this world, but be transformed by the renewing of your mind (Romans 12:2)."

The article and Bible verse were both good reminders. This was something I had never actively tried to do. I understood it intellectually, but was I living it? Not even close. My whole life, goals, desires... *everything*, was predicated on success and happiness in the world. *What are my attachments? What if I did fully release my attachments to the world? What if I solely focused on renewing my mind? What would that be like?*

I hesitated to make the list at first. I pushed through the resistance of my mind and made a list of as many attachments and bad habits that I could think of. I wasn't sure why I felt guided to write a list of the bad habits as well. When I looked over the two lists, it was clear that my bad habits were driven by my attachments to how the world perceived me.

- **Attachments:** Attention, recognition, successful career, looking good in the eyes of others, a high salary, being the perfect wife, my children being well-behaved, dressing nice, material things, my outer appearance.
- **Bad Habits:** White lies, pretending, inauthenticity, too busy, disconnected, isolation, yelling at my oldest son, spanking my oldest son when anger rises, consumed with work/career success.

The connection between my bad habits and attachments was unmistakable. After going through this exercise, I had no doubt that I needed to release my attachments. I wasn't sure how to do it, but I had the sense that this retreat was the first step in doing so. I felt a little lighter, even after simply acknowledging what I was attached to. Baby steps.

I arrived at the ashram around 1 pm with plenty of time to participate in some of the yoga and meditation sessions offered. The driver took me to a beautiful viewpoint on the property that overlooked the river. We got out the car, and I took in the magnificence of the surroundings. After taking a few photos, I stood there feeling the wind brush lightly against my face – the only part of me that was exposed to the winter air. I could have stayed there for hours, but we had to make our way to the main campus.

As I turned the doorknob and stepped inside the Guest Services reception area, a sense of calm and relief came over me.

I knew this was exactly where I was supposed to be. Following the lead demonstrated by the rows of shoes on the floor, I took off my sneakers and placed them alongside another pair. There was no one at the desk, so I rang the bell and patiently waited for assistance. I glanced around at the fliers and information on the wall about yoga classes, retreats, massage therapy, Ayurvedic counseling, Reiki sessions, and more.

The woman who came out to greet me was pleasant. She gave me my room key and registration packet with the following note on it: *Welcome Kandace! Please rest – then come to Guest Services to check in around 3pm (+/-). We look forward to meeting you! Om.* They prepared a map for me and had highlighted and labeled different areas of the property in relation to my room in the Lotus Guest House. What a warm welcome.

I arrived to my room and noticed the placard on the door: *Upon entering, kindly remove shoes and place near the door. Thank you.* I thought about how much I liked the idea of removing shoes prior to entering one's space. *Maybe we should consider that at home?*

When I opened the door, I was pleasantly surprised by the room. I was expecting it to be more dorm-like, but it was much more modern. While unpacking my things, I paused when I pulled out the books I had brought with me for the trip. I really hadn't been reading many spiritual books over the past few years, and all the ones I had were packed away in boxes. I had been reading books about education reform and other career-related success books and magazines. Thankfully, my cousin studied philosophy and religion in college, and had a large collection of books. While staying at his house, I pulled out the book *Radical: Taking Back Your Faith from the American Dream*,[3] by David Pratt and started flipping through it. I knew I had been drawn to it for a reason when I realized it was about giving up attachments to the things of the world.

The other book I brought along with me was *Siddhartha*,[4] by

Hermann Hesse, which I had read once in the past. *Siddhartha* is a beautiful story that details the spiritual journey to enlightenment of a young man living in India during the time of the Buddha. As I held the book in my hand, I reminisced on the first time I read it during our vacation in Laos years ago. It was an amazing experience to read passages from the book then go spend time in the elaborate temples. I remembered Siddhartha releasing his attachment to all things of the world. I was beginning to sense a theme to this trip.

I finished unpacking and plopped on the bed to do nothing for a bit (which didn't last too long; my mind was too busy for me to relax). I picked up the *Integral Yoga* magazine that was provided at check-in to read more about the ashram. I was intrigued by the bio of Sri Swami Satchidananda, the Guru who founded Yogaville. Satchidananda also founded the Light of the Truth Universal Shrine[5] (LOTUS), which was built at the ashram in 1986. LOTUS, a shrine open to people of all faiths to meditate and pray, is the first shrine ever built that features altars for every major faith as well as lesser known spiritual traditions. I couldn't wait to visit and meditate at LOTUS. I thought it was marvelous that this shrine had been built to honor all religious paths as it reflected my respect for all paths.

> "Truth is one.
> Paths are Many."
> ~Sri Swami Satchidananda

One of the ashram books on the nightstand started calling to me: *Yoga Sutras of Patanjali*[6] by Sri Swami Satchidananda. I opened the book to Chapter 3 and read, "You are not bound by the outside world. There's nothing wrong with the world. You can make it heaven or hell according to your approach... If you have controlled the mind, you have controlled everything. There is nothing in this world to bind you." These powerful words reminded me of the Course, a book that I hadn't cracked open since Kevin and I were going through the healing of our marriage. *Maybe I should revisit the Course,* I thought to myself. I knew it worked because of the amazing transformation experienced in our marriage, and I was looking forward to applying it to my present condition.

As it approached 3 pm, I set my books down and made my way to Guest Services. I walked slowly and took in the peace of the environment. It appeared as though all whose eyes met mine, met them with Love. No one was rushing. Everyone seemed to be fully present and resting in the peace of God. I wanted that.

"You must be Kandace! It's so nice to see you!" I looked at the desk; there was an older woman, maybe in her seventies, standing behind it. She had a cheerful demeanor that instantly reminded me of my grandmother. The thought of my grandmother brought a smile to my face. She introduced herself, but I didn't quite catch the name. I didn't even think to ask again because I was so overwhelmed with emotion. Being in her presence did something to me at a physiological level. I could feel myself being pulled into peace.

"So, tell me, what brings you to Yogaville, dear?"

"I am so stressed. I have a stressful job, and my life is going at such a fast pace that I can't keep up. I just needed a break to regroup and get myself together."

Without hesitation and still maintaining the peaceful smile that seemed to be molded on her face, she replied, "Stress is a matter of perception. Your situation is not stressful – it's how you perceive it... If you can do something about it, do it. If not, let it go... You are going to have a wonderful time here! Participate in as much or as little of the ashram activities that you prefer. You may also wish to do a silent retreat... that's okay too. Everything is okay."

"Thank you so much. I really needed to hear that."

"There is a scripture study class tomorrow night that you might be interested in. You are welcome to join. This evening, yoga class is at 5 pm, and dinner begins at six. Feel free to come to Guest Services if you need anything at all. We are here to support your stay here."

When I got back to the room, I looked up her name – Swami Gurucharanananda (no wonder my Western mind couldn't quite catch it the first time). Lovingly referred to as "Mataji," she is a senior monk-disciple of Sri Swami Satchidananda. According to the Integral Yoga program guide: *"She is one of the most popular teachers at Yogaville and abroad, leading guided meditations, Hatha Yoga classes, and teaching meditation workshops. She is also a beloved mentor/counselor to retreatants and guests. Mataji serves in many other capacities: She enjoys waking you up gently with her lovely violin music, she reads from Sri Gurudev's talks and teachings during lunch, and gives a joy-filled smile to everyone!"* I really liked her. Being in her presence brought me a peace that I was still trying to find words to express. I hoped to get to spend more time with her during my stay.

As I walked into the Restorative Yoga class, I was immediately thankful for being there. The atmosphere in the room was calm. The lights were dim, candles were lit, and there was light music playing to set the mood. The instructor gently welcomed everyone, pointed them toward a desirable location, and ensured they had all of the equipment necessary for the class (e.g. blocks, blanket).

I hadn't taken a Restorative Yoga class before, so I had little idea of what to expect. I did know that it was supposed to be relaxing and comfortable, which was exactly what I needed. Class began with some breathing exercises, which put me in a more present and tranquil state. Soon, all thoughts of the stresses of my life back in DC were in the background.

As I walked back to my room after class, I was in awe of how peaceful I felt. I didn't want to analyze it too much, as I didn't want old thoughts to creep back in. Instead, I took in everything around me. I focused on each step I took on the ground, each breath I released into the air, each person walking by. It was exhilarating! *Is it really possible that after less than a full day here, I feel this peaceful?*

Dinner was incredible. All of the food was locally grown, organic, vegan, and delicious. I decided not to sit at the 'silent' table at dinner the first night – I was open to meeting some of the other visitors. I sat at a table with a group of 'twenty-somethings,' all of whom were in the yoga teacher training program. They were immersing themselves not only in Hatha Yoga, but in many other yoga paths to develop mind, body and spirit. They had all left stressful situations back home to return to peace, and bring what they have learned back with them.

The conversation at the table piqued my interest enough to want to attend the interfaith scripture class. I walked in late, but just in time for the discussion. The scripture they focused on highlighted living a virtuous life. The class discussed what that meant, and what tends to get in our way of doing so. I remained fairly quiet during the discussion until we got to the topic of attachments. The teacher was discussing the importance of us releasing our attachment to all things – including our loved ones. At first I thought, *This woman is being ridiculous… I'm not giving up my attachment to Kevin and the boys.* Caught red-handed in my thought, she called on me to share. *Can this woman read minds?*

I shared about how stressed I was and the challenges I was having with my 2-year-old son's behavior in particular. I didn't understand how giving up my attachment to him could help me. I felt like I needed to be attached to the idea of helping him get better, and being a 'good mother' to him.

When I finished releasing my frustrations, she compassion-ately guided me to view the situation from another perspective. She asked, "What if you could not be attached to the idea of things being different than they are, and just be present and virtuous in the moment?" She left the question dangling, so I could allow it to sink in as she moved on to other students.

I went back to the room around 8:30 pm and was in bed by nine. I set my alarm for 4:30 am so that I could shower and head to meditation at five. I didn't know about getting up that early every day, but I was willing to give it a shot for the duration of the retreat at least. As I laid my head on the pillow the question asked of me earlier that evening popped up in my mind. *What if I could just be totally unattached to changing my circumstances and just be fully present and loving in each moment? Wouldn't that be something?! How do I do that?*

It had been years since I meditated, so I was glad that the first sitting of the day was a guided one. I grabbed a pillow and made my way to a spot that was not too close to the door, yet not too close to the front. I wanted to blend in. All I kept thinking before the session started was, *"Please* don't let me fall asleep."

The session lasted for one hour and consisted of chanting, breathing exercises, and silent meditation. The session ended with a brief audio of Sri Swami Satchidananda. Although my mind was not yet totally clear, the experience was beautiful. I noticed the thoughts were less invasive when I was engaged in the breathing exercises.

As I made my way to the morning Hatha Yoga class, I contem-plated making conscious breathing a daily part of my meditation. The yoga instructor was wonderful, and came over to me a few times to gently adjust my posture. I was grateful for her attention to detail, and the way she thoroughly explained each pose and what it was good for. The class ended with a meditation that took me even deeper than I was able to go in the early morning session. This gave me more motivation to keep going with my meditation practice, as my thoughts were becoming less and less of a distraction.

I felt an inner urge to spend the remainder of the retreat in silence, and so I did. During mealtimes, I sat at the 'silent' table, where I could no longer hide from the thoughts that were percolating in my mind. I sat and observed them. I didn't write about them. I didn't judge them. I didn't analyze them. I just allowed them to move through my mind without engaging them. It was a powerful lesson from the Spirit that I didn't understand the depth of at that time.

After breakfast, I had a three-and-a-half hour break to relax before Noon meditation at LOTUS. It was unseasonably warm (55 degrees at the end of January!), and I took that as an opportunity to spend some time in nature. I was told that the walk to the LOTUS shrine was about 20 minutes. I figured I would leave around 10:30 am so that I could enjoy some time outside. I was also looking forward to exploring the altars dedicated to various faiths.

After being in meditation and near silence for a day, I took a walk in nature that I will never forget. I had an incredible sense of calm about me. I walked slowly, soaking in the pure beauty of the trees, waterfalls, rocks, and the sounds of the crickets and other animals. I felt more alive than I had felt in a long time.

There was something incredibly powerful that I received from that time in the woods. Never had I walked that slowly in my entire life. I never knew slowing down could facilitate my return to happiness. I always thought I had to keep achieving, keep progressing. And now, in the stillness, with no makeup or business attire, and no fancy meetings to attend, I was completely content.

As I arrived at a lookout point, I could see the peak of LOTUS in the distance. It was one of the most beautiful places I had seen in a while. I sat on the small bench in front of me and meditated on its splendor. I could not believe that something this breathtaking had been right in my backyard all these years. I began to quicken my pace so that I could get closer to its radiance.

Tears welled up in my eyes as I got closer and closer. I could feel that this was a turning point for me. I couldn't grasp what was happening, but I could feel changes taking place within the deepest part of my being. I had been walking so slowly, taking in each and every tree and stone along the path that I arrived *just* after meditation had begun. I was unable to go in. I normally would have been frustrated, but I felt nothing at all. That rise of adrenaline that normally came rushing through my chest when I was running late was nowhere to be found. I was completely calm, and felt like whatever I did with the extra time was meant to be.

I decided to go into the interfaith room while I waited for the meditation room to clear and began writing down some of my favorite quotes from each faith. They were good reminders to me of the beauty that lies in all spiritual traditions. While many stand firm in their belief that their spiritual path is the 'right' or 'only' way, I truly believe there is one Truth that runs through them all. The tagline for the shrine is "Truth is one, paths are many" – indeed.

We are on a market trip on Earth, whether we fill our baskets or not, once the time is up, we go home.
~Ibo, Nigeria

Be thankful, be united, and love one another.
~Seneca Tribe

Faith is like a sacred fire; pass it from generation to generation without extinguishing it.
~Konko Daijin, Shinto

Do not judge your neighbor until you walk two moons in his moccasins.
~Cheyenne Tribe

As the mind, so the man; bondage or liberation are in your own mind.
~Sanskrit

After writing these down, I spontaneously wrote: *Be sure you care more for peace than things. If you don't have peace, nothing is going to make you happy. God longs to give you so much more than you have ever thought to ask for.* I didn't know where it came from, but I knew it was true.

After 30 minutes of absorbing the ancient wisdom displayed at the shrine, I noticed the meditation room was clearing out. I was grateful to be able to visit the room while it was empty. It was absolutely incredible. There were quotes about 'light' from each religion/spiritual path placed on wooden tablets around a circular room, and each display had a beam of light that met at the top of the room as one. The energy in that room was like no other – I could feel it radiate through every part of me. I reflected on how people from all faiths would pray and/or meditate there daily, together, in the way that worked best for them. *There should be more places like this all over the world. We are one,* I thought. The vibration of energy in the room was so comforting, I didn't want to leave. It was like a warm bath – soothing, calming and cleansing to my soul.

The remainder of the retreat seemed to fly by. I was consistent with the meditation and yoga practices, and spent most of the day in silent reflection and contemplation. An ocean of tears streamed from me, dissolving one of the many emotional layers I had built up between me and my true Self – the Self that God created.

Surprisingly, I was not sad about leaving. I had received so much, and was ready to return to my family in a peaceful state. On the three-hour bus ride home, I read one of the books I purchased from the Yogaville bookstore, *Meditation for Children: Pathways to Happiness, Harmony, Creativity, and Fun for the Family,*[7] by Deborah Rozman. I figured it would give me some practical tips that I could use to bring what I had connected with over the past few days back to my family.

I was stunned to find that the first two chapters of the book were like a mini-review of all that I had learned about meditation, the mind, ego, projecting thoughts onto others, and more. It was exactly what I needed to read before entering back into 'the world.' I had to put the book down to look out the window many times – I could not believe how perfect the timing of all of this was. I just sat and allowed the words I was reading to penetrate my soul.

> *Things outside neither bond nor liberate you; only your attitude toward them does that.*
>
> *If you control your mind, you have controlled everything.*
>
> *A fish cannot know what water is because it is always in it. Similarly, man does not know what the traps of the mind are because he's always caught in the mind.*
>
> *To know thyself is facing yourself as you are, not as society believes you ought to be... Getting rid of the ego is only destroying the false image of who we think we are so we can wake up to our true Identity.*
>
> *Meditation is developing your own hotline to the infinite.*

The last thing I wrote in my journal while on the bus was: I have mastered the pursuit of excellence, now it's time to master the pursuit of peace. I was ready to turn my focus from being successful in the world's eyes to being at peace, and being all that God created me to be.

As I pulled up to the bus station in DC, I remembered

something Mataji said to me at lunch on the final day when 'something' told me not to sit at the silent table: *When anything comes to you, first ask yourself, "Will I be maintaining my peace by getting this or will my peace be disturbed?" Always choose peace.* She spoke with such a quiet strength and conviction that the words leapt from her mouth and straight into my heart. *Always choose peace... Always choose peace...* my new mantra.

A Gift for You!

Click the following link to download a free Meditation 101 recording by Kandace to support your journey to unshakable peace! Keep shining!

www.kandacejones.com/meditation101

Chapter 4

A Vision from the Spirit

After the retreat, I started consistently doing the workbook and reading the text of the Course. I continued to wake up at 5:00 each morning to meditate and practice yoga. I also returned to counseling to help me continue to identify and release the old ways of thinking and being that were no longer serving me. Kevin noticed the difference immediately and wanted to know more about the retreat. I didn't know where to begin, and certainly didn't know when we would have enough time for me to share the richness and fullness of what I had just experienced. I figured the best thing I could do to share the experience with him was to *live* it. So, that became my primary goal.

A few weeks later, I serendipitously ran across advertisements for events being hosted by two spiritual teachers that I had learned from during the time of healing my marriage. I had become disconnected from their work during my period of stress. Marianne Williamson and Michael Bernard Beckwith were both holding workshops in DC, within one week of each other. They are based in California, and rarely come to DC. With them *both* coming precisely at the time I most needed to accelerate my spiritual practice, it gave me another clue that there was a Greater Hand involved in my healing process. Each teacher gave me the 'kick-in-the-spiritual-butt' that I needed.

First up was Marianne Williamson who spoke on the topic "Transforming Ourselves, Transforming Our World." Dynamic as always, she eloquently wove deep, spiritual teachings with relevant topics of today. She stressed the need to move away from "middle-class, self-help spirituality" where individuals become "awakened" and then do nothing to assist others or give back. She encouraged the audience to serve the healing of the world from a place of love and forgiveness. She reminded the audience of their true Identity as a "perfect idea in the mind of God" and encouraged us to view others that way. She referenced the Course several times, and even touched on one of my favorite quotes from it, "The presence of fear is a sure sign that you are trusting in your own strength."[1] Toward the end of the talk she reminded the audience of the four questions[2] (from the Course) that we can ask the Spirit as we begin our day: *What would You have me do? Where would You have me go? What would You have me say? And, to whom?* I sat there realizing that I had not asked those questions. I had been trying to run my life on my own. I hadn't cultivated a spiritual practice that allowed the flow of Divine guidance and required my surrender. I was focused on *doing* instead of *allowing*. Marianne's powerful talk stirred up some more of the spiritual teachings that laid dormant in my mind. I knew I was on the right path.

> "The presence of fear is a sure sign that you are trusting in your own strength."
> ~A Course in Miracles

During the Q&A session, I had a vision of myself on stage answering similar questions. I listened intently as she answered each question; somewhere deep inside I knew that I would be answering comparable ones in the future. I dismissed the idea as a meaningless fantasy, but continued taking notes.

When the session was over, I patiently waited in the book signing line while reflecting on the wisdom that had just been shared. I thought about what I would say to her, the woman whose books I was savoring when my marriage was at its lowest point. Her words transformed many old patterns of thinking and facilitated my internal switch from looking for what I was *getting* out of the relationship to focusing on what I was *giving* to the relationship. *What do you say to someone who unknowingly helped save your marriage?* I knew I needed to be short and sweet because they were trying to keep the line moving. No one was getting more than a couple minutes with her. Before I knew it, I was handing her my book.

"I can't thank you enough. Your words transformed me at the most difficult point in my marriage. They *truly* saved my marriage. You are such an inspiration," I said with composure. I was much more calm and collected than I thought I would be.

She looked me in my eyes for a bit then thanked me for reading. She looked up at me again with a look I still find hard to describe – it was like she *knew* something about me. "You are SO beautiful!" she said. "What do you do?"

"Wow! Thank you so much. YOU are so beautiful. Well, I work in education, but I really want to teach *this*."

She gave me a nod of approval as if to say, "Yes, that's exactly what you should be doing" and she wished me well. We took a picture together and I went on my way.

As I walked away, the comment that jumped out of my mouth sunk in. *Did I really just tell her I wanted to teach this? Where did that come from?* Up until this point, I hadn't thought about teaching this to anyone. Shoot, I hadn't even taught it to myself yet. All the excuses for why I couldn't be a teacher of God rose up in me, and eventually I pushed the idea out of my mind. *I get major butter-flies when speaking in front of large groups. I don't know enough of the Word. I have not lived a 'Holy' life. Why would anyone want to listen to me? I haven't mastered this yet.*

Michael Bernard Beckwith began the *Life Visioning* workshop with the same fire and energy that I remembered from attending

Agape years ago. "You're not living your life to GET something; you're living your life to LET something... let the Love of God flow through you!" He was not working his way up to the punch line – his words came out swinging. Ego could not stand a chance in the presence of his conviction. As I watched him I thought, "Man, I want to be *that* confident about God."

As if he had heard my soul's call, he began walking through the stages of the spiritual journey or "The Four Stages of Evolutionary Growth," which helped me to assess my progress along the path. I took notes like I was back in college and my grade depended on it. I was fully available to absorb all that was being shared.

Dr. Beckwith stressed that the four stages were by no means *all* of the stages of the spiritual journey, but a starting point to gaining access to the Mystery that surpasses what words can categorize. He also stressed that many individuals go back and forth between stages, and that the way in which they would categorize themselves may vary depending on the context (home, work, etc.).

- **Stage 1: Victim Consciousness**
  - Signs: Blame, frustration, anger, resentment, fear, doubt, worry
  - The belief that circumstances determine mood and actions
  - No consistent spiritual practice
  - A 'Why me?' mindset
  - In order to progress, need to replace blame and shame with forgiveness
- **Stage 2: Manifester Consciousness**
  - Signs: Intention setting, affirmation, law of attraction, creating your life, making it happen, vision boards
  - Spiritual practices: Affirmation and visualization
  - Feeling a sense of control over their life, and the circumstances

- ○ "I can use the law of manifestation to attract what I want in my life"
- ○ In order to progress to the next stage, need to surrender control, false sense of power, and the ego's agenda through daily spiritual practice
- **Stage 3: Channel Consciousness**
  - ○ Signs: Becoming available to the flow of the Infinite through you, make consciousness available to receive higher Wisdom
  - ○ Spiritual practices: Meditation, visioning, affirmative prayer
  - ○ "God expresses in, through, and as me" (Still, a lingering sense of separation from God remains)
- **Stage 4: Being Consciousness**
  - ○ Signs: A realization of oneness with God and all in existence
  - ○ Spiritual practices: In this consciousness of unbroken oneness with God, spiritual practices continue for the joy of it rather than out of necessity.
  - ○ From this point on the individual lives in the awareness of "I and my Father are One"

Due to shortage of time, Dr. Beckwith was moving quickly through the material (I highly recommend his book *Life Visioning: A Transformative Process for Activating Your Unique Gifts and Highest Potential*[3] to readers who are interested in exploring these stages further). During the break, I sat and looked at my notes and began assessing where I was on the spectrum. I realized that I was clearly in Stage 1 when I had the affair, but then moved to Stage 2 after that. I got very comfortable with the level of 'control' I thought I had on my life and the ways in which I was attracting goodness into my life. I didn't push myself to progress further. To be totally honest, I didn't even pay attention that there *was* more progress to make.

> "Spiritual practice cultivates the ability to think
> independent of circumstance."
> ~Michael Bernard Beckwith

I had slipped from Stage 2 to Stage 1 in my work and home life during the period just prior to the depression and anxiety setting in. I was blaming my emotions on work and my toddler's tantrums, and took no personal responsibility for my feelings. During the session, Dr. Beckwith said, "Spiritual practice cultivates the ability to think independent of circumstance" – something I was clearly not doing.

I've heard it said that, "When the student is ready, the teacher appears." This *Life Visioning* workshop came *right* at the time when I needed to cultivate the daily practices that would move me from trying to control my life to surrendering to God's plan for my life. I could see clearly that I was being trained in Stage 3 practices that would assist with this.

Immediately following the workshops, the teachers and learning opportunities were flowing my way faster than I could have imagined. The stirring that began at the retreat was intensified, and I dove deeply into the waters of spiritual wisdom. I began a seven-week spiritual boot camp called "Finding Freedom" and an eight-week "Living A Course in Miracles" class led by the Rev. Jennifer Hadley,[4] a joyful teacher of the Course. I simultaneously took a 12-week "Foundations for Spiritual Living" and an eight-week "Power of Your Word" course through the Centers for Spiritual Living.[5] These courses opened my eyes to universal spiritual laws, and the true essence behind scripture. I listened to every audio and read every book I could get my hands on by well-known teachers of the Course, and other spiritual teachers. I was learning so much and was bursting open with peace, love, joy, compassion, creativity, wisdom, and gratitude. I started to feel a yearning to share what I was learning, but didn't know how. *Maybe that comment I blurted out to Marianne Williamson wasn't so crazy. Maybe I **am** supposed to share this someday.*

∞

On March 25, 2012, I was in meditation and was using the *Life Visioning* technique I had learned in Dr. Beckwith's workshop. Up until that point, I had been mostly doing guided meditations, breathing techniques or using some form of meditation music. Dr. Beckwith encouraged us to sit in the silence after posing the following questions, among others, to the Spirit:

What is the highest vision for my life?
Who must I become to manifest that vision?

I sat and listened in silence for a little while, and the answer came pouring through me so fast I had to grab a pen. I could not believe what I was writing. I was being guided to share my life story and spiritual journey publicly. *Me? The one who spent her whole life concerned about looking good in the eyes of others?* Yes, me. A blog was the first thing that came to mind.

Shortly after, I had the overwhelming urge to listen to the song *Live in the Light*[6] by Fertile Ground, which I hadn't listened to in years. As I listened to the words, tears began to flow. I knew exactly what to name the blog: Living in the Light.[7] *Was this really happening? Was I hearing from the Spirit already?*

I didn't hesitate to follow the guidance. Later that day, I began creating the blog with the expectation that every step would be revealed to me along the way. That was indeed the case.

In the following months, I was guided through and experienced a series of life lessons that I applied all of my learning to and shared publicly. This was an intense period in which I gave my full attention toward living in alignment with God. I was clear that there could be no half-stepping this time. It was one thing to study and know about spiritual ideas, but what I hadn't done before was live it fully in every area of my life.

To me, "Living in the Light" meant that total non-judgment, compassion, forgiveness, honesty, unconditional love would have to replace all of my judgment, resentment, inauthenticity, doubt, fear, and any other habits that were not serving me (or those interacting with me for that matter). This also meant to live in perfect peace, to remember myself and others as reflections of God, to show compassion toward those who are not acting according to their innate Divinity, to express gratitude in each moment, to consistently extend forgiveness, to love unconditionally, to trust wholeheartedly in the Divine plan, to lean on spiritual understanding versus the thinking of the world, and to rest confidently in the Truth with no need to defend myself. I was not there yet, but it was my aspiration to be. I had a feeling that writing this blog would accelerate the process of living it fully.

Each time I had a new insight or increased level of awareness about a spiritual principle, I spontaneously wrote a new entry on the blog. None of the entries were pre-planned or calculated. I also shared openly about my struggles with the ego throughout that period. A couple months into my writing, I weaned off of counseling and continued to follow the guidance of the Spirit to facilitate the healing process. At the time, I could not even fathom the peace that this process would lead me to.

If someone had told me five years ago that I would be sharing intimate details about my life with the world via a blog, and ultimately a book, I would have told them they needed to go take their meds. Never in a million years would this have been what my ego-self would have chosen for my life. I am so grateful for this turn of events, even the depression and anxiety, because I now realize it can serve a Higher purpose. *All* of our life challenges can serve a Higher purpose if we allow them to.

Part II

Living in the Light

Note: The remainder of this book highlights the lessons learned along the journey to surrendering my identification with the ego (or, sense of an individual self that is separate from God), and the acceptance of the Self that God created. It describes the daily practices I used to reverse the thought patterns that led me into destructive behaviors. It is honest. It is intimate. And it is a reminder that no situation, circumstance, person, or dis-ease can keep us from the Love of God that resides within.

You will note that some of the spiritual principles I briefly introduced in the earlier chapters that describe the beginning of my healing journey are discussed again throughout the journal entries. The following Zen proverb sums up the reason for this: "To know and not to do is not yet to know." While I understood a lot of these spiritual truths intellectually, it was the act of applying them to real-life situations and learning to embody them that made all the difference in moving *From Stress to Peace*.

I encourage you to keep a journal handy to pause and reflect on how each lesson may apply to your life. Each chapter has within its pages the wisdom learned, the daily practices implemented, and the breakthroughs experienced along the way, which served as a sort of preparation process for the revelation that is unveiled in Chapter 11.

I have included a sampling of reflection/discussion questions at the back of the book. You can find more at

www.kandacejones.com/discussionguide.

I encourage you to read each chapter successively so that you, too, can apply the lessons and experience the life-changing and mind-blowing shift that the *Living in the Light* blog and, ultimately, this book was preparation for. My prayer is that, through sharing my story openly, others might find healing and return to the Peace of God. Savor. Reflect. Apply. Repeat.

Chapter 5

Breaking Old Habits

I n my opening post for the *Living in the Light* blog on Monday, March 26, 2012, I wrote the following thoughts of introduction and introspection, moving toward inner peace and God's love:

This blog is about my journey to finding and maintaining peace of mind. I know the road to true 'enlightenment' and 'non-attachment' to the world's view of happiness and success can be challenging, but I am willing to share my ups and downs publicly in hopes that it encourages even just one person to join me in "Living in the Light."

What do I mean when I say "Living in the Light?" I mean living a totally non-judgmental, authentic, loving, peaceful, forgiving and healthy life. I mean completely releasing negative thoughts that ultimately manifest themselves in physical disease in our bodies (like the pneumonia, depression, and anxiety that I have experienced over the past six months). I mean giving the ego the boot. I mean loving all people unconditionally. I mean completely surrendering to allow God's Love to shine through all the dark corners of ourselves. That's a radically different life than what's promoted on TV, social media, etc., so we have to support each other in staying focused on the path. Ultimately, my prayer is that individuals sharing real-life examples of Living in the Light and finding true peace will become the norm. It can be done. It WILL be done. Keep shining!

What follows in this chapter through Chapter 10 are the primary lessons I learned and shared on the journey to inner peace. They were the primers for the awe-inspiring direct encounters with the Divine that are described in Chapter 11 and beyond. Enjoy and keep shining!

The Opposite of Complaining is Gratitude – March 27, 2012

After my personal retreat, I went deep into meditation, spiritual readings, audiobooks, therapy, and anything else I could find that would help me stay focused. One of the things I couldn't shake was the negative thoughts I was having about people or situations in my life that I wasn't happy with. And then I watched a sermon online by Dr. Beckwith that was live streamed from the Agape International Spiritual Center. He said something that slapped me in the face: *The opposite of complaining is gratitude.* He went on to say that, before you go to bed each night, you should (1) forgive yourself for anything that *you* said or did that may not have been aligned with who you know you really are (the image and likeness of God); (2) forgive others for anything *they* said or did that may not have been aligned to who you know they really are (the image and likeness of God); (3) name as many things as possible that you are grateful for; and (4) pray for God to show you what your next move should be.

It sounds so simple and it was not new news to me, but I had to check myself on how often I actually practiced that on a daily basis. I asked myself, *Do my thoughts about what I am grateful for outweigh the thoughts I have about what I don't like or want to change? Do I go to bed forgiving everyone who has frustrated me? Do I go to bed forgiving myself for the things I didn't complete? Do I go to bed forgiving myself for the areas where I made mistakes?* Absolutely not.

I started to think about how many years I have gone to bed with 'stuff' on my mind that I should have released. I had gotten better at forgiving others, and my husband and I made a pact to never go to bed upset with each other, but what about myself? That's where I was messing up. I was holding myself to a standard that was impossible to meet. I wanted to give more at work, and not get so frustrated with my 3 year old, and save more money, and volunteer in the community more, and exercise more... and... and... and.

I have started to practice the process described above, and what a profound impact it makes! In addition, I got serious about practicing the lessons in the Course workbook daily. Prior to that time, I had been inconsistent in doing it, and picked it up whenever I remembered to do so. Doing it consistently has already transformed my thought patterns and connection to God in such a profound way. I have been smiling every day (sometimes at embarrassingly random times because I'm full of so much joy) and I know it's because I am thanking God on a regular basis for *all* things (having two hands, two feet, eyes, the ability to walk, two healthy boys, a home, etc.). I am even finding myself being grateful for the situations I don't like because I know, no matter what I see in front of me right now, they will work out and ultimately make me stronger. Nothing is too hard for God... nothing.

On this beautiful day, my 32nd birthday, I am grateful for so many things. I am not holding myself to impossible standards. I am not complaining about the small stuff because I know that God walks with me everywhere I go – I don't have to do it all by myself. Every day, I remind myself how blessed I am. When I get caught up or really frustrated with something, I am taking it to my meditation session, my yoga mat and pray about it. I do whatever I can do to change it, and then I let it be. Because of that, I have more Love and Light to give to everyone else which is the true reward.

Releasing Attachments – March 28, 2012

In order to stay on the path to *Living in the Light*, I knew there were going to be some things I would have to let go of. I spent some time, while on my personal retreat, writing down everything I was attached to in *any* way. During this exercise, I was reminded of the following quote by Buddha: *The root of all suffering is attachment.* As I looked down at the long list of things, stories, habits, thought patterns, outcomes, and dreams that I had listed on the page I felt anxiety rising in me again. On that sheet of paper laid my whole identity and vision for my life. I know the anxious feeling in my gut stemmed from not wanting to fully release my attachment to each of them. I started rationalizing why certain things were impossible *not* to be attached to. I immediately asked myself an important question: *Do you want peace of mind more than you want these things?*

I certainly can't say I have fully let go of my attachment to everything, but I am practicing releasing on an almost daily basis through daily prayer and meditation. The *awareness* that I'm attached has shifted my perspective in a major way on some of the items on my list. One of those items was my attachment to having well-behaved children (which I think is tied to my attachment to 'having it all together'). My son was going through 'terrible twos' and I was so embarrassed and frustrated when he would have tantrums in public. I knew it was a phase that kids went through, but it was incredibly annoying to me and made me feel like an inadequate parent. I was stressing myself trying to get him to act 'right' and I was getting tired of dealing with him. This in turn made him act out more to try to get my attention. I decided in that moment to release that attachment and replace it with the following affirmations. (Thanks to my therapist who reminded me to replace negative thoughts with affirmative ones. I was a little rusty on affirmation writing, but these definitely helped.):

I will ask for help when I need it.
I will enjoy life, regardless of the circumstances.
I will give my all in each moment, and release my attachment to the outcome.

One of the ashram members, who had lived at Yogaville for over 30 years, was listening as I shared some frustrations with her about what was going on in my life. She said something to me that I'll never forget: "Whatever has to come will come, and whatever will not come, will not come." Simple, but powerful. What use is worrying or doubting when you know it's all going to work out eventually? Has there been anything in my life that *didn't* turn out to be good for me even though it didn't live up to the outcome that I was attached to? No, definitely not.

This morning, I had an enlightening conversation with my husband. He is very attuned to energy and mentioned that he could literally feel the sense of calm in my body. It was a calm he hadn't felt in me since we met in Spain nine years ago. His observation reminded me of another attachment I had: the idea that living abroad would make me happier. Our time traveling the world together was *so* peaceful and I was convinced that it was impossible to live in America *and* have real peace of mind. I used to say all the time, "People in Spain [or insert whatever other country] know how to slow down and enjoy life."

We always talked about living abroad again and I envisioned that 'one day' we would get overseas and I would get to live my peaceful life. What I 'got' in that moment was that I don't have to go anywhere or get anything else in order to feel better – the peace and sense of calm I was seeking is my innate nature. I can tap into it through making time for contemplation, meditation, prayer, and just *being* with myself. Letting go of my attachments to my negative thought patterns can free my mind. Letting go is not based on anything outside of myself, but is based on my decision to take control of my peace in each moment. Wow. What an incredible shift. Now, I can consciously make decisions about next steps (even living abroad), but I will not be attached to how I think they will make me feel. Now THAT is *Living in the Light*!

What is it that you're attached to? Be honest with yourself. Being in the know? Being right? Perfection? Outcomes? Impressing people? Attention? Food? Looking good? Clothes? Negative thought patterns? The Internet? Social Media? Entertainment? Saving your happiness for later? Alcohol? Your attitude? Waking up late? Caffeine? Giving all of yourself to others and leaving none for yourself? I could go on and on, but you get the picture. Many, if not all of us, have some attachments that don't contribute to our well-being and can keep us distracted from really getting in touch with our True Nature. *Are you willing to release them in order to regain your peace of mind?* I know I am! Keep shining!

Straight, No Chaser... With Love – March 29, 2012

I had the pleasure of attending a seminar a couple weeks ago featuring one of my all-time favorite authors and spiritual teachers, Marianne Williamson. As always, she said SO many things that resonated with my desire to be more loving and peaceful in my daily life. There is one thing she said that day that has been replaying in my mind on a daily basis since the seminar:

Honesty without compassion is brutality.

I really needed to hear that. Some people have absolutely no problem telling the 'whole truth and nothing but the truth' at all times, but *delivery* is everything. I have always had a hard time with people who gloat about "keeping it real," but the way they tell their truth is totally unloving and judgmental. The word "brutality" really stuck with me because I have certainly been on the receiving end of that, and it makes my heart ache when I hear people speak rudely to others. My distaste for the way people do that has led me to the other extreme: holding my tongue in situations that could have used a loving, kind word of Truth from me.

I was always afraid of coming off as rude (or 'brutal') even though that was not my intention. This was something that had been a daily struggle for me. I held in my thoughts for so long about things I was unhappy with that I would start to blow up inside. The built-up frustration also made me feel like there was no compassionate way to share what I thought (because I was boiling hot by that point), so I decided to not say anything at all.

Bad idea. This decision to keep it all inside is what led me into depression, anxiety, pneumonia, and unrest in general.

Since becoming aware of this truth about my old self, I have tried to be lovingly honest as situations arise throughout my day (particularly with *myself*). This morning, for example, we woke up and got ready much later than normal. Since I've been working from home, I normally drop off my husband and the boys then come back home and start my day. I hadn't meditated yet, and I had a two-hour morning meeting that I needed to prep for. The old me might have told myself to "work it out" or lied to myself and said, "I'll meditate later," knowing full well I wouldn't. I then would have had an attitude with my husband and boys about being late, drop them off, and rush into my meeting with no preparation.

Instead, I paused for a moment and was lovingly honest with myself and thought, "You really need to meditate and pray before this meeting and busy day... you don't have to just suck it up and do everything... you don't have to be superwoman." I then asked Kevin if he would mind dropping off and picking up the boys today because I had a busy day and really needed to meditate before getting started. He was super supportive and added, "Always let me know what would be helpful to you." I love that man. All it took was me being completely honest about what I needed.

Another area where I had not always been compassionate and honest with myself and others is about how much I can take on and/or the time frame in which I can complete things. I would say "yes" to a new project or meeting a certain deadline knowing full well that it would mean staying up late, getting up early and working through lunch in order to make it happen. Now, I simply pause and ask myself, *What's a reasonable time frame for me to complete this?* I then respond to whoever is requesting something of me with what I can complete and by when. Sometimes, I have to say "no." I no longer feel bad about saying no to something I know I don't have time or the desire to do.

There are a few relationships (friends, family, coworkers) in which I had not been fully open about what I think. I didn't want to come off as critical or judgmental, and I definitely didn't want to make anyone feel bad. However, I am now feeling empowered to share my thoughts with compassion and love. I have been speaking up more and it has produced miraculous results and even closer bonds in a short period of time. I look forward to the conversations to come.

Where are you not being honest with others or yourself? Or, where are you being brutally honest in your relationships? Something to reflect on until next time. Keep shining!

P.S. One of my favorite jazz songs inspired the title of today's entry: *Straight, No Chaser*[1] by Miles Davis and John Coltrane. Take a listen when you have a moment. Enjoy!

Be A Rainbow in Someone Else's Cloud – March 30, 2012

> "Be a rainbow in someone else's cloud."
> ~Maya Angelou

I used to think that in order to continue to progress on my spiritual journey, I would have to release the 'negative people' in my life. I wanted to surround myself only with people who were positive and weren't going to bring my mood down. There have been a few messages that have come my way this week that have completely turned around my thinking in that area:

When people are gossiping or speaking negatively, that is your opportunity to be a light bearer in that situation.
~the Rev. Sylvia Sumter, Unity of Washington, DC

YOU are the representation of God in your life.
~Iyanla Vanzant

There is another way of looking at this.
~A Course in Miracles

I tried a new church on Sunday, Unity of Washington DC,[2] and it felt like the minister was speaking directly to me on this issue of whether to remove people from my life. Her sermon was titled "Be a Light Bearer." Then, during *Oprah's Lifeclass* on Monday, Iyanla Vanzant said, "YOU are the representation of God in your life." On Tuesday, my lesson in the Course was: "There is another way of looking at the world." The lesson's focus was on shifting one's perception of situations and saying in each difficult moment, "There is another way of looking at this." Okay, okay... I hear you, God.

> "If you are filled with light, with no dark corners, then your whole life will be radiant, as though a floodlight were filling you with light."
> ~Luke 11:36

In every situation I have a choice: Am I going to contribute to bringing Light or darkness in this situation? I have to make the conscious effort to *choose* Light. And, whenever I backslide, I must remember to forgive myself and try again. I know it will take some work, but eventually my way of being will be "Light" in all situations and relationships. Who *doesn't* want that?

Let's *Be a rainbow in someone else's cloud*[3] today and every day! Much Love and Light! Keep shining!

Just Do It! – April 2, 2012

I woke up this morning thinking about how good it feels to move from theory to practice. I logged into Facebook and the first thing I saw was this quote:

> *Your beliefs don't make you a better person, your behavior does.*
> *~Anonymous*

PRECISELY! I recently started a seven-week spiritual boot camp that's focused on helping individuals walk the talk. For many years, I sat in churches, visited spiritual communities, read tons of spiritual and self-help books, and still couldn't shake some of the negative thoughts I had about certain people or situations in my life. I really wanted to feel peaceful and be loving toward everyone, but it wasn't playing out like that in my life.

> "Be the change you wish to see in the world."
> ~Mahatma Gandhi

Last weekend, during the *Life Visioning* workshop I attended, Dr. Beckwith said, "Your a-ttention must be aligned with your in-tention... where are you focusing your attention?" That was an 'Aha!' moment for me. I was always good at developing project timelines and action plans for my work life, but didn't do the same regarding the qualities I wanted to nurture in myself. If I say my "in-tention" is to experience and give more love (or more peace, joy, harmony, etc.), but focus my "a-ttention" on listening to and spreading gossip, judging people, harboring unfor-giveness, and picking and choosing when I want to follow the 'Word,' then I'm being hypocritical and making it impossible to reach my goal. If I want my true desires to come to fruition, I have to align my thoughts and actions with that intention. Period.

How am I going to do that? By *being* what I say I want to have.

I know it will take serious discipline and practice to align *all* of my thoughts and actions with my desire to give and receive love, forgiveness, peace, patience, kindness, joy, harmony, compassion, empathy, and all the other spiritual qualities that are innate in us all. I am so excited about the boot camp and am going 'all in' this time. I know that it doesn't matter if I can quote scripture, spiritual text, excerpts from the speeches/writings of famous 'enlightened ones' (Jesus, Buddha, etc.), if I'm not working toward actually making it my way of being. I am prepared to forgive myself along the way anytime I slip. Using tips from the Rev. Jennifer Hadley's spiritual boot camp, I created a spreadsheet to track my progress, and hold myself accountable for completing my daily spiritual practices until it becomes habit. As I once saw in a sports advertisement, "You play like you practice."

Research has proven that it takes between 21–28 days to create a habit. What habit do you want to create in your life over the next month or so? To download your free, customizable, From Stress to Peace 21-day Challenge[4] spiritual practice tracking sheet, go to:

http://www. kandacejones.com/spiritualpractice.

Love is Always the Answer – April 4, 2012

On the 44th anniversary of the assassination of Martin Luther King, Jr. (April 4, 1968), I am renewing my commitment to *Living in the Light*. I saw a video titled *Iranians We Love U: A Message to Iran from Israel* that went viral this morning and I teared up. The people in the video were iterating that, while their leadership may be promoting hate and fear, they had nothing but love in their hearts. It was so moving. This is the type of love that can drive away hate, as Martin Luther King, Jr. so poignantly stated in the following quote:

Darkness cannot drive out darkness; only light can do that.
Hate cannot drive out hate; only love can do that.
~Martin Luther King, Jr. (From the book "Strength to Love")[5]

I have found in my life, especially recently, that love is *always* the answer. No matter what situation I find myself in, when I choose love (or compassion, forgiveness, etc.) instead of hate, I feel a sense of peace and joy that I know would not have come by choosing hate. There can be so much pressure from society to retaliate when someone offends or hurts us; but when we choose love and forgiveness instead, we free *ourselves*. We free our hearts and minds from any resentment, bitterness, or hate so that we can give and receive more love. *I know I have not been perfect in my actions, so who am I to hold others accountable when they are not perfect in their actions? When I make a mistake, I want others to forgive me, so why would I deny them of the same unconditional love I am seeking?*

This is easier to put into action with the minor day-to-day situations that come up in life, so my challenge to myself now is to forgive and love *all* people unconditionally – no matter what they did. I am no better than anyone else. We are *all* God's children and have equal potential.

Something that has been on my heart for a while is working with youth in the juvenile justice system. I'm excited to start volunteering at a local youth detention center that houses young men and women that are involved with the system. We are *not* our mistakes. I want them to know that, no matter what they did, they are forgiven, and can go on to have the life they choose to. The same goes for all of us. Keep shining!

Let's Get Social!

For daily inspirational messages as you read, visit the Living in the Light Facebook page at www.face book.com/livinginthelight, and connect with me on Twitter @coachkandace or Instagram @iamlivinginthelight. Share your 'Aha!' moments as you read using the hashtag #stresstopeace. Leave a comment or question on the Facebook page anytime. I will monitor these, and will respond to as many as possible! Keep shining!

Chapter 6

Walking the Talk

Jesus: The Way-shower – April 6, 2012

I have heard, "The Kingdom of God is within you (Luke 17:21)," over and over throughout my years, but it is resonating with me on a whole different level as I go through this transformation and healing process. As I reflect on this Good Friday, I am reading a book by Eric Butterworth, *Discover the Power Within You*.[1] In it he states:

> *[Easter] is not just a day when we recall how Jesus rose from the dead. It is a time to take a new look at ourselves and contemplate the Divinity within us, the depths of our own innate God-potential. It is a time to reappraise the principle that makes all overcoming possible... We downgrade Jesus and the Great Demonstration when we think of Easter 'happening' as a miracle of God instead of the revelation of the depth-potential of man.*
> *~Eric Butterworth*

Jesus was a true Way shower when it comes to self-mastery and total oneness with God. Another recent favorite verse of mine is John 14:12, which states: "He that believeth in me, the works that I do he shall do also; and greater works than these shall he do." In other words:

> *If you have faith in the God-potential locked within man as I have faith in the power within Me, then you can do all I have done and more... because I have made this great discovery.*
> *~Eric Butterworth*

I am excited this Easter, not because I have a cute outfit to wear to church (which I spent way too much time shopping for in the past) or because I got an Easter basket with bunnies for my boys to open, but because I finally 'get it.' I have that same power... the power to heal... the power to love unconditionally... the power to activate the Christ-potential that is already within me. For that, I am grateful. For that, I will celebrate this day and EVERY day. I don't believe Jesus wanted to be worshipped as the great 'exception,' but rather celebrated as a Way shower. To 'follow' Jesus means to know, unwaveringly, that you are one with God; to know that there is no place where He ends and you begin; to love oneself and others unconditionally; and, to know there is *nothing* you cannot do. This is indeed the greatest discovery of all time – the Power that resides within.

Black Sheep – April 10, 2012

I am JAMMIN' right now! Black Sheep was one of my favorite groups of the early 90s Hip-Hop era and the song *The Choice is Yours*[2] has been playing over and over in my mind all day. When I got home this evening, I finally had a chance to put the video on and am now on the fifth rotation. I am happy to say that I still know most of the words. But I digress...

My real reason for writing this entry is because I am feeling like a 'black sheep' right now because of my new walk in life. The dictionary defines a black sheep as "a person who stands out because of deviation from the accepted standards of his or her group." Unfortunately, the "accepted standards" of modern society include judgment, blame, retaliation, vengeance, dishonesty, vanity, unforgiveness, impatience, greed, etc. As someone who is committed to love, peace, compassion, non-judgment, harmony, forgiveness, etc., I constantly find myself in situations where I am the oddball because everyone else is operating under the "accepted standards" of society. I find myself wanting to interrupt the conversation with something like, "Well, that's one way you could look at it, but another way is [insert positive viewpoint here]." Although I know doing this would ruin the judgment/pity party, it's what I feel the need to do in order to be true to myself.

The other option is staying silent which dishonors who I am at this point in my life. Further, it hurts me to see so many people accepting that, "This is just the way things are now, and there's nothing we can do to change it." I wholeheartedly disagree, but I can see how one could easily come to that conclusion based on what we see happening in the world. I used to feel that way. I used to believe the only way to get through to certain people was to raise my voice, or that the only way to respond to the attack of another was retaliation. As I slowly reverse this pattern in myself, I am keenly aware of what a dramatic shift this is.

I can't even escape via TV, like I used to. Almost every show seems to be operating under the same low standards (with the exception of a few channels or shows that are intentional about leaving the viewer better than before they watched the show, like Super Soul Sunday or *Lifeclass* on OWN). I now watch less than one hour of TV every day (most days I don't turn it on at all). I constantly feed my mind with positive talks, books, music, and other uplifting material to keep me focused on the path. I have a laser-like focus on reversing my negative habitual patterns right now, so it is absolutely essential that I go to this extreme. Until it becomes second nature for me to see the best in everyone I meet (no matter what they have on, how they smell, how they talk, how their hair looks, what they say, what their title is, what they do, what race they are, etc.) and to forgive myself and others for what I perceive to be wrongdoings, I cannot afford to continuously entertain and contribute to the negativity I say I don't want to promote.

What made me feel better today was reminding myself that all of the GREAT individuals of our time, and before our time, that stood for the very ideals I stand for were *not* walking in lockstep with society (e.g. Jesus, Martin Luther King, Jr., Gandhi). In fact, they were radical *non*-conformists. I feel honored to be walking in the footsteps of those that paved the way for me and I pray that I can inspire even a fraction of a fraction of the people they did to do the same. As Black Sheep would say, "You can get with *this* or you can get with *that*." I choose this: *Living in the Light.* What about you?

A Healing for my Soul – April 11, 2012

Depression has been heavy on my mind. When I was diagnosed in January of this year, I was resistant to taking antidepressants because I was afraid of the long-term effects. I was afraid I would be addicted to them and not be able to get off. If I'm really being honest, I was concerned about how it would make me look to be on 'meds.' Eventually, I was convinced by my doctors that medication could support my recovery efforts. I have been on the medication for the past couple months.

Since I started consistently integrating daily spiritual practices and going deeper into my scriptural studies, I feel there is no reason to continue taking the medication. My perception of myself, and the world, has transformed profoundly. My connection to God is stronger than it has ever been. I have meditated twice daily since the retreat (two and a half months straight without missing one day), practiced yoga a few times per week, prayed, practiced gratitude and forgiveness daily, read spiritual texts daily, and more.

Although I felt confident I am on the right path, I was worried about going 'cold turkey' without consulting my doctor (who recommended I remain on my current dose through June of this year and *then* reevaluate next steps). Then, over the weekend, I went to church and was reminded of the scripture I mentioned the other day:

He that believeth in me, the works that I do he shall do also; and greater works than these shall he do.
~John 14:12

I started thinking to myself: *Jesus healed the sick, and raised the dead. If He said I can do all of that, and more, then surely my healing from depression and anxiety is possible.* I prayed about it and decided that night to break my pill in half to lower my dose. The following evening I didn't take the pill at all. Yesterday, I started experiencing depression symptoms again. I had read that this is a normal part of the withdrawal process. The symptoms came back with a vengeance, too! I felt like a dark cloud had come over me, and wouldn't pass. Depression is not something I would wish on anyone. The emotional paralysis that ensues makes it difficult to do even the most basic daily tasks.

I started reading about depression medication and withdrawal symptoms and discovered there were tons of stories of symptoms similar to mine. I read that these symptoms typically last for about four weeks. I almost decided to go ahead and continue on the medication because I couldn't imagine another four weeks of feeling this dreadful. Instead of giving in to that urge, I decided to pray, reread my lesson for the day in the Course ("God goes with me wherever I go"), and meditate. Afterwards, ALL of the symptoms were gone!

It has been a day and a half, and I *know* I am Divinely healed of the symptoms of depression! There are so many warnings about getting off this type of medication without the consultation of a doctor, and so many warnings about the withdrawal symptoms. Well, I consulted the No. 1 Doctor, dwelling within me, and what a mighty Doctor He is! What a blessing!

While I never was a non-believer, I have always been unsure of my own healing power. I heard people claim 'Divine healing' before and have witnessed people 'laying hands' on the sick and healing them, but I always thought that was something I wasn't gifted with. I thought I wasn't spiritually mature enough to do it. If 'little old me' can do it with my mustard seed-sized faith, I *know* we all can. The Kingdom of God dwells within each of us; all we need to do is believe.

Although the symptoms are gone, I know I still have work to do to treat the cause – my thought patterns. The work continues, but I am celebrating the small wins along the way to true peace.

Disclaimer: The information shared in this entry is not medical advice. If you are currently on medication, please continue to consult your medical professional(s) regarding the right next steps for you.

P.S. The title for today's entry was inspired by the song *Healing*[3] by Kelly Price.

The Greatest Love of All – April 18, 2012

> "You can't have a better tomorrow if you can't stop thinking about yesterday."
> ~Unknown

The theme of this week for me has been forgiveness. On Sunday, I was feeling stuck when I started thinking about what to include in my forgiveness letter, which was an assignment for my spiritual boot camp. On Monday, *Oprah's Lifeclass*[4] was focused on forgiveness. Then, on Tuesday, my lesson in the Course was "God is the love in which I forgive."[5] One of the things that stood out in Tuesday's lesson was:

After you have applied the idea to all those who have come to mind, tell yourself:
God is the Love in which I forgive myself.
Then devote the remainder of the practice period to adding related ideas such as:
God is the Love with which I love myself.
God is the Love in which I am blessed.

My hesitation in doing this assignment was based on my initial thought that I didn't have anyone that I needed to forgive. My participation in *The Landmark Forum* years ago helped me work through my forgiveness issues and mend relationships that had been broken for years. Since that time, I had made forgiveness a regular practice. I had become complacent and a bit arrogant about my ability to forgive. What I realized after reading my lesson for that particular day, and after giving my homework assignment a thorough reading, is that I had not forgiven *myself!* This was a powerful breakthrough for me, and I'm only beginning to see the benefits of it.

I started to make a list of everything I never forgave myself for and, before I knew it, the list was four pages long (it's a small journal, but still… it's *a lot* of stuff!). The list brought tears to my eyes and I thought to myself, *How can you see the God in you if you're carrying all of these judgments about yourself?* I knew I had to let all of this go and affirm for myself that **I am not my mistakes**.

During *Lifeclass*, Tony Robbins led an exercise in which you close your eyes and remember a time when you were most grateful… he then led a brief, guided meditation in which you fully experience how it felt in that moment and really allow that awareness to fill your heart and mind. What came up immediately for me was when Kevin forgave me for my affair. One of the things he said when he got to a place of forgiving me (and it took some serious work, on both of our parts, to get to that point) was that he realized it was a mistake. He knew that it was not my intention to hurt him, and that I was acting out of insecurity and fear based on things I hadn't resolved within myself. It was definitely my most grateful moment – I will NEVER forget it. I had been feeling so terrible about myself, what I had done, and who I had done it to. When he forgave me, I realized something: My past mistakes do not define who I am in this moment. Since that time, I have felt empowered to pay forgiveness forward. The one person I forgot to pay it forward to was myself. I carried around guilt, shame, insecurity, defeat, etc., for this mistake, and many others throughout my life.

> "I don't forgive people because I'm weak. I forgive them because I'm strong enough to know people make mistakes."
> ~Unknown

On this day, I am finally forgiving myself. I am experiencing that same profound feeling of gratefulness that I felt when my husband forgave me six years ago. I am releasing my thoughts of resentment, guilt, shame, blame, anger, bitterness, doubt, judgment, and insecurity that I have directed toward myself based on my actions throughout my life. Below is a list of some of the things that were on my four-page forgiveness list. I hope those of you that have not forgiven yourself for something you've done in the past will join me in releasing them. Once we release our judgments about the past, we can be fully present to all that's available to us in this moment. All of those judgments were blocking my view of the Light. I am grateful for finally beginning to be able to see the Divinity in me.

Kandace, I forgive you for...
- *lying to try to fit in*
- *using intimate relationships to temporarily satisfy your need for love and attention (which can only be found via your connection with God)*
- *getting pregnant in college and making the tough decision not to move forward with it*
- *not speaking up regarding how you really feel in many situations throughout life*
- *not trusting in God's plan and trying to 'make it happen' instead of 'let it happen'*

- *being jealous and insecure in many relationships*
- *taking friendships for granted and not putting the time in to keep them flourishing*
- *spending too much money on clothes, particularly in your 20s, to satisfy your need to appear to 'have it all together'*
- *not sharing your true feelings in order to avoid conflict*
- *judging people and their actions*
- *gossiping about people just because that's what the crowd was doing*
- *not asking for help when you needed it*
- *holding back on implementing some of your dreams due to fear*
- *trying to be 'perfect' based on the world's standard instead of recognizing your inner perfection as the image and likeness of God*

Just looking over this list (and the other things on the list in my journal) has me completely blown by how much was bottled up inside of me. No wonder I 'acted out' in so many ways throughout my life (particularly in my teens and 20s), and no wonder I experienced depression and anxiety. I felt *terrible* about myself and didn't know any other way to pacify my need to feel better other than keeping it inside and covering it up. Now, I know better. As Maya Angelou says, "When you know better, you do better." Thank God for another chance!

P.S. The title for today's entry was inspired by the late Whitney Houston's version of *The Greatest Love of All*,[6] which was one of my favorite songs as a little girl. The lyrics still speak to me today, and remind me of my passion for helping the next generation live authentic, fully expressed lives!

When the Going Gets Tough… Keep Loving! – April 20, 2012

I mentioned when I started *Living in the Light* that I would be sharing the ups *and* downs on my journey. Well, today started off as a down day. I woke up with a heavy heart due to judgment and opinions from *some* family and friends who disagree with my transparency, and do not believe I should be putting all of my personal business out there for others to see. I thought I was 'over' being affected by the judgment of others, but I really couldn't shake the hurt feelings (even after prayer and meditation).

"No weapon turned against you will succeed. You will silence every voice raised up to accuse you. These benefits are enjoyed by the servants of the Lord."
~Isaiah 54:17 (NLT)

Thank God for my sister-friends who always know the exact thing to say to lift my spirits and remind me of *Who and Whose* I really am. They reminded me that no one on Earth has the authority to judge me. They reminded me to be patient, loving, and kind despite the actions of others. They reminded me *not* to be judgmental and to choose love instead. They encouraged me to keep being authentic. They reminded me that my healing comes from God and not from the acceptance of others. They prayed that those who judged would find compassion and forgiveness in their hearts. They prayed for me and my strength to press on. Amen!

I am SO grateful for such amazing sisters (blood and spirit). Their words lifted my spirits and I now am back to experiencing my natural state of wholeness and oneness with God. Sometimes when you can't lift yourself back up, it's great to be surrounded with those who can remind you of *Who* you really are and what really matters. They helped me to respond with love instead of vengeance.

During lunch today, I was listening to Rachelle Ferrell on YouTube (getting ready for tomorrow night's concert, which I am SO excited about!) and I ran across a video that reminded me of my sister-friends. It was a video of Rachelle Ferrell singing with

Ledisi after a concert, and they are just being silly and showing their love for each other as friends. It reminds me of how my friends are when we're together (laughing one minute... crying the next... loving always). I love them more than they know!

Random Thoughts on Spirituality and Karma Yoga – April 24, 2012

> "The best way to find yourself is to lose yourself in the service of others."
> ~Mahatma Gandhi

On Monday morning after meditation, the blog topic that came to me was "Karma Yoga." I wrote the idea down, but I didn't do anything with it all day. I turned on *Oprah's Lifeclass* that evening and there she was telling the world about karma (which is her favorite of *The Seven Spiritual Laws of Success*[7] by Deepak Chopra). I was incredibly happy to hear her start off the show by breaking down religion versus spirituality. She spent a good amount of time on this and I think that was a potential pivotal moment in television history.

Spirituality and religion are two different things and, in my opinion, are not mutually exclusive. I used to limit my openness to some spiritual ideas because I thought they went against the religion I grew up on. I now know that is not the case. Oprah defined spirituality as, "Living your life with an open heart," and added qualities such as compassion, love, harmony, and peace. Deepak Chopra defined spirituality as: "A journey to self-awareness that includes love, compassion, joy, creativity, choice, free-will, imagination, etc."

The reality is that we are all spiritual beings temporarily in human form. Our purpose here on Earth is to extend the Love of

God and fully express our God-given gifts. If we take off our 'social masks,' we are all the same at the core – individual expressions of God (or the Creator, the Most High, the Universe, Source… whatever you want to call it). All of the spiritual teachings discuss this connection, albeit in different ways.

My recent return to living with an "open heart" has exposed me to many new paths and practices that have transformed the way I *live* each day. It has also helped me see the ones I had already been exposed to, but in a new light. (All because I opened my mind to ideas that I used to think were outside of what I believed in.) It was one thing to memorize scripture and *believe* in God; however, it was an entirely different thing to work toward *completely* undoing the ego and live my life with a pure and open heart, in service to others and the world. That's the essential difference between religion and spirituality, at least in my observation thus far. I don't believe it has to be an either/or, but I have come to discover that religion without spirituality is theory without practice.

I have sat in churches all my life and have journals filled with notes on sermons. In my experience, church alone didn't get me to the point where I could shake my daily thoughts of fear, lack, attack, blame, etc., in order to live my life as Jesus did. The 'how to' has come through my spiritual practices, which have given me the daily tools to undo my ego-driven thinking and quiet my mind in order to see the Light in everyone and everything.

Practicing spirituality is helping me *be* and express the qualities that Jesus mastered as well as undo the ego. As the Course puts it, "Salvation is undoing." Undoing what? The sense of separation from God. I read that years ago when I was first introduced to the Course, but it wasn't until now that it really sunk in. Now that my ego is fading into the background, and my social mask is peeling away, I can see how freeing it is. The other day someone asked me, "How does it feel now that everything is out there?" I responded unhesitatingly, "I feel free." Free at last.

Back to the topic that crossed my mind for today's entry (I got on a little tangent with the spirituality discussion). The words 'karma yoga' translate to *selfless* service. I saw this concept in action during my stay at the ashram while on my retreat. The ashram has a month-long program called *Living Yoga* that combines spiritual practices and daily activities of service. The program participants would perform duties around the ashram without attachment to the fruit of their labor. They would look for the Divine in everything as they did this work. It was powerful to see in action, as they practiced harmoniously serving others each day. As they went deeper into the program, the ego was less and less in the way, and they were able to stop judging the work they were assigned to do (e.g. "I shouldn't be picking up trash along the side of the road, I should be selling books in the bookstore") and just be of service. It made me think about how I really wanted to build in a regular practice of serving others and my community instead of just doing service when I feel like it (or when my 'busy schedule' allows).

Over the weekend, Kevin and I attended volunteer orientation for an organization in our neighborhood that we're going to start working with on a weekly basis. We vowed that our family will represent service and the love of *all* humanity (we're still refining our family mission statement, but service will definitely be in there), and it feels good to be putting that into action by committing to weekly service together in an organization we both are passionate about. I used to get *so* caught up in focusing on achieving my dreams and career goals that I barely had the time to fit in service activities. I was lucky if I did something once a month (other than donating money). I also used to make myself feel better by saying to myself, "What I do for a living is making a difference," because I work in education. Yes, it is indeed a nice feeling to do work day in and day out on something that makes a difference in the lives of others, but I don't think it replaces giving selflessly (in a way that is not related to me paying my bills and advancing my career). I am committed to being of service not only through my daily spiritual practice (or, "living with an open heart" as discussed above), but also through the practice of karma yoga. I pray that our family will always be a blessing to others and continuously give more than we take in this world. Keep shining!

Without being attached to the fruits of activities, one should act as a matter of duty, for by working without attachment one attains the Supreme.[8]
~Bhagavad Gita

It is more blessed to give than to receive.
~Acts 20:35

The Boomerang Effect of Judgment – April 27, 2012

Earlier this week, I was in a situation where a bunch of people around me were in 'judgment mode' and were feeding off of each other in putting someone down. I allowed myself to forget my commitment to *Living in the Light* for a moment and joined in with a couple of comments. Afterwards, I felt terrible. When I left, I thought about all of the things I could have said and done differently in that situation to steer the discussion in a different direction and to "*Be* the change I wish to see in the world." In the past I would not have even thought twice about it. I used to feel like my negative comments somehow pierced the person I was talking about and/or that the comments were justified due to how terrible I thought their actions were. Quite frankly, I was not spending even a few minutes assessing my actions and thinking about how I could have been more loving in my daily interactions. Thank God for my change in perception about the world. Now I step back and assess my thoughts and actions multiple times a day so that I can make a more loving choice the next time. There were a few messages that came my way through my readings and spiritual development classes this week that really drove this point home for me:

Mercy exults victoriously over judgment.
~James 2:13

Judgment is like taking poison and waiting for the other person to die.
~Unknown

Judge nothing, you will be happy. Forgive everything, you will be happier. Love everything, you will be happiest.
~Sri Chinmoy

If you kick a stone in anger, you'll hurt your own foot.
~Korean Proverb

Do not judge, and you will not be judged. Do not condemn and you will not be condemned. Forgive, and you will be forgiven.
~Luke 6:37

I am grateful for the opportunity to 'dust myself off and try again.' I am also grateful for getting the message loud and clear that I'm only hurting myself, not the other person, when I judge. I had read quotes similar to the ones above before and understood them intellectually, but never really put them into practice. Now that I am aware of my tendencies and conscious of my power to choose between love and hate/fear *in every moment*, I can more quickly adjust myself (which is a major step forward for me). In the times when I am not perfect in my spiritual walk, I am grateful for God's forgiveness. I am also grateful for the example Jesus set for living a life filled with love and compassion for others – he has become my Master Teacher and guide on my journey to live in alignment with God.

As I was centering myself through meditation yesterday, I felt the Holy Spirit surrounding me – an incredible feeling. I sincerely felt like I was covered by God. After I finished my "Be still and know time" (which is what I recently started calling my meditative moments), I logged in to Facebook to share a quote with friends, and the first status update I saw was the one below from Marianne Williamson (definitely not a coincidence):

According to A Course in Miracles, *any time we've deflected a miracle (thought or behaved lovelessly, sending an opportunity away), the miracle that we could have had is "held in trust for us by the Holy Spirit until we are ready to receive it." As long as we atone for our error and seek now to be the people we weren't when we made the mistake, then we can rest assured that the opportunity will come around again in another form.*

That was exactly what I needed to hear. I am grateful for a 'God of a second chance' (or third, fourth, fifth... however many it takes). One of the things I committed to doing is praying prior to going into any situation to keep my mind focused on the Truth about everyone and everything. I also think my next class assignment will help me with the way I look at others. In my spiritual boot camp, one of our assignments for this week is to read the Rev. Dr. Martin Luther King, Jr.'s *Loving Your Enemies*[9] speech out loud (with 'oomph'... really feeling what he was saying). I encourage you to join me in this assignment and, while doing it, think about anyone that you have chosen to make your enemy (anyone you've spoken or thought negatively about). On that note, I'll leave you with a great quote from Dr. King:

We must develop and maintain the capacity to forgive. He who is devoid of the power to forgive is devoid of the power to love. There is some good in the worst of us and some evil in the best of us. When we discover this, we are less prone to hate our enemies.
~Martin Luther King, Jr.

Chapter 7

Redefining Self

Queen Bee – April 30, 2012

Over the past week I have had a number of interesting encounters with bees. At first I considered it coincidence, but after the third encounter I started to believe there was a message there for me.

I was sitting in my office last week and two bees appeared seemingly out of nowhere. I say "out of nowhere" because the door and windows were closed and I had been working in the office for hours. They began buzzing around the window and weren't bothering me too much. Still, my old reaction to bees kicked in and I went searching for something to 'get' them with. I came back in the office with a spray bottle filled with water and proceeded to spray the bees. As soon as I sprayed them, they fell down and I left them there. I didn't want to touch them. I sat down at my desk to get back to work when a swarm of bees came outside my office window. They seemed to say, "How dare you spray our family!" They were buzzing so intensely that I thought they were going to make a crack in the window. That evening, I shared the experience with Kevin. We had a good laugh and left it at that.

The following morning, while getting the boys ready for school, my 3 year old screamed "BEETLE, Mommy... Daddy [that's what he calls ALL bugs]!!!" I ran over to look and there, crawling slowly across the hallway, was a bee. I was in reaction mode and stepped on the bee to 'save' my son. After I did, I felt bad and thought to myself, *Man, I should have just picked it up and put it outside.* I didn't want to set a bad example for my son. (*Side note: I know what some of you may be thinking... is she seriously that worried about killing a bee? Yes, I really am. My recent emphasis on my spiritual development has helped me see the Divinity in ALL life. I think bees are incredible and serve a great purpose in nature.*)

As I mentioned in my previous entry, I am so grateful for second chances. The next day, I was focused on the computer screen and, all of a sudden, I heard buzzing around my ear. I looked around and there were two more bees in my office. This time around I sprayed them with a little water so they wouldn't sting me, placed them in a cup and set them free. It felt SO good! The next day I was riding in my car listening to an audio program on the Course titled *Fearless Love*[1] by Gary Renard and he briefly mentioned animal symbolism. Shortly after that *another* bee appeared in my car. Again, there were no windows open and I hadn't heard any buzzing prior to that moment. The bee was right on the driver's seat window, which would have sent me into a complete panic in the past. I sat there for a moment and looked at the bee, said a little prayer, let the window down and set it free. At this point, I couldn't wait to get home and look up what bees meant.

I did some research on bees and came up with the following meanings:[2]

- *Symbol of the original source of all life and inspiration (God)*
- *Used as an emblem of those who wish to associate themselves with the inspiration of God*
- *Immortality and resurrection*
- *Diligence and effort*
- *Hope*
- *Healing*
- *Inspirational power*
- *Word of God/Divine breath*
- *Royal emblem/Regal*
- *Supernatural power*
- *Secret wisdom*
- *Poetry/Intelligence*

For me, this was confirmation of the Divine direction my life is taking. I feel more connected to God than I ever have before, in a way I never have experienced before. This also reminded me of the source of my name Kandake (the title for queens that was used in the ancient African Kingdom of Kush – also known as Nubia and Ethiopia) and the nickname that followed me in college, "Queen." While I was depressed, I started to dislike the nickname. I felt like everyone was looking at me as 'queen-like' and perfect, and I believed that was part of what caused me to push myself so hard. Now I know the truth – it was my *thoughts* that caused me to push myself, not anyone or anything else. I am re-embracing the nickname (and the source of my name) after my recent experiences with bees and see nothing but beauty in it. I am grateful and proud of it now. What a blessing!

An Instrument in the Arms of God – May 2, 2012

I have loved music since I can remember. My dad still holds the record for the largest record collection I've ever seen in person. I grew up loving many types of music, but had a particular affinity for jazz. I used to want to play like the great musicians my dad exposed me to, especially master musicians like John Coltrane, Miles Davis, and Thelonious Monk. I knew I wanted to play some type of instrument and, after some thought, landed on the clarinet and the piano (well, to be honest, I didn't have a choice regarding piano). I played in elementary school, but quit as soon as I got to middle school because I didn't think it was 'cool' to be in band anymore. I never really got great at it because I didn't put the time into honing my craft. I haven't picked up an instrument since that time, but lately have been feeling the itch to learn to play something.

A new instrument craving emerged a few weeks ago when I was listening to one of my favorite artists, Roy Ayers. I suddenly wanted to learn to play the vibraphone. I thought it would be a fun instrument to learn and that my sons would have fun playing it with me. Then I discovered how much they cost (the cheapest one I found was $1,500). I put that on the backburner for now since we just bought a house and have *lots* of other things to purchase before I can buy a vibraphone. Over the past week, the instrument craving emerged again while listening to some light music during meditation. I've been listening to Nawang Khechog during some of my meditations for the past couple weeks and am mesmerized by the sound of the native flute. I thought about taking flute lessons and, ultimately, working on a flute meditation album. While I believe I can do anything I put my mind to (my grandmother used to always tell me that and it definitely stuck with me), I heard the following message during my meditation time and it stopped me in my tracks:

You are an instrument in the arms of God.

I had written this very statement down in my journal during my retreat in January, but it popped up in my mind again today. I was reminded of something I read in the book *The Science of Mind*[3] by Ernest Holmes last week about being a "transparency for God." There was an exercise in the *Foundations of Science of Mind*[4] workbook that instructed the reader to close their eyes and imagine their body being completely transparent. Once everything was transparent, the reader is then guided to bring their attention to God while inviting the Spirit to flow through them into the world. It was a powerful exercise that significantly shifted my daily experiences and interactions.

Relax and let this flow of God pour through every inch of you into the world, as if you were a clear window, a conduit of the Divine. And as this essence pours through your being, set your intention in love, knowing that this is [living in] Grace.
~Joel Goldsmith

While I still believe there may be something else I am meant to do with my music passion, I have my marching orders... learning to *consistently* play in tune in the Divine band. To radiate the love, compassion, peace, joy, serenity, forgiveness, kindness, harmony, abundance, etc., that God is (and that I am because I am made in His image). Whenever I play off-key (judgment, resentment, bitterness, unforgiveness, etc.), I will get back to practice (through meditation, prayer, affirmation, etc.), tune up, and play again! Let's make music together. Keep shining!

> "They can shoot a soloist, but they cannot shoot a song...
> we need to start singing."
> ~Marianne Williamson

Redefining Prayer – May 15, 2012

I had an amazing Mother's Day spending quality time with my husband, the boys, and my parents. I have SO much to be grateful for!

One of the most memorable parts of my day came at the end of the night when the boys were asleep and the house was quiet. I had an assignment for a course I am taking and it required having a partner. It was an hour-and-a-half long meditation and reflection 'workshop.' Kevin agreed to do it with me. Normally I would have read through the workshop outline ahead of time and maybe even listened to the meditations in advance just so I would know what I was getting him into, but I didn't make time to do that. I was forced to go with the flow and I'm glad I did.

I began by giving him some more background on what we've been learning about, and spent a little time walking him through each of the five elements of the prayer technique I was introduced to a couple weeks ago. The technique is designed to help move students from praying to God as an external 'Santa-Claus-in-the-sky' presence to aligning their minds back with the spiritual qualities of God (which is our true nature). The technique was designed to assist individuals in removing the internal blocks that hinder them from seeing the divinity in everyone and everything, while reminding that the qualities of God are already *within* them (love, peace, wholeness, abundance, joy, compassion, etc.). It was a powerful process, and very different from the way I had been praying.

> "We are moved away from an empowering relationship with God when we go for the form without assessing the experience or qualities of life we are also seeking."
> ~Ernest Holmes

The workshop consisted of four guided meditations (approximately 10 minutes each) with breaks in between for readings, journaling, and time to answer specific reflection questions about the meditations. The first one began with this reading:[5]

Ernest Holmes said that we must "enter the silence." The silence is within us, not in the outer world; it is up to us to find the silence and experience it. It is in the silence of our being that we come to recognize the distinction between the forms, or physical wants and needs in our lives, and the ultimate purpose and meaning for our lives. Thus we free ourselves to [pray] for that which will bring us peace, joy, love, harmony, true prosperity, etc.

It was so good to meditate together again and just 'be.' The entire workshop was powerful for the both of us, but the third meditation had the most profound impact. This meditation focused on realizing what we *really* want. So often we have desires, but we don't ask ourselves what it is that we hope to *experience* from having that which we desire. We are disappointed when we finally get the new home or the relationship we've been praying for because we're still not happy. The issue is that we didn't assess what it is that we *really* want: to experience love, to feel secure, to have peace, etc. Most times, we will not be happy once we get the material things we want because they are cover-ups for our deeper desires.

The third meditation asked the individual and his/her partner to take turns asking each other three questions repeatedly for three minutes: *What do you really want? What form do you see this taking? What specific experience do you desire from what you want?* This is a powerful exercise; one that I encourage anyone who wants anything to do. I find it interesting how disconnected our wants can be from the experience we desire. Moving forward, Kevin and I will continue with this meditation practice – individually, collectively and as a family. My deep desire is to know and experience peace, love, compassion and joy in every moment – starting with our home and then rippling into the world. *What's your deepest desire?* Something to think about until next time. Keep shining!

> *The process of [prayer] is to bring into alignment that which we know to be true and that which we are not experiencing. In this process we are surrendering any idea of separation between the inner and outer realms of our being. We are surrendering any idea or feeling of separation between the Creator and Its Creation... between the Intelligence and Wisdom, the Peace and Harmony of the Creating power and our own life.*
> *~Ernest Holmes, The Anatomy of Healing Prayer[6]*

Reflections on my Shadow – May 30, 2012

As I mentioned in an earlier entry, I don't watch much TV but something led me to pick up the remote today. I ended up landing on Oprah's *Super Soul Sunday* from a week ago on the documentary *The Shadow Effect,*[7] featuring Debbie Ford, Marianne Williamson, and Deepak Chopra. I had heard of the film, and had even bought it for someone who was going through a difficult time, but I never watched it for myself. I thought I already knew what my "shadow" was and had already healed it. Well, I was wrong about the latter.

Our shadow is the dark part of ourselves that we try to keep hidden from the world. The documentary gave some examples of how it shows up in our lives: claiming someone else's work as your own, yelling at your children, bouncing checks, lying, shoplifting, drinking too much, overeating, thinking negative thoughts about other people, harming ourselves and/or others, recurring anger, etc. The film brilliantly illuminates where the shadow comes from and shares many examples of how to release it and/or use it in a more positive way. One example of this is a little girl who is made fun of at school. The little girl develops a mean attitude and hard exterior to protect herself from the comments of her schoolmates. Throughout life, this girl-turned-woman holds onto that hard shell and it becomes who she is. She is trying to protect herself from harm, but doesn't connect it back to the root of where it came from. Deep inside, she wants to be loved but doesn't know how to be vulnerable anymore because of what happened so many years ago. Until she uncovers this pattern (shadow), she will not understand why she can't find love or hold onto relationships (or whatever other challenges she's facing due to her negative attitude).

Many of us have a similar storyline: something happened in the past that we then used to form an outer persona – the way we present ourselves to the world. Some of us have even tricked ourselves into believing it was a good thing. I was one of those people. I tricked myself into believing that I was a go-getter, determined, strong, hard worker, etc., and that I was the epitome of 'success.' What I didn't realize was how hard I worked over the years to maintain the 'perfection.' It was eating away at me on the inside. It was causing me to choose career over more important things, to be upset when things were not perfect, to aggressively manage my 'image,' to take on way more than I could manage, to never ask for help (because that would let people know I didn't have it together), to lie to look good, to spend too much… you get the point. It was *not* a good thing.

I blamed my dad, and a few other childhood incidents, for the inner feelings I had of not being good enough, and the pattern I had developed of trying to appear perfect to everyone around me. One of those childhood incidents was experiencing racism. My middle school guidance counselor assumed that "students like me" would *not* take the most advanced math courses so that I could be on the college 'track.' She scheduled me for a lower level class; my mother had to work incredibly hard to get me back in the correct one.

From that moment forward, I was determined to change the perception of black students – starting with me. Some would say that's a good thing, but when you're so wrapped up in proving yourself, it becomes detrimental to your well-being. I found that out the hard way in January when I had finally pushed myself to the limit.

When I first started watching *The Shadow Effect*, I was thinking, "Yeah, yeah, I know this already," but then I was hit with the truth. Although I knew what my shadow was, I had not completely mastered it. Even in my spiritual practice, I find myself wanting so bad to be perfect in my walk that I sometimes forget to forgive myself when I make mistakes. I was expecting myself to be perfect even though I just started actively practicing *daily* meditation, prayer, study, etc. On the professional side, I find myself holding back because I don't have that 'perfect' idea to share instead of just allowing my raw thoughts to flow.

Although I know intellectually that I am a spiritual being in human form that will make mistakes every time I forget who I *really* am, I don't always keep it at the forefront of my mind.

Every time I forget that I was made in the image and likeness of God, I will make mistakes, feel fear, and see myself as small, weak, and vulnerable. What I have to remember is that every challenge or mistake is an opportunity to extend forgiveness and Love. I still have some work to do on *Living in the Light*, but I am grateful for being one step further out of the darkness of my old, ego-driven self.

We're often afraid of looking at our shadow because we want to avoid the shame or embarrassment that comes along with admitting mistakes. We feel that if we take a deep look at ourselves, we'll be too exposed. But the thing we should actually fear is not looking at it, for our denial of the shadow is exactly what fuels it. One day I looked at something in myself that I had been avoiding because it was too painful. Yet once I did, I had an unexpected surprise. Rather than self-hatred, I was flooded with compassion for myself because I realized the pain was necessary to develop that coping mechanism to begin with.

~Marianne Williamson

Soul Costumes — May 31, 2012

Kevin called me and asked me out on a spontaneous lunch date yesterday. I happily accepted, and even got dressed up, did my hair, and put on a little makeup (I work from home, so this is not my daily routine anymore). We had a great lunch and talked about everything imaginable, including our Will. The subject came up because we're going out of the country on vacation this summer and will be away from the boys for a week. Since we're both going, we thought we'd better revisit our Will – *just in case*.

During the discussion, I mentioned that I'd recently decided I would like to be cremated. I went on to share that I was reminded of my grandmother's death during the last *Living A Course in Miracles* class which discussed "Life, Death, and the Illusion."[8] During the class, the guest speaker talked about his father's death and shared how he felt when he saw his father's body. He said he felt no connection to it, like it wasn't really him. That was *exactly* how I felt when I saw my grandmother's body. I almost wanted to laugh when I finally worked up the nerve to go look in the casket because she looked so different to me. I was clear that it is the soul that animates the body, and that the body itself could do nothing. Reminding myself of that moment helped me reconnect to the idea that we are *not* our bodies.

Kevin said, "Yeah, it's like we have on costumes." Exactly! God has created each and every one of us in His image. We all look different on the outside, but we all have the same Light within us. The problem is we forget that we are connected to something WAY bigger than our temporary costume; we are connected to the Love and almighty Power of God. The soul that lights us up and illuminates the costume we have chosen (our body) is not of this world – it *is* and *forever will* be of God. I now look back at my grandmother's death and don't feel as much sadness because we are still connected. She has rejoined with God and is now a part of the Source of my strength.

For some people, this idea of 'not being a body' makes them feel disempowered and care less for their body (because it's only temporary, and does not fully represent *Who* they are). It does the opposite for me. It makes me want to care for it (eating right, exercising, meditating, etc.) because this is the vessel God blessed me with to express Him. If I don't care for it, I'm not accepting the blessing that it is and I'm not fully living up to my potential and purpose here on Earth. Even though it is not *Who* I am at the core, it is what has been given to me to use as a tool to express the Infinite. I can't freely give and express the Love that God is if I'm tired, weak, and unhealthy. For me, daily meditation, prayer, and regular yoga practice keep my mind focused on being an immortal soul who is temporarily in costume with the sole purpose of outwardly expressing all that God is: Love. I am toning my spiritual muscle, inwardly *and* outwardly, in order to build the stamina to share the Light with the world for as long as I am here in this form. When my time on Earth is complete and my soul returns home, there will be no need for this costume. I don't want my loved ones to celebrate who I was on the outside, rather *Who* I am (and *Who* we all are) on the inside. Keep shining!

> "Let go of the idea that you're a body that's destined to die, and instead seek an awareness of your immortal Self. Affirm: 'I am eternal, and that means that I showed up here from the infinitude of spiritual intention to fulfill a destiny that I must act on.'"
> ~Wayne Dyer

P.S. The song *Spiritual*[9] by Donald Lawrence was playing in the background as I finished this entry – perfect complement to this blog! *You're not a natural being having a spiritual experience... but you're a spiritual being living this natural experience.*

Chapter 8

Shift in Perception

Welcome Home – June 4, 2012

This morning when I went out the door, I couldn't help but pause when looking at our 'welcome' mat. I see it every day, but today it had a different meaning to me. I started thinking, *Who is not welcome here?* At first I wasn't sure why this strange question popped up in my head, but then I thought back to this morning's message in the Course that stated:

My grievances hide the light of the world in me.[1]

Right after I read my lesson for the day, I started searching my mind for any grievances I've held in the past and any that I still can't seem to let go of. This was a powerful exercise and it reminded me of my commitment to *Living in the Light*. If I honestly want to see the Light in everyone and everything, then I have to be willing to release *all* of my judgments, opinions, and grudges – period. This is not a new concept to me (I even wrote about it the other day in my entry about *The Boomerang Effect of Judgment*), but what *is* new is my bold willingness to actually do it *all the way*.

Today, I am overwhelmed by a feeling of love toward everyone and everything. As I searched my mind in this moment for who would *not* be welcome in my space, I couldn't think of one person. I am releasing all of the grievances that I've cherished for years about people, places, corporations, corrupt politicians, lobbyists, slavery, celebrities, murderers, terrorists, etc. I am seeing all of these things through the lens of God: the lens of love, compassion, forgiveness, kindness, peace, harmony, and non-judgment.

We are literally attempting to get in touch with the salvation of the world. We are trying to see past the veil of darkness that keeps it concealed. We are trying to let the veil be lifted, and to see the tears of God's Son disappear into the sunlight.
~*A Course in Miracles*

What a profound shift this has had on my thinking! When I started this writing process a few months ago, I had more than a few judgments that I didn't want to release. I felt justified in my opinions and wanted to argue my point anytime someone brought these topics up. When one of those same topics came up today, I noticed how radically different my response was. I am responding with more compassion for the person being talked about. I notice that I increasingly view people's 'sins' (or, mistakes) as a cry for help or a cry for the Love of God instead of arguing the 20 reasons why they are dead wrong for what they did.

God loves **all** of us equally. Someone who is considered a murderer receives the unconditional love of God just as much as someone who loves all people. My greatest desire is to love like this, and be at peace with everyone. I used to have strong opinions about the horrible things occurring in the world and held grievances against them while forgiving the seemingly 'small' mistakes of others. Looking through this lens of Love feels SO much better. I feel so much lighter already!

What if we all viewed everyone and every situation with a loving heart? What a peaceful world we'd create by choosing forgiveness and 'welcoming' everyone into our space with love. That is Heaven on Earth. We *can* do it! We *are* doing it... one by one. The shift starts with us *being* the Light in each and every moment of our lives. Even in the darkest of situations, we can be the glimmer of Light that reminds those around us of our 'Home Sweet Home.' Keep shining!

P.S. This post made me think of the song *Home* from *The Wiz*. (One of my favorite versions[2] is one by Jazmine Sullivan.)

Let it Go – June 15, 2012

I have been super excited this week for a number of reasons. One of the biggest reasons is an AMAZING vision that was shown to me by the Spirit. It is one that ignites my passions, and will take me in completely new directions. It came to me about a week ago, and is far beyond my wildest dreams. I am a natural dreamer and visionary – it's one of the gifts I am blessed with in this lifetime. *But* sometimes being a dreamer and visionary can lead my mind *way* out in the future and I miss the present moment. I'll spend hours working on a plan, thinking about who I can partner with, dreaming about what my life will be like, thinking about potential obstacles, etc. *Have you ever had that experience? Have you ever been SO excited about something that it consumed the majority of your thoughts?*

I was writing down some of the new ideas that came to me in my journal earlier, when I noticed a ladybug crawling across my *A Course in Miracles* book. I picked it up, took it outside to release it, and almost went back to writing but something told me to look up the meaning of ladybugs. Below is a list of the meanings[3] my search led me to:

- Spiritual enlightenment
- Rebirth/Renewal
- Regeneration
- Fearlessness
- Protection
- Good Luck
- Wishes being fulfilled

I went on to read that a ladybug showing up in your life foretells a time of luck and protection, where wishes start to come to fruition. The ladybug reminds you *not to force things or try hard to fulfill your wishes and to, instead, go with the flow and let things take their natural course.* Your wishes will come true in their own time.

When it appears in your life, it's telling you to let go and let God. *As a messenger of promise, the ladybug teaches us how to restore faith and trust in the Spirit. It initiates change where it is needed most. When a ladybug appears it is asking us to get out of our own way and allow the Spirit to enter.*

WOW. If that isn't the Spirit speaking to me, I don't know what is. I really needed that message today. I need to remind myself on a regular basis to let go and let God. I can't plan every step of the way or manipulate things so they turn out the way *I* want them to. *When has God's plan ever been less than what I envisioned?* Never! God has the absolute highest vision for my life if I would just get out of the way and let the Holy Spirit work through me.

Today I am working on letting it go. I'm not going to say it's easy for me to do, but it's my lesson for today and I'm taking it seriously. I am reminding myself that *ALL things work together for good to them that love God* (Romans 8:28). With that reminder I know that, even if it doesn't look the way I envision it right now, it will be spectacular and orchestrated by God. Whew. What a release! *What future idea are you attached to that is keeping you from enjoying what's in front of you right now?*

P.S. A friend of mine posted a song on Facebook earlier today that is SO fitting for the message I received today – *Let It Go*[4] by Jazzanova. Definitely take a listen… you can't *not* "let it go" after listening to it. Keep shining!

Eternal Life: June 18, 2012

Last week in my "Foundations for Spiritual Living" class, we discussed immortality. We read some interesting passages and shared our own visions of what happens after we leave our bodies. Everyone had a unique vision of what happens next and how the transition takes place, but one thing was consistent with all of us – the belief that we are eternal beings having a temporary human experience. One of the passages we read from Ernest

Holmes' *The Science of Mind* really stood out to me, as it was very similar to what I envision happening when we transition:

> *When we came into this life, we were met by loving friends who cared for us until we were able to care for ourselves. Judging the future by the past, we can believe that when we enter the larger life, there will be loving hands to greet us and loving friends to care for us until we have become accustomed to our new surroundings.*
> *~Ernest Holmes*

It was confirming to read this and hear from others who have a similar vision. Throughout the week, a few people mentioned the book *Dying to Be Me*[5] in which Anita Moorjani recounts her experience losing consciousness and leaving her body when she was in the final stages of cancer. In her Near-Death Experience (NDE), she was able to connect to the source of the pain in her life that she believes caused the cancer. When she woke up from the coma, she was able to heal herself completely of cancer and was out of the hospital within *weeks* – amazing! I haven't read the book yet, but have added it to my wish list (I am reading *way* too many things right now). In addition to this one, there were a few other NDEs like this that I read about last week and was inspired by.

All of this was going on in my mind when it hit closer to home. On Saturday my parents visited a friend of theirs who was released from hospice care after being in a coma. He described his experience leaving his body (mind you, he was pronounced 'dead') and being greeted by friends and family members who had passed on. He said he told them that he was "not ready yet" and that he wanted to go back. Shortly after, to the amazement of the hospice workers, he opened his eyes! Not only that, he pulled out his tubes because he was completely healed from his pain (migraines for which he was receiving shots of morphine *every 10 minutes* prior to the coma)!

He shared his experience with the priest by his bedside who

shared that he has heard *countless* experiences like this while working in the hospice (he has even had people say things like, "Don't you see my grandmother right there?" while pointing to what seemed to be an empty space in the room). My parents' friend said he is experiencing more peace than he has ever experienced – he now knows *without a doubt* what is *Real*. All of the petty things of this world that he used to get frustrated by weren't worrying him after this experience. There's more to the story, but you get the gist. Powerful!

> *And so we prepare not to die, but to live. The thought of death should slip from our consciousness altogether; and when this great event of the soul takes place, it should be beautiful, sublime… a glorious experience. As the eagle, freed from its cage, soars to its native heights, so the soul, freed from the home of heavy flesh, will rise and return unto its Father's house, naked and unafraid.*
> *~Ernest Holmes*

This week's reminders completely healed me of any fear of 'death' that was left in me. After my pneumonia, I was really struggling with this fear. I worried about leaving too soon and even developed a fear of losing my kids before 'their time.' I am now remembering that, regardless of when we leave our bodies, we will continue to live on in the Spirit forever and ever. This life on Earth is not, and will never be, our permanent home. Keeping my *real* Home at the forefront of my mind has brought me an indescribable peace and joy. All I have to do is *remember* and not get caught up in what I can see in front of me. I hope this helps others who are struggling with the fear of 'death' (for themselves or loved ones) as well. Keep shining!

Perfect Storm – June 25, 2012

This weekend felt like a roller coaster ride… thrilling… scary… heart-pounding… and definitely had lots of ups and downs!

Here's the rundown of events and the lessons I learned from it all.

In preparation for my husband being away for a week-long business trip, I went 'big' grocery shopping on Friday. I wanted to have enough food for the week for the boys (now ages 3 and 1½), and did not want to have to run back and forth to the store with both of them in tow. I was feeling good because I thought I was ahead of the game.

Before I left the house to pick up the boys from school, something told me to turn the air conditioning down to a lower temperature so that the house would be cooler.

Friday evening, while I was cleaning up after dinner with the boys, the sky got very dark and the wind started blowing like crazy. It started pouring and the wind was so fierce that debris was flying into the windows. My 3 year old was *super* excited and my one and a half year old was just staring bug-eyed at the window. I hustled the boys to their bedroom to put on their nightclothes and, shortly after, the electricity cut off.

I was on the phone with my husband when this happened (thank God!), and he reminded me of where the flashlight was and told me how to use it (it can be switched from a flashlight to a lantern). I tried to turn it on but the light was very faint. The battery was almost dead and we didn't have any more 'D' batteries. Shoot!

At this point, I was frantically scrambling to get the boys in their nightclothes, get their teeth brushed, and to read them a bedtime story while there was still a little bit of light outside. My youngest was cooperative, but my 3 year old did *not* want to go to sleep especially without his nightlight, which was not working. I didn't want to leave the flashlight on in their room because I knew the battery would die, and we wouldn't have any light at all. He gave me a *seriously* hard time, but eventually went to bed. He was excited about his first day of soccer camp, so I told him if he didn't go to sleep he wouldn't be able to go – worked like a charm.

On Saturday morning, I dropped the boys off at the babysitter so that I could run some errands before taking them to play soccer. Turns out I didn't get to do half of the things I wanted to do; the roads were cut off because of downed trees in the area. I was upset about that because that was going to be my only free time by myself for the weekend. I was hoping to lift my spirits by going back to the house and finding that the power was back on, but I pulled up and noticed that the outside light was still off (I turned it on so that I could just drive by to see if it was back on). I went inside to check the temperature and it was *extremely* hot in the house, so we definitely could not stay there that night.

On my way to pick up the boys from the babysitter, I was praying and thanking God in advance for providing a cool, comfortable resting place for us that night (silently wishing for it to be my home). I was also thinking about what to do with the boys after soccer practice if the power was still not back on. *I was hoping it would be back on... for comfort... and to save all that food that I had just purchased.*

We went to the place where soccer camp is held. We were running about 10 minutes late so I was expecting to see a bunch of little kids running around on the field, but no one was out there. We got out of the car and went inside the gymnasium to see if they were playing indoors because of the heat, but there were no kids in there either. My 3 year old becomes very upset at this point because he was SO excited about playing (and I promised that if he went to bed the night before that he would get to play). He asked, "Where are the kids? Where are the soccer balls, Mommy?" He started running through the building and screaming, "I WANT TO PLAY SOCCER!" I called the group that organizes the soccer camp and no one answered. Finally, I checked online and realized that it starts *next* Saturday. I felt SO bad!

To make up for the soccer mistake, I decided to take the boys to an indoor play area and get some ice cream. I figured this could help buy us some time since the place was a half hour away from where we were. We had some great mini-sundaes and then the boys played for a while. When it was time to go, my 3 year old had a meltdown and ran out of the play area while I was getting my youngest ready to go (putting his shoes back on, etc.). I left all of my stuff in the playroom (except for my little guy) and ran after him, losing my flip-flop in the process. Who knew I could run like that with a baby in tow! We finally got out of there, but it took a lot of kicking and screaming. At this point, I started to feel myself lose my cool. I tried to counter the feeling with positive thoughts about the power being back on when we got home.

I drove home and was praying that the power would be back on. I was on the phone with my husband trying not to tell him every little thing that was seemingly going wrong that day. I didn't want him to feel bad about being away. He was encouraging, as always, and suggested that I get a hotel. He called the power company and they didn't estimate that the power would be on until Monday. I really didn't want to believe that, so I was resistant to booking a hotel (we decided on a hotel versus staying with friends or family so that the boys could just run freely). He still searched options for me and found a location near church so that it would be convenient for me in the morning. I thought, *I prayed about this… it's going to work out!*

The power was NOT back on when we got home. I went in the house to pack our things as fast as I could so we could get settled at the hotel.

On the way to the hotel, I picked up some fast food for the boys so they could eat in the car and almost be ready to go to bed by the time we checked in. This was the third fast food meal they had over the weekend, and I was feeling bad about that. My youngest was crying the whole way there. I think he was frustrated with being in the car seat and stroller most of the day. Poor baby (and poor mommy's ears).

That evening and the following morning at the hotel were

challenging, a bit frustrating, and expensive for me. Valet parking was $29 which I thought was pretty crazy. We got to the room and I thought I'd be 'nice' and let my 3 year old play the video game in the room (we typically only allow him to play educational games); it was $8.50 for an hour of play time. Despite my 15- and five-minute warnings, getting him to stop playing the game was terribly challenging. We were in for another round of kicking and screaming.

The boys didn't want to go to sleep. They were bouncing all over the room, throwing things (they only broke one thing, a cup, thankfully), and play-fighting each other. They thought it was hilarious. I thought I was going to burst with frustration. (At this point, I was exhausted and ready for meditation and sleep.)

In the morning, I got them ready and we went down for breakfast. My 3 year old thought it would be fun to run away from the table and out into the hallway of the hotel. Once again, it was a wild goose chase involving me losing my flip-flop and, this time, my cool. I pinched him very hard, got on his level, and told him not to ever run away from me like that again (mind you, my youngest is still at the table in the restaurant). Oh, and did I mention breakfast was $28? I thought surely breakfast was included, but apparently not. SIGH.

It was still early (maybe 8:30 am) and church wasn't until 11, so we had some time to kill. We went back to the room and watched cartoons for about 30 minutes, but the boys were antsy and ready to go. We made it out of the hotel without causing too much havoc, but my 3 year old had another meltdown on the way out; he didn't want to hold my hand. He was screaming and yelling, "I CAN DO IT MYSELF! " Oh the joys of toddler independence. We went to the airport to watch planes take off for a while, but that didn't keep them focused for as long as I hoped. Finally, we started to make our way to church.

I needed gas, so I pulled over. While at the gas station, I pulled out the Course and started reading. Then I read a little bit of *This Thing Called You*[6] by Ernest Holmes. I also read through the latest quotes I posted on the *Living in the Light* Facebook page[7] to lift my spirits. Yes, I was ministering to myself! I needed to renew my spirit and release the negative energy that was building up inside me. What came to me during that reading, meditation, and prayer time was the word "acceptance," which was exactly what I needed to hear! I needed to accept the situation for what it was and not hope it was different and try to change it. I needed to just let it be.

> *The Mind within me, being God, is not afraid of anything. It does not remember any unhappy experience, nor does it anticipate any. At the center of my being there is complete poise, perfect faith and confidence.*
> *~Ernest Holmes (This is the quote that I read while at the gas station. What a great reminder!)*

> *Praise and blame, gain and loss, pleasure and sorrow come and go like the wind. To be happy, rest like a great tree in the midst of them all.*
> *~The Buddha (One of the quotes I read on the Living in the Light Facebook page that helped me with 'acceptance' of what is)*

With my lifted spirit, I went to church and received a super-warm welcome from the minister which felt nice. This was only our fourth time going to this spiritual community. I had a feeling the message would be perfect for me today. I went up to the kids' room to get the boys settled in. No matter how hard I tried, and what snacks I gave him, my youngest was *not* staying in there. I tried for about 15–20 minutes with no success (all the while missing service). Finally, I brought him with me. I caught the tail end of service. One of the things the minister was talking about was being the "Chief Possibility Officer" of your own life. I needed to hear that. I started thinking about the possibilities I could create for myself – even in this stressful time.

We got settled in the car, after some struggles, and I immediately called my husband for a word of encouragement. After driving about 10 minutes I realized I left my journal (Seriously?)! My heart dropped. I turned around to get it and, at first, no one could find it. I was trying to keep my cool, but this was my journal with all my notes from the spiritual development classes I'd taken over the prior six months, ideas, brainstorming for future projects, etc. I took a few deep breaths and went back in to look a few more times. There it was, sitting on a chair on the side of the room. Thank you, God!

The electric company still hadn't called to say our power was back on (we set up an automatic notification), so I decided to take the boys to the movies. On our way there, I was still feeling like I could use a mood-lifter, and I thought about a song I used to play when I was going through rough times – *I Told the Storm*,[8] by Greg O'Quinn. I played the song and I cried. I sang every lyric and really felt what the song was saying – the storm will not last! I needed that release so bad and especially needed the reminder that the storm is only temporary.

Even though your winds blow
I want you to know
You cause me no alarm
Cause I'm safe in His arms

We went to the movies and had only a few meltdown moments then went home only to find that the power was *still* off (sigh). I repacked our bags and booked another hotel room – this time one with breakfast included.

Finally at 1:00 am, I received a call from the electric company to let us know the power was back on! I got the boys ready in the morning and was just about ready to take them down for breakfast when I noticed my youngest was soaking wet on one side. I have no idea where it came from because it didn't smell like urine. At this point, I just had to laugh. I asked myself, "What's next?"

After dropping the boys off at school, I went home and proceeded to throw away all of the food that spoiled (easily $100 worth of food). I went to my office and settled into a good work groove for a few hours, and then the power went *back* off. I knew *something* had to be next. Thankfully, it went off right after I sent a time-sensitive proposal to my coworker. My mind almost went to, "Oh no, not another night of hotel and eating out!!" I called the power company and they said they expected it to come back on by 6 pm this evening. As I type this, it is back on. Whew!

Needless to say, after all of this, I was more than a little bit flustered. One of the things that helped me to lift my mood throughout all of this, though, was my gratitude practice. See below for some of the things I am grateful for after this experience:

- Having power in the first place.
- There was no damage to our home (I drove by houses with windows broken, trees on their roof, etc.).
- Two healthy boys.
- The financial means to cover hotel costs, food, and entertainment.
- Remembering my lesson in 'accepting what is' instead of trying to push to have things be the way I want them... going with the flow!
- My husband is coming back and doesn't have another business trip for the remainder of the year!
- My 3 year old being understanding about me mixing up the day for his first day of soccer camp once he calmed down – "Oh, you forgot, Mommy... it's OK."
- Playing a game with my 3 year old and him saying, "This is so fun, Mommy!"

- Delicious free cookies from the hotel (I used to order tins of these cookies – they're that good!).
- Our waitress at breakfast who gave me two more free cookies "for the boys" (nope... for mommy!).
- The woman at church who rubbed my back and said, "You're doing great," when she saw me dealing with one of my 3 year old's tantrums (sometimes you just need a little encouragement).
- My youngest being the star of church service when the choir was singing. He was clapping and dancing... it was SO cute! He was *really* feeling it. There was definitely a reason for him not staying in the playroom.
- The show *Pequeños Gigantes* on Univision which had the boys doing some hilarious dance routines before they went to bed.
- Fun bath time with the boys splashing and playing with their happy meal toys.
- My youngest giving me kisses and smiling at me as he fell asleep next to me.
- The person in the room next to us that went to the bathroom at 11:45 pm last night and woke me up (I had fallen asleep with my clothes and makeup on).
- The 12 am, 20-minute yoga routine I snuck in when I couldn't fall back asleep.
- Blackout curtains at the hotel helping the boys sleep in a little. (Note to self: buy some blackout curtains *immediately*.)
- The woman at the hotel this morning who said, "You have such well-mannered boys." (Bless her heart for seeing the Light in them!)
- The power is back on!!
- The beetle that appeared in my bathroom and what it symbolizes (beetles symbolize gradual, steady progress; remind us to appreciate the simple things in life; and to build the best opportunities even among the 'dung' in life).

The beetle really sums this all up. Our response to the trials that come up in life is everything. There's no question that ups and downs will come our way. In fact, if we don't get the lessons from them the first time they will reappear in a different form for us to learn from. I think I got my lessons this time. Slowly, but surely, I will become a constant 'calm in the storm.' I don't have to beat myself up for not always feeling happy or responding peacefully. Like the beetle symbolizes, I am making "gradual, steady progress" and that's OK. I'm ready for the next challenge. I know I'll do even better next time, as I'm continuing to build my spiritual muscle. Until the next perfect storm... keep shining!

Living in the Overflow – July 12, 2012

On Sunday, we attended church service and the topic was "Interconnectedness." It was a great message and reminder that we are not separate from one another. I seem to need that reminder daily. One of the things the minister said that really struck a chord with me was, "We can only be of service from the overflow." She went on to talk about the necessity of maintaining our regular spiritual practice so that we can renew our spirit by reconnecting with the Divine presence within. When we do this, the "overflow" (our thoughts, words, and actions) reflects the love, peace, joy, kindness, and abundance that are God. When we *don't* do this... well, you know what happens. But, for those that need a refresher – all hell breaks loose! We're frustrated, angry, bitter, resentful, tired, judgmental, and more – like I was at the beginning of this year. Because we are feeling this way and are forgetting the divinity within our brothers/sisters, our words and actions come from this place of negativity and separation.

"Out of the overflow of the heart, the mouth speaks."
~Luke 6:45

Kevin was so full of love and gratitude after service that he said he had a special lunch activity for me and the boys. On our way out he thanked the minister for such a powerful message, told her he had a surprise in store for the whole family, and that we would share it with her later in the week. I couldn't wait to see what we were doing!

We pulled up to a deli, and he went inside and ordered 20 sub sandwiches. We then went to the grocery store, where he got about 40 bottles of water. We proceeded back into the city; I drove while he and our oldest son delivered food and water to anyone in need of it. It was over 100 degrees outside that day. To say everyone was grateful would be an understatement. It was such a beautiful experience of living in the overflow!

If we hadn't heard that message on Sunday, or otherwise spent time remembering Truth, I'm not sure that we would have felt inspired to do that. We have so much more love to give when we take the time to commune with God.

Which "overflow" are you living in? Love, peace, joy, kindness, gratitude, abundance, and compassion, or resentment, bitterness, guilt, lack, judgment, fear, doubt, and shame? If you find yourself experiencing the latter, for the next week be vigilant about spending five minutes in the morning and evening quietly communing with God in meditation and affirmative prayer. If you do this consistently, you are sure to be living in the overflow of the Spirit!

Outpouring of Truth – August 15, 2012

A powerful word of Truth came to me this morning after meditating on Lesson 130 in the Course. I sprung out of bed at 5:15 am. As I read through today's lesson, the following statement struck me: *Truth has a power far beyond defense, for no illusions can remain where Truth has been allowed to enter. And it comes to any mind that would lay down its arms, and cease to play with folly. It is found at any time; today, if you will choose to practice giving*

127

welcome to the Truth. This is our aim today. And we will give a quarter of an hour twice to ask the Truth to come to us and set us free. And Truth will come, for it has never been apart from us. It merely waits for just this invitation we give today.

This is the Truth that came to me after meditation...

The Truth becomes perfectly clear when you release all attachment to the world of illusion. It is indeed possible to live IN the world while knowing you are not OF the world. You are eternal, and nothing in the world can threaten that. That is the key to lasting peace and joy. All fear is laid aside when this Truth sets you free. Freedom is always available for you to choose in each moment. The alternative is the misery that comes from believing this world is the 'end all be all' of your existence. What are you choosing today?

I know that these words did not come from my ego-self. This came from the Self that God created. I had been praying to receive the Truth, and to be set free. It feels like that simple prayer turned up the faucet to the flow of God through me. It removed some of the blocks that were in the way of Truth flowing freely to me in a way that I could receive in that very moment. I tried it again later in the day and asked for the Spirit to speak through me as I sat down to write something I had been procrastinating on. Not only did the language flow through me with ease, but it was WAY better than I imagined. I thought it would take a long time to get it written. Today I was shown that, if I stop being stubborn and *ask* to be used for God's highest purpose through my words, I will be given the language to speak to the hearts and minds of others through the Spirit. It now doesn't feel as daunting to complete this particular project that I initially envisioned would take years to complete.

I had been praying to be a vessel for God to flow seamlessly through so that I may be a 'space' for the healing of others. I believe it; I receive it; and know that it is already done! The signs

I saw today were more proof that there is indeed a Power greater within. If I just surrender to it, and stop trying to be in the driver's seat myself, exactly what needs to be done in each moment will be done *through* me, with the Spirit right there to guide me. I willingly surrender to the grace of God knowing that I will be guided to the best outlet for this outpouring of Love flowing through me. So grateful for this beautiful lesson in Truth today!

Forgiveness Opportunities – August 17, 2012

This week, a few incidents happened that would have previously sent me right into anger, frustration, upset, and stress. This time, instead of viewing each occurrence with resistance and dread, I noticed the speed at which my mind went to viewing them as *forgiveness opportunities*. I noticed my body calmed down much quicker, my breath was normal, and my forehead and eyes were serene – despite anything that was going on around me. To continue to build my forgiveness muscle, I decided today that I am starting a new weekly tradition. On Fridays, I am going to journal on the forgiveness opportunities that were presented to me throughout the week. Anything that brings me upset in any form is the perfect forgiveness opportunity (annoyance, frustration, anger, guilt, regret, judgment, resentment, etc.).

I have a sticky note by my bed with "forgiveness" written on it, but I have to admit that I am not always good at letting everything go the same day it happened. There are times when I have more releasing to do in order to let it go. This weekly journaling opportunity will afford me the chance to release. Eventually, I will not need to do this and I will just automatically forgive everything right away.

This week provided me with plenty opportunities to practice releasing intentionally through journaling. On Tuesday, my computer started going really slow and I had a hunch it was not a typical slow Internet moment. Menus started flashing across the screen, everything went black, and the computer shut down. When I powered it back up, it did the same thing. Before, my mind would have started to assess all of the things I had on the computer (documents, photos, music, etc.), and all of the work I needed to get done. Instead, I calmly thought, *Oh, looks like I have a virus.*

I called IT and they informed me that it was not a virus: My hard drive failed and needed to be replaced. They were not certain if my files could be saved and would not have my computer back to me for at least four to five days. Meanwhile, I was working on a grant proposal that needed to be submitted the following day. After a brief 'Aw, man' moment, I sent my boss an e-mail informing him of what was going on and that I would still have the document complete the following day. I dropped my computer off to get it fixed, and that was that. There was nothing else I could do. As I drove away, I started forgiving myself. I forgave myself for not saving all of my files someplace else (I had many of the files on a thumb drive, but not all of them). I forgave myself for not turning my computer off each night. I forgave myself for not noticing signs of my computer's hard drive failing. I forgave myself for having to rewrite the proposal for work. I forgave myself for *anything* that was causing me upset in that moment.

Anytime someone or something is causing you upset, it's an opportunity to forgive.

On Wednesday, my youngest son was playing on the playground at school and fell *forehead first* on the concrete. He had fallen about a month ago at school and had another large scar on his head already. The first time it happened, I was livid. I felt that the teachers weren't watching him, and I was sad that he would have a very large scar on his head. (All of the skin came off on a circular shaped area of his forehead about the size of a quarter;

he is brown skinned, so he has a large, light spot on his head now.) Every time I looked at him, I would notice the scar and tears would come to my eyes. I was finally getting 'over' that incident, only for the school to call and let me know he had *another* one on his head just as big as the first one? I couldn't believe it. I called my husband right away and told him I was on my way to the school to pick him up. Initially, I was ready to transfer him out of the school and have a serious talk with the director (let's just say, I wasn't exactly going to say how much I loved the school).

I sat for a minute and prayed that I would respond in love. I sent my husband the following text: *Trying to remember this is a forgiveness lesson (like everything else). Praying before I go in there.* When I got to the school, the teacher admitted she wasn't watching when he fell. She was also nonchalant in her explanation of the event. I let her finish telling me the story and said, "Thank you for letting me know." I signed the incident report, and left the school. I decided not to have the talk with the director that day so that I would be sure to respond from a calm place. The assistant director called later that night to express her sincere apologies, and I accepted.

On Thursday, the daycare called me and I remember thinking, *What now?* They said my youngest was stung by a bee on his face. Seriously??? All I could do was crack up laughing when I got off the phone. What a week. Nonetheless, I am grateful for all that occurred. I was reminded that I need to practice forgiveness until it becomes a way of living. I know that whatever I *don't* forgive now will come back up as a future lesson for me to learn so I might as well do it now! I have made the decision to live in the Love and Light of God, which means I cannot harbor unforgiveness. Unforgiveness and unconditional love cannot coexist. I'm sure there are more tests to come. With practice, I will be armed and ready to forgive on the spot. Then, and only then, will I experience the constancy of inner peace.

What forgiveness opportunities did you have this week? May this excerpt from the passage "What is Forgiveness?"[9] in the Course bless you as much as it blessed me. It reminded me to forgive as I have been forgiven.

An unforgiving thought does many things. In frantic action it pursues its goal, twisting and overturning what it sees as interfering with its chosen path. Distortion is its purpose, and the means by which it would accomplish it as well. It sets about its furious attempts to smash reality, without concern for anything that would appear to pose a contradiction to its point of view.

Forgiveness, on the other hand, is still, and quietly does nothing. It offends no aspect of reality, nor seeks to twist it to appearances it likes. It merely looks, and waits, and judges not. He who would not forgive must judge, for he must justify his failure to forgive. But he who would forgive himself must learn to welcome truth exactly as it is.

Do nothing, then, and let forgiveness show you what to do, through Him Who is your Guide, your Savior and Protector, strong in hope, and certain of your ultimate success. He has forgiven you already, for such is His function, given Him by God. Now must you share His function, and forgive whom He has saved, whose sinlessness He sees, and whom He honors as the Son of God.

Choosing Happiness – August 26, 2012

I didn't start off the day in a great mood. I was super tired. My boys woke up at 5:50 am during my meditation/prayer time, and were not listening at all. My meditation was weak, even before the boys woke up. My stomach was bloated. My hair needed to be washed (I have a thick afro so it takes a while to comb through). I had known all week that my husband was going to have to work this Sunday, but I didn't plan anything to do with our boys. The list goes on and on. I can't even pretend that I wasn't frustrated. Today could have easily been 'one of those days' if I had given in to the negative thoughts I was having. I would have had an attitude with my husband, been disengaged when talking with people, and felt annoyed with the boys all day. I would have had a bad day overall.

While in the shower, I listened to Gary Renard's *Secrets of the Immortal*[10] audio program, which started to get me back on the right track. I was feeling a bit of resistance: I was still being stubborn and holding onto some of my frustration. In that moment, I decided what today's activity would be: We would visit a spiritual community that we hadn't visited in over a month. I had a feeling that today's message would be exactly what I needed to hear. I was feeling better already. Then I heard screams from the other room.

My oldest son thought it would be 'fun' to play in my grapefruit essential oil (which, ironically, is supposed to be a mood lifter), and got it in his eyes and his brother's eyes. They were screaming at the top of their lungs, and I felt horrible. I was upset with myself for leaving the bottle within their reach, and I was upset with them for 'always getting into everything.' My husband and I got them cleaned up, and ready to get out of the house.

The drive over was uneventful. We arrived to the spiritual center about 15 minutes early, and walked in to the blissful sound of the musical inspiration. I was still in a 'blah' mood and was praying that the boys wouldn't act up. Them acting up would have been all I needed to set me off. They sat quietly and cuddled with me as we listened to the music (normally they would have been jumping up and down).

When I went to drop them off in the toddler room, they stayed there with no fuss at all (which also was not normal). I got back to the sanctuary just in time for prayer and meditation. Unlike earlier this morning, I was able to sink into the sweetness of the presence of God without interruption. As the minister began to introduce the guest speaker for the day, I felt a little disappointed that she wasn't going to be speaking. I still believed the message was going to be *just* what I needed.

After a brief introduction, the speaker introduced his topic: Happiness is an Inside Job. I almost fell out of my chair. I had seen this *exact* line multiple times over the last week via Facebook status updates, my Twitter feed, and an inspirational e-mail newsletter I subscribe to. I barely paid attention to it because the ego was telling me, "You already know that." In that moment, even before the guest speaker uttered another word, I realized what the Spirit was trying to remind me of.

While I have been immersed in the study of the power of the mind and understand intellectually that our thoughts are creating our experiences, I don't always remember to actively choose another thought that *is* aligned with Truth when in the thick moments of frustration. *My happiness is not dependent upon external circumstances; it's dependent upon my **perception** of those circumstances.* Or, as today's speaker said, "You will be happy when you make the decision to be happy."

If I remember these words in those moments of frustration, it will make *all* the difference in my day-to-day experience. *I* have the power to change my thoughts and, thus, change my life (as so many great spiritual teachers have said). One of the most powerful thought-shifters for me is, "All things are working together for my good." I believe in a Power greater than myself. I know that there is *no* challenging circumstance that hasn't turned around and worked out for the highest good *for* all involved. *How could I not be happy knowing that everything is working together for my good?* The challenge, however, is remembering. Thankfully, this is where the Holy Spirit comes in to consistently guide me to gentle reminders of Truth like the one I received today.

I'm so grateful that opportunities to change my mind – or "choose once again" as the Course states – never cease to present themselves. When I miss the message or choose to think negatively, another opportunity to realign myself with the unconditional love and forgiveness of God is around the corner. Everything lined up in perfect order today so that I could fully receive the message that had been trying to penetrate my mind for the past week. We have the power to choose to align with the ego *or* God in each and every moment. I release the guilt, shame, blame, judgment, and anger that the ego had me fixated on this morning.

I choose to align my thoughts with the peace, joy, compassion, kindness, and gentleness of God in response to all that is causing me any sense of frustration. The result of this choice is happiness – now.

Every time I am *not* happy, I know that I have made the wrong choice in my thinking and that I have the power to change that. I don't have to wait for circumstances to change; I only have to change my mind.

You always choose between your weakness and the strength of Christ in you. And what you choose is what you think is real. Simply by never using weakness to direct your actions, you have given it no power. And the light of Christ in you is given charge of everything you do. For you have brought your weakness unto Him, and He has given you His strength instead.[11]
~*A Course in Miracles*

The Little Things – September 4, 2012

> "Do small things with great love."
> ~Mother Teresa

Tomorrow will mark the 15-year anniversary of Mother Teresa's transition. For weeks she has been on my mind, and I couldn't figure out why. I knew a little about her story (enough to be inspired by her), but hadn't spent much time studying her work. A couple of weeks ago, I was in the drugstore picking up a card for a friend's birthday when I saw a magazine on the stand with a striking photo of Mother Teresa on the cover. I knew I needed to pick it up. It was *TIME* magazine's special edition titled, *Mother Teresa at 100: The Life and Works of a Modern Saint*.[12] Around the same time I bought the magazine, I stumbled upon a book about her life that I purchased years ago but never finished, *Reaching Out in Love*.[13]

After reading the magazine, and some more of the book, I am very clear on why the Holy Spirit was reminding me of her. She is such a powerful example of living life with the sole intention of expressing the unconditional love of God – the very way I am now focused on living my life. She spent her life caring for 'the least of these,' and modeling her life after the Master Teacher, Jesus.

Around the time that she was first placed on my heart, I passed a homeless man and had the overwhelming urge to stop and talk to him. To the dismay of the drivers behind me, who were rushing off to work or other appointments, I pulled over and said, "How are you doing today?" He said he was doing alright and asked me if I liked jazz music. I responded affirmatively and he went on to tell me that he plays the bass and had heard about Esperanza Spalding. (For those of you who don't know her, she is an amazing, young, upright bass player and jazz singer.) We had a good conversation about what an amazing jazz artist she is, and talked about other artists he likes. Finally, I left him with some money and told him I'd see him soon. He said, "It was nice talking to you." I agreed.

The next day, I went back and rolled down my window to say, "Hello." I asked him if he had eaten anything that day. He said he hadn't, and that he would love some water. I went to the store to get him something to eat and a couple large bottles of water. He couldn't believe I did that, and was smiling from ear to ear. He asked me what I did for a living and I told him that I work in education. He asked me if I knew of any General Education Development (GED) programs. I told him I would research some programs and bring him back some options the next day. I did just that. I was able to find some free programs and talked with the coordinators to find out the schedules and requirements. I went back the next day with everything clearly written out for him and gave him some money to take the bus to get to the locations. He shook his head in amazement and was SO grateful. I am tearing up just writing about this experience because it took very little of my time, but blessed both of us immensely. I have not seen him on that corner since.

This is what Mother Teresa did EVERY day. She helped those that most people passed by every day. She only saw the Christ in everyone, and denied the existence of anything that countered that. Because of her relentless awareness of the Truth about all beings, 'miraculous' healings took place in her presence. One of her sayings was "one, one, one" and it represented her commitment to doing one small thing at a time. I really needed to hear that because I am a big dreamer. I have a passion for helping others, but am always thinking so big that it sometimes paralyzes me.

Mother Teresa started out helping one community and her ministry expanded to help millions around the world. She was not pushing for that to happen; it was a natural extension of the unconditional love and undivided attention she gave in each community in which she worked. Here's something that she said to someone who wanted to come volunteer in Calcutta, where she started her ministry:

Stay where you are. Find your own Calcutta. Find the sick, the suffering, and the lonely right there where you are – in your own homes and in your own families, in your workplaces and in your schools. You can find Calcutta all over the world, if you have the eyes to see. Everywhere, wherever you go, you find people who are unwanted, unloved, uncared for, just rejected by society – completely forgotten, completely left alone.

I am incredibly inspired to start small, and right in my own community. I have so much to give that doesn't cost a lot of money nor require the formation of a large organization. I am so ready. As Mother Teresa would say, "Let's do something beautiful for God."

I never look at the masses as my responsibility; I look at the individual. I can only love one person at a time – just one, one, one. So you begin. I began – I picked up one person. Maybe if I didn't pick up that one person, I wouldn't have picked up forty-two thousand... The same thing goes for you, the same thing in your family, the same thing in your church, your community. Just begin – one, one, one.
~Mother Teresa

Forgiveness and Politics – September 5, 2012

While I typically don't write about politics, I had to share this story because of the powerful lessons I learned last week. For those who disagree with my political position, I pray that you can see past that to the message this entry is intended to share. Much Love and Light!

The political season is in full effect. I tend to get very frustrated and worked up around this time. Instead of expecting the worst, I decided to watch last week's Republican National Convention (RNC) with an open mind. I wanted to look through the lens of unconditional love and compassion, instead of the judgment and anger with which I watched in the past. I wish I could say it was a breeze, and that I did it perfectly, but that was not the case.

I had a really tough time listening to some of the speeches. There were many moments in which I had to pause the television and give Kevin an impassioned speech about why I get frustrated when they say this or that. The night after the Republican candidate's speech, I was feeling especially bitter. As I went into prayer and meditation that evening, I spent some time realigning myself with the qualities of God and trying to release the ego-driven thoughts that were running rampant in my mind (resentment, judgment, etc.). I asked that the Holy Spirit help me see this in a different light. I knew I needed help, and was certain I would receive it once I surrendered my perspective.

Shortly after prayer, I started thinking about the root of my anger. Because of the work I've been doing this year to grow spiritually, I know that when anger comes up in me that it has *nothing* to do with what someone else did and *everything* to do with how I perceive what has happened. I thought hard about the statements made by the Republicans that pushed my buttons. The ones that came to mind were: *Anyone can make it in America if they just try hard enough; We all came to America looking for greater opportunity and a better life; I pulled myself up by my own boot straps and so can you;* and *We built this.* At first glance, these statements seem empowering. After some reflection I finally reached the source of why they pushed my buttons so much, and it wasn't what I expected.

I realized that my greatest frustration with those statements stems from the experience of my ancestors, later labeled "African-Americans." My ancestors did NOT come to America looking for greater opportunity, but were brought here in chains and forced to do hard labor to build this nation. They were viewed as less than human, and were treated as such. For generations, my ancestors had to work twice as hard to be on 'equal' footing with white Americans. Yes, America is supposed to be the land of great opportunity but, unfortunately, we are *still* not at a point where all people view African-Americans as equals. We have certainly come a long way since slavery, and we have a lot of success stories, but we are not there yet.

I won't spend a lot of time on recent – and sometimes tragic – examples of racism. Nor will I recount the number of times I have directly experienced or been witness to the inequalities that are still present today as that is beyond the scope of this entry. I will say that we are certainly not in a color- and class-blind utopia that the Republicans often paint. And, I'm not sure we would be as far along as we are today without some assistance being provided to help level the playing field.

It felt good to have acknowledged the root of my anger and frustration as it wasn't about the Republicans. What I felt was something much deeper – bitterness towards the difficulties that generations of African-Americans have faced since slavery. I was also saddened that people think it's OK to let others (particularly those less fortunate) fend for themselves and are completely OK with *not* providing support. I was frustrated by feeling the need to lay aside my African heritage in order to conform or 'look the part' throughout much of my life. And I could not stand that *all* people receiving government assistance were being labeled as 'lazy' or 'not working hard enough.'

I was annoyed by the stories that were shared at the RNC of people who "pulled themselves up by their own bootstraps" because they made it seem as if they didn't benefit from any type of assistance along the way. I felt like the African-American experience (and the experience of other marginalized groups), in particular, was being totally disregarded in the comments made by the Republicans and *that* is why I was angry. I certainly believe that anything is possible with hard work, but I also believe in assisting others along the journey. In that moment, I knew I had some serious forgiveness work to do if I wanted to be at peace.

The next day, I was led to turn on the parts of the RNC that I recorded but hadn't yet watched. The first thing that came on was the Republican candidate's campaign video. Hearing his story really helped me see a different side of him. The videos of him with his children... the story of how he and his wife met... the stories about his father's political career... All of this helped remind me that his opinions about life were formed based on his life experiences and what he has been exposed to up to this point. He did not grow up in a family like mine and did not experience the same struggles I experienced (or that my ancestors experienced), so it is natural that he wouldn't understand that perspective.

I was reminded of a time that a former boss shared with me how her ancestors immigrated to the United States from Ireland and Poland. She then asked me where mine were from. I paused for a moment to think about how best to answer that question. I finally emerged from the silence and said, "I don't know." I paused for a moment still trying to figure out the right way to put this (and trying to calm myself down because I was angry that she would ask what I viewed as an ignorant question). She looked very puzzled. Finally, I said calmly, "Most African-Americans don't know what countries in Africa their ancestors came from because they were separated from their families, forced in boats, stacked on top of one another, brought over to the US in chains, forced to give up their names and traditions, and sold to slave owners who gave them names and forced them to do hard labor for no money." She apologized profusely and stated that she didn't realize that. She knew a little about slavery (whatever brief lesson she learned in history class back in elementary school), but she never connected those dots. She didn't know any better.

I believe that if people understood the day-to-day experiences of people who have life struggles different from their own they might begin to see things in a different way. Who knows, they might even find more compassion for those who have had less fortunate life experiences. Instead of getting angry, I'm choosing to forgive. And I feel lighter already. What a release! I had been holding onto that bitterness for *years*, and I'm so happy to let it go. That bottled up anger was only disturbing *my* peace – not the peace of those to whom my anger was directed.

I also needed to remind myself to see the Light in *all* people. We are all creations of the Divine. We are all one in God, and cannot be separate from one another. If I can remember this, regardless of the actions of others, I will be able to extend the Love and Peace of God to all whom I encounter. I'm so grateful for this situation reminding me of this simple Truth. My forgiveness is not really directed toward anyone except myself because *I* am the one who forgot to see the Light and chose, instead, to focus on perceived darkness.

The light in them [our brothers and sisters] shines as brightly regardless of the density of the fog that obscures it. If you give no power to the fog to obscure the light, it has none. For it has power only if the Son of God gives power to it. He must himself withdraw that power, remembering that all power is of God. You can remember this for all the Sonship. Do not allow your brother not to remember, for his forgetfulness is yours. But your remembering is his, for God cannot be remembered alone. This is what you have forgotten. To perceive the healing of your brother as the healing of yourself is thus the way to remember God. For you forgot your brothers with Him, and God's Answer to your forgetting is but the way to remember.[14]
~A Course in Miracles

Before I got to a place of self-forgiveness and remembering the oneness of all life, this quote from Mother Teresa really helped me heal the deep-rooted resentment I had carried so long and directed toward certain groups of people. (Note: I think the word "poor" in this quote could be replaced with "marginalized", "homeless", and many other words that represent those who have been looked down upon.)

The trouble is that [some] rich people, well-to-do people, don't really know who the poor are; and that is why we can forgive them, for knowledge can only lead to love, and love to service. And so, if they are not touched by them, it's because they do not know them.
~Mother Teresa

Chapter 9

Detaching from the Ego

If You're Happy and You Know It – September 9, 2012

I wish you could have been a fly on the wall in our home yesterday. There was lots of singing, dancing, and being silly. I felt like a kid again. The day certainly didn't start off this way though. I was doing fine for the first few hours then things took a turn for the worst. I felt like my sons made a vow to do the *opposite* of everything I told them to do. They thought it was hilarious. I was about to pull my hair out. I totally lost my cool. I felt that I had done all I could to get them to settle down. I was exhausted and ready to give up. I eventually let them watch some TV (which I intend to limit, but many times use as a crutch when I get annoyed).

In that moment of seeming defeat, my Inner Voice said, "If you're happy and you know it clap your hands." I started singing it immediately and, within minutes, felt a significant shift in my mood and noticed a shift in theirs. I kept singing it over and over, and by the time I got to, "If you're happy and you know it, shout 'hooray,'" I was smiling from ear to ear. The boys were having so much fun and didn't want to stop singing. We went on to sing a few more songs together (e.g. *Head and Shoulders, Knees and Toes*) until we were all tired.

I was present. I completely let go of any thoughts about what I needed to read and chores that needed to be done around the house. I let go of my desire to have them sit down and be quiet. And I let go of my embarrassment about the boys not listening to me. I went from exasperation to elation in less than five minutes just by simply being present and positively affirming a new feeling – happiness. I wish I could say this was all intentional, but this definitely came from deeper within. I am so grateful for hearing, and adhering to, the Voice for God in that moment.

This all happened just a few hours after I live streamed a workshop led by Louise Hay and Cheryl Richardson titled, *You Can Create an Exceptional Life.*[1] It reminded me to affirm what I want to create in my life. Looking back, I see that I unconsciously created the mood I wanted to experience in that moment. It worked then and I know it will work in any moment.

What situation in your own life is draining your energy? What can you affirm now to help move to a state of happiness, peace, joy, and love?

> *"Deny the ability for anything not of God to affect you."*
> ~*A Course in Miracles*

I must disclose that I have had an issue with being consistent with affirmations in the past. I used to feel that I was lying to myself and would pretend that I felt differently after the affirmation when I didn't. Since my counselor reintroduced affirmations to me, what has helped me is forgiveness of myself for whatever negative feelings I was experiencing. I, *then*, coming from a place of peace, affirm what I want to replace the old thought with. That has made them feel much more authentic. My affirmation after this situation yesterday was:

Like fireworks, I am bursting with Light. I bring joy to all I encounter. I let my Light shine!

Later in the day, I was feeling drained and the boys were getting a little out of control again. I turned on the Music Choice channel and declared it was "dance party time." I was going back and forth between the Throwback Jams and Hip-Hop Classics channels, which are two of my favorites because they play the songs that were popular when I was growing up. We were jamming. I tried to teach my 3 year old the "Roger Rabbit," the "Running Man," the "Cabbage Patch" and "the Wop" (all popular dances in the 1980s). It was hilarious! My husband even joined in the fun.

The old me would have had an attitude for the entire day, and been a drag for the family to be around. I'm so grateful for yet another reminder to continue *Living in the Light*! Keep shining!

Pool of Tears – September 12, 2012

Sometimes you just need a good cry. Today was one of those days for me. Tears began streaming on my way home from running errands and didn't stop until I reached the bathroom floor (don't ask). I knew exactly what this was about: It was time to shed another layer of my past that was no longer serving me. This time it was guilt and shame.

Guilt and shame are cousins on the ego side of the family. I have entertained them almost my entire life. Shame came into my life at a young age when I started comparing my family life with what I perceived to be the perfect home life of others. I was ashamed of not having the perfect family, not realizing at the time that almost every family had challenges of their own. Guilt began tagging along when I began to seek love and acceptance in all the wrong places. Counseling, spiritual development, self-help courses, and even writing on the *Living in the Light* blog have helped me to see how guilt and shame have hurt me through the years. Recognition is one thing, but now it is time to disown them.

Yesterday, I was practicing the *Life Visioning* technique and seeking God's highest vision for my life. I have been receiving flashes of visions of me helping thousands, and even millions, of people by sharing the lessons learned on my spiritual journey. To be honest, it scares the crap out of me. Ego is telling me I'm not ready, I don't have enough experience on this topic, I'm still ashamed of parts of my past, I don't have my 'five-step plan' together, etc. Excuses! During my visioning session, I asked for help in releasing whatever is blocking me from expressing full confidence in His vision for my life.

I was led by the Spirit to listen to a talk[2] by Iyanla Vanzant and, in it, she said, "Call in the Queen." *Did she really just say my nickname?* Even though the talk was given years ago, it was like she was speaking directly to me. She went on to say, "The Queen's job is to take care of the kingdom, and the kingdom is your life... whenever you feel like you can't do it alone, call in the Queen in you who is *always* connected to the King." I wanted to jump through the screen and give her a high five!

Dr. Beckwith asks in his *Life Visioning* process, *"Who do you need to become in order to manifest God's highest vision for your life?"* Later in the day, I turned on the CD player in the car and, sure enough, it was his audiobook talking about this exact thing. *What skills do you need to develop? Describe the person that has manifested that vision? Who do they surround themselves with? What do they sound like?*

Those two pep talks helped me feel better in the moment. They got me thinking about the things I can do to prepare myself to live my purpose. But, they still didn't help me connect with what was blocking me from *being* who God is calling me to be. This morning, the answer drowned my ego through my tears, and helped me hear the voice of the Spirit within me ("the Queen"). I came face-to-face with the reality and had two choices: (1) call forth the Queen; or (2) stay stuck in the ego's small view of who I am and what I can be. The ego was trying hard to make me feel like I am not worthy of the goodness that God is preparing me for because of the guilt and shame I was carrying from the past. I will not let the ego win again. I disown the ego and its cousins, guilt and shame. As the Course says repeatedly, "I am as God created me." Nothing can change that.

Affirmation: I am a Queen. In each moment, I manifest God's goodness in the Kingdom of my life. I am a bold witness to the grace of God. I share His Love wherever I go.

Have you been shrinking from moving forward on a dream or a vision for your life? Has the ego been trying to tell you that you aren't good enough or that you aren't ready? What can you affirm in place of the ego's lies in order to begin manifesting what God has for you?

5 Steps to Releasing Negativity – September 17, 2012

I spent so many years living a beautiful exterior life and miserable interior life. I had all of the things a woman could dream of: a wonderful husband, healthy children, a high-paying job, a roof over my head, disposable income to travel the world, and more. So, why the heck was I unhappy? I have been reflecting on my old ways a lot lately, as I am noticing the dramatic shift in my way of moving through life.

From the time I was about 8 years old until earlier this year, my self-talk sounded something like: *You're not good enough; You're not pretty enough; You're not smart enough; You need to work harder; You're not as good as _____ ; I can't believe you did that; You don't do enough around the house; You're not successful enough; Am I enough for him; What are people going to think?* I could go on and on.

My thoughts about other people weren't any better. They sounded something like: *I can't believe they did that; She needs to get a life; She is such an attention seeker; They are so annoying; I hate_____; He/She is such a hypocrite; It's all their fault; They can't do anything right.* Once again, I could go on and on. I was a 24/7 judgment and blame machine.

I used to think I was alone in thinking about myself like this. I thought most people were totally happy with themselves, and I was one of a few who felt trapped by the desire to be perfect and look good in the eyes of others. In terms of my judgment of other people, I had never stepped back to observe it. It was a mental habit. This habit was something I had no idea was keeping me trapped in the cycle of judgment. This changed once I began being mindful of my thoughts.

In January of this year, when I was diagnosed with depression and anxiety disorder, I was absolutely determined to get to the root of what was causing the insanity that was my mind, and to reverse it once and for all. And, yes, I am deliberate about my use of the word insanity. As Einstein once said, "The definition of insanity is doing the same thing over and over again and expecting different results." *How could I expect to experience happiness and peace if my thoughts were 90 percent negative and judgmental of myself and others?* It's impossible. No wonder I wasn't happy.

> "The judger always feels judged. The lover always feels beloved."
> ~Rev. Jennifer Hadley

Aside from beginning the Course again, one of the most helpful things I did to release the negative thoughts was an activity from the spiritual boot camp I participated in. During class one night, the Rev. Jennifer said, *How long do you want to hold onto your negativity? Set a date to release it!* I love that.

Listed below are five steps that helped me most in releasing negativity in my life. They sound so simple, but it's amazing how unconscious we can be about the effect our thoughts have on our internal and external experience. This made ALL the difference in replacing my regular experience of frustration and upset with a regular experience of peace and love in a *very* short amount of time. I pray that it helps others struggling with recurring negative thoughts as well.

5 Steps to Releasing Negativity

1. Observe your thoughts
Set a time period to observe your thoughts and write down the ones that come up the most. Include thoughts about yourself as well as thoughts about others. I suggest doing this for a minimum of seven days (longer is better – remember, it takes between 21–28 days to form a habit). You can do this throughout the day; however, I also recommend setting aside quiet reflection/meditation time daily for this.

2. Decide which thoughts are *not* contributing to your peace
Spend some time reviewing the list of your most frequent thoughts and put a circle around the ones that are not contributing to your peace of mind and/or peaceful interactions with others. Write these on a water bottle or a balloon – or some other item that will allow you to release it when the time comes. To ensure it will fit on the bottle/balloon, I suggest using broad categories. For example, my list included things like: self-hatred, blame, judgment, guilt, uncertainty, shame, and gossip. (I used a water bottle in the boot camp, but used a balloon for a fear exercise at a women's retreat a few years ago – both work great!)

3. Affirmative prayer
Take each negative thought on your list and create an affirmation that you can use whenever these thoughts arise. For example, one of my negative thought patterns was "unworthiness" and the affirmation I used was, "I am as God created me. All the gifts of God are mine." In addition to the list of affirmations, I began to practice affirmative prayer. Instead of praying to an external God to fix something, I prayed to the indwelling presence of God (the Holy Spirit) and called forth all the qualities of the Spirit that are my natural state of being (joy, peace, kindness, love, gentleness, etc.). I used my affirmations during prayer time to

realign with the Truth about myself and others. In addition, as a student of the Course, I find the prayer below to be incredibly helpful when I'm feeling out of alignment with the Spirit:

> *I must have decided wrongly, because I am not at peace.*
> *I made the decision myself, but I can also decide otherwise.*
> *I want to decide otherwise, because I want to be at peace.*
> *I do not feel guilty, because the Holy Spirit will undo all the conse-*
> *quences of my wrong decision if I will let Him.*
> *I choose to let Him, by allowing Him to decide for God for me.*[3]
> *~A Course in Miracles*

4. Set a release date

I pose the same question that the Rev. Jennifer did during boot camp, "How long are you willing to hold onto your negative thoughts?" Set your own timeline. I felt a dramatic shift after one month. After about two months, I could catch myself mid-sentence when I was about to say something negative and would redirect myself. To date, it has been about six months and I am a new woman. (*That just randomly reminded me of the song, (I've Got a)* New Attitude[4] *by Patti LaBelle, which can also lift your spirits.*)

5. Let it go!

I have to admit, I didn't take the Rev. Jennifer's advice at first on setting a date. I kept letting it linger and, as a result, kept falling in and out of my old ways of thinking for a while. There is something about the ritual of releasing all of the negativity (setting the balloon free or pouring out the water) that really gives wings to the intention for living in alignment with the Peace and Love of God – *Living in the Light*. Do I slip up from time to time? Absolutely. When I do, I forgive myself and get right back in the game.

I was going to end this here, but I just got an internal nudge that someone is asking, "What if everyone around me is negative? How can I get everyone else to stop being so negative so that I can feel peaceful?" This is a question I really struggled with when I first started actively focusing on *Living in the Light*. The question answered itself when I completed the above process. I'm so grateful for the peace that I am now experiencing more and more *despite* the day-to-day life circumstances. Whenever I have moments of upset, I can get out of them in less than a day (whereas before it would have taken days, weeks, months, or years for me to let it go). Experiencing peace has nothing to do with external circumstances and everything to do with our internal response to them. Try it; you won't be disappointed. Keep Shining!

The Key to Releasing the Past – September 19, 2012

After my last entry, I received a few questions about releasing attachment to the past. Readers mentioned that many of the thoughts they were having trouble releasing were replays of negative experiences in the past and/or predictions of negative experiences in the future.

> "The journey is much easier when you are not carrying your past."
> ~Unknown

Isn't it 'normal' to think about the past? Shouldn't I use the past as a guide to predict the future? Shouldn't I be 'on guard' with people who have hurt me? These are some of the questions that used to run through my mind as it relates to the past. In answering these questions, it helps to start with what seems to bind us to the past in the first place. I have learned that this has so much to do with who you identify with. What do I mean by that? Well, I used to think that the thoughts that were flowing in and out of my head *were* me. I thought that it was just 'normal' to remember the past, and for it to keep playing over and over in my mind. It wasn't until I really began to step back from the thoughts and observe them (as described in *5 Steps to Releasing Negativity*) that I realized that *I am not my thoughts... I am the observer of my thoughts.* This was big. I was no longer a slave to the thoughts that ran through my mind. This realization gave me back my power.

If you are indeed the *observer* of your thoughts, then you have the power of choice. This means that your natural state is the peace that lies beyond the thoughts. In each moment you can choose whether to carry the baggage of the past forward, or to release it and be present to what is available in the moment. You can choose whether to see the past mistakes of others, or see the person that's standing in front of you today. You can choose to express love, or withhold it based on negative past experience. The quote below from the Course hits the nail on the head on this topic:

> *If you remember the past as you look upon your brother, you will be unable to perceive the reality that is now. You consider it 'natural' to use your past experience as a reference point from which to judge the present. Yet this is unnatural because it is delusional. When you have learned to look on everyone with no reference to the past, either his or yours as you perceived it, you will be able to learn from what you see now. For the past can cast no shadow to darken the present, unless you are afraid of light. And only if you are would you choose to bring darkness with you, and, by holding it in your mind, see it as a dark cloud that shrouds your brothers and conceals reality from your sight.*[5]

When I first read that I thought it was harsh. *Am I really delusional?* Then I sat for a moment, meditated, read it again, and asked for Divine understanding of this idea. The answer came almost instantly. The Voice within said, "When you go on a trip, do you pack dirty clothes and spoiled food?" I had to laugh out loud at that. Of course I don't. Then *It* said, "How do you want others to see you? As you are now or as you were in the past?"

I paused again, and even began to tear as I remembered a time in my life when I was feeling particularly guilty – after the affair. All I wanted was for Kevin to see me as I was in the moment, but that took time. I remembered the pain and hurt of that experience. All I wanted was for the good in me to be recognized. All I wanted was to be forgiven and loved. *Isn't that what we all want?*

The miracle enables you to see your brother without his past, and so perceive him as born again. His errors are all past, and by perceiving him without them you are releasing him. And since his past is yours, you share in this release. Let no dark cloud out of your past obscure him from you, for truth lies only in the present, and you will find it if you seek it there.[6]
~A Course in Miracles

Forgiveness is the key to releasing the past. When I say forgiveness, I'm not referring to the world's definition of it where people say, "You're wrong and a 'sinner,' but I forgive you anyway… but I'm better than you." The forgiveness I am speaking of is forgiveness of the Spirit that says, "I see *Who* you *really* are, beyond any past mistakes you have made… I forgive myself for not seeing the *Light* in you." If you choose to see beyond all appearances to the ever-present Light within everyone, the past becomes irrelevant. As all of the great spiritual teachers tell us, *all that ever exists is now.*

I am still a work in progress on this, but I am light-years ahead of where I was. I am now clear that I have a choice in each moment – to live in the present or live in the dream world of the past. More and more, I am choosing the present. It makes all the difference in whether I am living in fear or love… darkness or light. My intention is to solely see the Love and Light that exists within me and others, and to help others do the same. *What about you? What's your biggest struggle in releasing the past? What seems to be the biggest obstacle you face when trying to seeing the Light in others?*

The present offers you your brothers in the light that would unite you with them, and free you from the past. Would you, then, hold the past against them? For if you do, you are choosing to remain in the darkness that is not there, and refusing to accept the light that is offered you... Child of Light, you know not that the light is in you. Yet you will find it through its witnesses, for having given light to them they will return it. Each one you see in light brings your light closer to your awareness. Love always leads to love.[7]
~A Course in Miracles

When in Doubt, Pray it Out – September 25, 2012

I am dizzy from the roller coaster of emotions I have experienced over the past few days. The ego is not going down without a fight, that's for sure. In some moments, I'm experiencing the perfect peace of God within myself and in all things. In other moments, some of my old ego-driven tendencies pop up and are blocking me from experiencing the perfect peace that I *know* is my natural state of being.

The ego-tendency-of-the-week has been the need to be liked and approved of. This was such a strong tendency of mine throughout my life. It popped up again recently because of the direction I'm going spiritually. My beliefs have shifted a bit, and I was feeling sad about what that may mean for some of my friendships. While I have many friends that are open to spiritual paths that are not the same as their own, there are also some who are not.

This fear of loss of friendship was heightened when the number of friends who "liked" the *Living in the Light* Facebook page decreased by a few people (silly, I know). The ego started running wild in my mind with things like: *See, I told you that you were going to lose friends over this; I told you people weren't open to these ideas; Maybe you should take a more balanced approach to your posts; Are you sure you're ready to share more of what you really think?; Maybe you should just stop sharing your spiritual journey publicly; This new path is going to be lonely,* etc.

Right when the ego was in the thick of its rant, and my eyes were welling up with tears, the phone rang. It was a good friend who shares similar spiritual beliefs (tolerant of *all* spiritual paths, and more focused on spiritual living versus dogma). Talk about Divine timing. He listened to me share what was on my mind with compassion, and then he mentioned a book he ran across years ago called *The Ways of Mental Prayer*[8] by Domitry Vital Lehodey. I looked it up while we were on the phone and, after reading a few of the sample pages, realized it was very similar to a prayer technique I learned about in one of my courses earlier this year, Spiritual Mind Treatment. Essentially, through prayer, you are realigning to the presence of God within. It's less about the words, and more about *feeling,* and attuning yourself to, the Spirit. I SO needed that reminder.

> "Prayer will draw down into your soul the omnipotence of God."
> ~Domitry Vital Lehodey, The Ways of Mental Prayer

As much as I am immersed in this material each day, I totally forgot to apply it to this situation. I was allowing myself to get frustrated instead of pausing, breathing, and reconnecting to the Spirit. After we got off the phone, I had the most powerful prayer/meditation session I have had in a while. I *felt* my oneness with God. It was also a beautiful reminder that we are *all* one.

The Spirit reminded me that "As you see him, you will see yourself"[9] is not just a nice saying – it's the Truth. Our brothers and sisters are reflections of ourselves. I realized I still had some judgments about religion that *I* needed to release so that I wouldn't feel judged for my spiritual path.

That was a big shift. I went from being at the *effect* of everyone else's judgments to being at the *cause* of it. I was actually projecting my own judgments on them, and then was feeling like *I* was the one being judged. I am so grateful for the reminder. When I remember to pray (through affirmative prayer/spiritual mind treatment), it keeps me connected to the truth about myself and others. No matter how different we may appear to be in this world, in God we are all one. That is all that matters. That's all I'm trying to see. Everything else is an illusion. Back up, ego... the Queen is coming through!

P.S. A song that just came to mind is one by India Arie and Idan Raichel called *The Gift of Acceptance*.[10] It's such a beautiful song about tolerance for all spiritual paths that I absolutely love.

If you are interested in learning more about prayer techniques to support the release of negative thoughts and the return to peace-of-mind, visit:
www.kandacejones.com/classes

The Gift of Acceptance – September 26, 2012

The song, *The Gift of Acceptance*, is still on my mind. In fact, it has crossed my mind multiple times throughout this year. I finally understood why this week. I first heard the song earlier this year when I became more vigilant in my spiritual walk. It really resonated with me, along with the mantra I learned from my ashram visit earlier this year: Truth is one, paths are many.

I genuinely believed I was more tolerant and open-minded

than I have ever been in my life – especially since I was reading more than I ever have about different faiths and spiritual walks. I saw clearly the Truth that was woven through them all, and thought I was accepting of all of them. However, I recently caught myself judging others. This happened when I felt like I was being judged by some friends for my transition toward spirituality. What I realized was that *I* was actually judging *them*. I was feeling like I was right about my beliefs, and they were wrong about theirs. I was doing the very thing I didn't want done to me – judging. Somehow my old mantra, "Truth is one, paths are many," shifted to "I'm right, you're wrong."

How could I expect for my spiritual walk to be accepted when I wasn't accepting of the walk of others? How could I expect to constantly experience oneness, when I was holding onto the idea of separation? I ran across the following quote while on my personal retreat back in January. It's particularly relevant for this post.

So, let us resolve not to fight in the name of religion. When the understanding comes that essentially we are one appearing as many, then all the other problems – physical and material – will be solved. Until then, they will never be solved because the basic cause for all the world's problems is the lack of understanding of this spiritual unity. Wherever you go say, "We look different, but we are all one in Spirit. Hello, brother; hello sister." No religion is superior and no religion is inferior... We should learn to live together and work toward one goal: to share and care, love and give.[11]
~Sri Swami Satchidananda

If this isn't *Living in the Light*, I don't know what is. I am incredibly grateful for this refresher lesson in acceptance, and pray that it helps others who have also found themselves judging the spiritual walk of others.

We all want the same things from life,
We want peace, love and prosperity.
But can we give up our need to be right?
Give the world a present; give the gift of your acceptance.
~India Arie and Idan Raichel, The Gift of Acceptance

Testimony on Faith – October 3, 2012

I announced to friends and family on Facebook that I received some great news at the end of last week, but I haven't shared what it was with everyone. I am brought to tears of joy just thinking about it.

After nearly collapsing at work in January, and being diagnosed with depression and anxiety, my 'New Year's Intention (what I call *resolutions*)' was to work from home by October of this year. Initially, I only shared this intention with Kevin, who was very supportive. I selected October because Kevin's benefits enrollment period would be open again so we could transfer our healthcare and dental benefits to him. It would also have given me one year with my new employer, which I felt was important at the time. I had NO idea how this would happen, but believed it was possible.

Since mid-January when I nearly collapsed at work, I have been home. I was on medical leave for about a month, and then I officially stepped down from my leadership role. I transitioned into another role that my boss allowed me to do from home. My boss was clear that this role was temporary and would expire on September 30, 2012. I was grateful for the opportunity to stay in a full-time position and work from home while I determined what was next for me. But, what *would* I do next?

I prayed, and asked the Spirit to reveal my next step to me. The next day, I was inspired to reach out to a former colleague who I hadn't spoken to in months. In that flash of inspiration, I remembered that she was now consulting on her own. She is someone I respected greatly, and knew that I could learn a lot from. She was *thrilled* to hear from me, and mentioned that she was working on a grant proposal that she would love for me to be a part of.

Over the summer, we worked incredibly hard on the proposal with a team of consultants. We submitted it in early August, and were to hear back by September 30 (the day my position was to expire). I felt great about the work we put into it, and believed it would stand out among the rest. I prayed about it and, for the first time in a long time, *truly* let it go. Normally, I would have interviewed for other positions, and would have been very worried about what I would do if it didn't come through. That fear would have crippled me in the grant writing process, and I would not have produced my best work. This time, I had an overwhelming sense that I would be fine – regardless of the outcome. I took the necessary steps from a position of strength instead of weakness. I had faith.

Now, I must admit that as the final week was approaching I started feeling some butterflies in my stomach. My faith was *really* the size of a mustard seed at that point. I thought, *Oh shoot, I really don't have a backup plan.* Then the first miracle happened on Monday, September 24. My boss asked if I'd be interested in staying on beyond September 30. I now had a cushion that I wasn't even expecting to come through. Nothing but the grace of God!

Then, on Friday, September 28, just after 5pm, I got a call from my former colleague stating we won the grant. Elated does not even begin to describe how I felt. I was thinking, "God is SO good... God is SO good!!!" I now have a five-year consulting contract that pays well, will allow me to work from home with minimal travel, *and* will allow me more time flexibility than I've ever had.

Once again, God's plan was *way* bigger than my plan. Surrendering to His grace has been the best decision of my life. I am incredibly grateful for this opportunity, and will continue to write with the time flexibility I have been gifted with. All it takes is faith the size of a mustard seed. That seed I planted with my intention at the beginning of the year has come to fruition – *right on time!*

"Because you have so little faith. I tell you the truth, if you have faith as small as a mustard seed, you can say to this mountain, 'Move from here to there' and it will move. Nothing will be impossible for you."
~Matthew 17:20

What seeds have you planted this year? Are you standing firm in your faith that all things will work together for your good? I pray that this is a gentle reminder not to be shaken by what you see in front of you, and to know that it will work out according to His purpose.

There is no problem in any situation that faith will not solve... you call for faith because of Him who walks with you in every situation.[12]
~*A Course in Miracles*

Calm in the Storm – October 11, 2012

Have you ever seen someone totally lose their cool in public? Have you ever felt a slight twinge of embarrassment for that person because you thought they were making a fool of themselves? OK, we all have. In fact, some of us have been that person a time or two (just me?). In the past, my reaction to episodes like this was to judge and gossip about the crazy person I witnessed that day. Not anymore. After experiencing a breakdown of my own, albeit in a different form, I know that those outbursts don't just come out of nowhere. They come from days, weeks, months, and even years, of built-up anger, guilt, resentment, and shame that have not been released. Eventually the breaking point is reached, which causes people to 'snap.'

I felt a rush of compassion earlier this week when I was on a plane with a mother of four who had reached her breaking point. She was like a shaken-up soda can that had just been opened – exploding all over the place for the entire plane to witness. She was sitting in the row in front of me, and I could tell something was not quite right shortly after I got settled in my seat. I began to observe her interactions with her family. She was yelling at her children (*Do your homework; Don't ask me for another thing; Sit down and shut up*), and was incredibly frustrated when asked to pass anything to them. She was snappy with her husband. What made it worse is that she was LOUD, *really* loud.

Instead of jumping to judgment, my heart genuinely ached for her. I wanted to walk up to her and give her a big hug. I thought about how this could have very well been me. I, too, have felt overwhelmed and underappreciated as I could tell that she did. All she wanted to do was sink into the book she brought to read on the plane, but the family kept interrupting her. Her reactions to their requests really had nothing to do with the interruption to her reading time, and had everything to do with built-up anger and frustration over time.

Witnessing this was a great reminder to me about the importance of taking time for self. I used to feel bad about asking my husband to watch the kids while I took time for myself. I would ask him to watch them while I went grocery shopping or to run errands, but rarely just for 'me time.' When I did do it, I felt guilty about it the entire time and didn't really enjoy the experience.

After dedicating this entire year to my well-being and spiritual growth, I can certainly say that my reaction to stressful situations has improved. I also noticed significant improvement in my reaction to my children's outbursts. So, what has been the key to this improvement?

There are five things that I have consistently done this year that I know contribute to whether I experience calm amidst the storms in life or whether I get swept up in them. They are not complicated, and they are certainly not new ideas. They are things I knew were good to do, but I was not consistent in doing them, which led to my breakdown. Being consistent in doing these daily is what has made all the difference in my day-to-day experience:

1. Daily meditation/contemplative time

This is an absolute must. When I go without it, I am more irritable and easily annoyed by daily challenges. When some people think of meditation, they think of sitting for an hour on a mat in what looks to be uncomfortable position (e.g. lotus posture) but there are many ways to meditate. For me, the length of time varies (generally between five minutes to 30 minutes) and so does the form. Meditation does not have to be long to be effective. The American Medical Association even reports that just five minutes of meditation each day can dramatically reduce stress levels. (Note: The American Medical Association estimates that over 60% of all illness and disease is caused by stress.)[13]

2. Prayer

I have mentioned prayer many times because it's such a crucial element in maintaining a calm mind. As I have mentioned before, I'm not talking about prayer that asks God to fix things, but prayer that realigns us with our innate Divinity; prayer that connects us to the Kingdom within. I've found the prayer process outlined in the *Song of Prayer* pamphlet of the Course to be a tremendous resource for this type of prayer. In addition, Spiritual Mind Treatment, or Affirmative Prayer, has also been useful to me.

3. Daily inspirational reading/listening/writing

Filling myself up with inspirational words on a daily basis has contributed tremendously to my peace of mind. I listened to them and read them repeatedly in order to allow the words to seep into my subconscious. No matter your faith, this type of daily reminder of the Truth beyond the world we see can be a great contributor to peace of mind. In addition, writing and reflecting on what you've read and how it can apply to your life can assist in making it more practical.

4. Make time for what you love

Each of us has something that makes our hearts sing. Making time for that on a consistent basis is so important. One of my favorite things is music, so I weave it into my day and it's such a mood lifter (even now, I have some light jazz playing in the background). In addition, one of my favorite things has become spiritual development. As a result, I am now taking classes and making space in my life to grow in this area. I have let my family know that this is a priority for me, so they are supportive when this takes precedence over things we used to do in the past. No matter what your favorite thing is, let those around you know that it's important to you. You'll be a better friend, coworker, parent, spouse, etc., because of it!

5. Gratitude

Spending time in the morning and evening reminding yourself of what you are grateful for keeps your cup full. No matter what is going on in your life, there's always much more to be grateful for. When you are operating from a state of gratitude, *no* situation can overcome your joy!

These all sound so simple, but the key is really sticking to it. Just like many of us faithfully watch our favorite TV shows, we must faithfully make time for ourselves. We must make time to reconnect to our true Self. Nurturing our mind and spirit will help prepare us to be unshakeable by the inevitable storms of life. We will be firm in our conviction that "God is good, ALL the time!"

What Did I Do To Deserve This? – October 19, 2012

What did I do to deserve this? That is a question that plagues many of us when the worst happens in our lives. It's a question that, I hate to admit, crossed my mind just last week, and during portions of this week. On Friday of last week, I wrote briefly on the *Living in the Light* Facebook page about a car accident that I was in last Thursday. The other driver ran a red light and hit the driver's side of my car.

The very next day I was hit by yet *another* driver and this time I was injured. This makes THREE car accidents in the last month and a half. These are also the first car accidents I've been in while I was the driver (well, aside from a minor bump of another vehicle while parallel parking... don't act like it's just me).

Immediately following last Friday's accident, I was running on adrenalin and was able to take care of all of the details with surprising ease. Then the post-adrenalin crash set in. I felt like I had been hit by a ton of bricks. The left side of my face, left shoulder, and left arm were numb for days, and I had significant pain in my back. Meanwhile, my two boys were going full speed and my husband was trying to take care of an ill family member who is staying with us for a month (and arrived the day before the accidents took place). To be completely honest, I was irritated – all I wanted to do was lie down and close my eyes for a while.

I made it through the weekend, and started feeling a bit better on Monday, but then had to deal with the details of the car accident (times three). I had to deal with the insurance companies, rental car company, city government, auto body shop, car dealerships, etc. In addition, there are a few other things occurring simultaneously with my work transition and home repairs that I was allowing to suck me in and stress me out.

Taking my own advice from my last entry, I continued my morning and evening meditation/prayer time, but it was kind of dry and I wasn't feeling as connected to God. When I finally had some extended down time, I picked up an inspirational book I'm reading for my Practical Mysticism class called *Entering the Castle*[14] by Caroline Myss. I heard the Spirit speak to me through her words.

> *Your goal is to transcend the controlling influence that the false gods of the outside world – like stress, money, and peer pressure – have on you and your relationship to God.*
> ~Caroline Myss

Even after being given a clue to the lesson in all of this through reading *Entering the Castle* (and other inspirational readings, including my daily lesson in the workbook of the Course), I still had a *Why me? What is this all for?* moment. Beyond wallowing in thoughts about how this could be happening to me, I really wanted to learn and grow from the experience. I was thinking, *I have been reading the Word, giving, meditating, praying, keeping my mind in the Spirit, trying my best to see the good in others, etc., and now everything is crashing down in front of me... what message am I supposed to learn from this, God? Help me see this with New Eyes.*

Then, today, not long after I ran down the list of 10 plus things that are annoying me to Kevin, I logged in to Facebook. The very first thing that popped up was the following quote from a well-known teacher of the Course, Ken Wapnick. Talk about Divine timing. There was the answer I had been waiting for.

> *We may feel victimized by what seems to be happening to us in our lives, but that interpretation of victimization is nothing but that – an interpretation. And if we're willing to accept our role in giving that interpretation to external events, then we can join with Jesus and allow him to offer a different interpretation in which no one is guilty, including, and especially, ourselves.*[15]
> ~Ken Wapnick

I read on, and the following quote was embedded in a response from Ken to a Course student that was feeling victimized by her circumstances in life. She had a recurring pattern of negative events that were showing up in her life and she was wondering if there was something she wasn't getting right in her spiritual walk because the negativity kept returning (sure sounds familiar to me!). In his response, Ken shared one of my favorite lines from the Course that I totally forgot to apply when all of this was going on:

> *The Course itself says that "trials are but lessons that you failed to learn presented once again, so where you made a faulty choice before you now can make a better one, and thus escape all pain that what you chose before has brought to you." But it is always and only ever talking about the content of our own perceptions of others [and situations], and the pain those judgments bring, and not the specific form of events as they seem to play out in our lives. And there is nothing in the Course that says you must repeat the cycle of pain and suffering until you get it right, as if there were some kind of karmic debt to be paid. This may be true within the ego thought system, but the whole purpose of the Course is to expose the insanity of the ego so we can make a choice for sanity against that thought system.*
> *~Ken Wapnick*

Then, to put icing on the cake, I looked back at Caroline Myss' book, and reread this passage (a little long, but really brings the lesson full circle). Just in case I still was allowing the ego to make me feel entitled to only 'good' life experiences (clearly I still was), the Spirit led me to read these words – again.

> *The word 'deserve' causes immeasurable pain. Beliefs about what we deserve are rooted in social-superstitious creed that suggests bad things should only happen to bad people. Most people believe that if*

they are good, God will reward them with protection from all undeserved suffering. This is human logic, but not divine logic. Pain and pleasure, suffering and abundance, are two sides of the coin of life experience. The divine asks you to learn through your life experiences. Yet we struggle with the concepts of deserving because we continually strive to see the logic behind events that occur to us. We cling to the belief that goodness is a shield of protection against having to experience the injustice or unfairness. But all sides of life [can been seen from the perspective] of the divine; the unjust side tests our capacity to trust in a Wisdom greater than our own. Without that trust, we often end up feeling betrayed by God, believing that somehow the wrong things happened to us. Such illusions give rise to bitterness and an inability to forgive.
~Caroline Myss

I hope that these words, which ministered to me during this difficult time, help someone else who is also dealing with multiple challenges in their life right now. I pray that you are able to tune out the ego and world, and tune in to your true Self, in order to experience the state of peace that is your inheritance – no matter what life sends your way. I pray that you can rise above any worldly appearances and see only the Love of God. I pray that we can help each other remember *Who* and *Whose* we are. Much love! Keep shining!

The Power of Choice – November 5, 2012

Over the past week, a message kept coming to me through different people, situations, and even dreams. I didn't recognize the central theme at first, but looking back at my journal entries for the past few weeks, I can see the meaning. Each of the forms in which the message was revealed to me were sent in order to help answer questions I had about how to stop allowing myself to get triggered by certain situations (in particular, toddlers that want to do the opposite of what their parents say). The answer centered on my own power of choice in each moment.

My journal entries from October 25–30 were mostly summaries of moments in which I noticed I was triggered and had responded in a less-than-kind way (to put it nicely). My entries in the past have not necessarily been focused on that, but that particular week I felt an overwhelming urge to get to the bottom of it and stop it. While I had definitely shortened the time that I stay angry about something that upsets me, I still didn't like the way I responded to my little ones not listening. There were moments in which I totally lost it, and was embarrassed by my tone when I reflected on the situations afterwards. Finally, I pleaded in my prayer/meditation time, "Help me to see this another way! Help me to respond in love!" I am so grateful that my plea was not only heard, but answered faster than I would have imagined. It was the 'little willingness' the Holy Spirit needed in order to show me another way.

"Any way I've been unkind,
Please let it fade into my love for You.
Holy Spirit glowing strong,
within your arms I am forever.
Any good that You got done,
is only You inside my willingness."
~Rickie Byars Beckwith (from the song, Innocent Love)

I won't run through each example of how messages were revealed to me, but I will share one. The first one happened a few days after I brought home my new car (my car was totaled in the accident). I set my keys in the place where my husband and I always put them, and in the morning they were nowhere to be found. While I do have 'senior moments' in which I can't remember things, this time I was absolutely *sure* I put them there.

My husband went out to the store the evening before and I was sure he must have picked them up by mistake. My mind was racing to what could have happened (*Did he drop them in the store? Did he drop them on the street?*) and I was upset about losing the keys so soon after getting the car.

When I got in the car to drop the boys off at school, using the extra set of keys I had, my car's Bluetooth audio system connected with my phone and automatically turned to a talk by Gary Renard, *Secrets of the Immortal*.[16] It's normal for my audio system to automatically connect to my phone, but it typically connects to the last thing I was listening to. This time, it connected to something I hadn't listened to in at least a month and it was *exactly* what I needed to hear. Renard was saying things like, "We have the power to choose between the ego and the Holy Spirit in each moment... the source of your upset is not what happened, but it's your reaction to what happened."

> "Would you be hostage to the ego or host to God? You will accept only whom you invite. You are free to determine who shall be your guest, and how long he shall remain with you."
> ~A Course in Miracles

In just a few minutes I had my power back. I had given my power to the situation, and allowed the ego to lead me to frustration and anger. I was reminded that what happens doesn't matter one bit – all that matters is my response to it. As I learned many years ago in *The Landmark Forum*, "The world is empty and meaningless." As the Course puts it, "Nothing in this [insert place or thing] means anything... I give everything all the meaning it has for me." Everything is inherently neutral. I can choose to perceive through the eyes of the ego, which will see everything from the perspective of fear (anger, resentment, blame, judgment, hate, etc.), *or* I can see through the eyes of the Holy Spirit, which will see with the eyes of Love (forgiveness, compassion, kindness, etc.) and behold the Truth about everyone and everything. This lesson clicked in my mind in a way that it hadn't in the past. I felt like I was about to shed another layer of my ego-self.

This shedding was confirmed by a vivid dream I had the next day. It was a very graphic, violent dream and I woke up in a sweat. The meaning of the dream was clear for me – some of the anger that had built up in my subconscious mind was being released. Since waking up from that dream, I have found myself in a state of pure joy. I have never felt so carefree. My mother was visiting over the weekend and even said, "You seem so happy... like your spirit is in a good place." Indeed. My interactions with my boys have been *so* much better over the last few days. The change has nothing to do with their actions but how I am consciously choosing to look at their actions: through the eyes of the Holy Spirit.

As I was observing the shift in my responses to my boys, I noticed that instead of *immediately* reacting to anything they did, I effortlessly paused and chose how I wanted to respond. I had been practicing this, and it was working in most areas of my life, but it was going out the window all too frequently when it came to my boys. I am grateful to have begun to take my power back in this situation. I just have to keep practicing and remembering that *I* have the power.

I know this is possible for everyone in *any* situation. We are so much more powerful than we can imagine. All it takes is a willingness to surrender – the Holy Spirit will guide you through the rest. Love is our natural state of being – we just have to let go of all of the internal barriers we have placed in its way. When we choose to *be* the Love that we are, it not only benefits us but those around us (and everyone they interact with, and so on). The

Prayer of St. Francis[17] reminds me of the power of choice that we all have. We can be taken in by the negativity that seems to surround us and respond in fear, or we can choose to respond in Love, remembering the Oneness from which we came.

Lord, make me an instrument of your peace.
Where there is hatred, let me sow love.
Where there is injury, pardon.
Where there is doubt, faith.
Where there is despair, hope.
Where there is darkness, light.
Where there is sadness, joy.
O Divine Master,
Grant that I may not so much seek to be consoled, as to console;
To be understood, as to understand;
To be loved, as to love.
For it is in giving that we receive.
It is in pardoning that we are pardoned,
And it is in dying that we are born to Eternal Life.
Amen.

P.S. The keys showed up the next day (my husband had gone down in the basement before he went to the store and the keys fell out his pocket down there). I also apologized to my husband for my attitude right after I listened to the Gary Renard talk.

Trying to Fly With One Wing – November 11, 2012

A couple months have passed since I wrote about messages I received via animals or insects. The last couple times, I received a powerful message about my true Self via a bee, and a reminder to 'Let go and let God' from a ladybug. Every time I notice these messages, it's at a moment when I'm feeling unclear about something in my life. This time was no different.

One of my passions has become helping others return to inner peace. I had been going back and forth between whether I wanted to become a certified life coach or a spiritual practitioner; something about it just wasn't feeling right. I even got in a car accident on the way to one of my practitioner classes, which felt like a sign that I may not be on the right course.

Part of me also started feeling like I should study on my own. I was falling back into my old pattern of trying to do everything myself and pretending I didn't need anyone. I was saying, "I got this... I don't need any certification... I don't need anyone's help." Ego was creeping back in.

I was so confused, and really wanted to make the right choice. I was on the Web site looking around and reading about a spiritual life coach certification program, when a fly started buzzing around my office window. I thought it was strange because there normally aren't a lot of them around when it's this cold outside.

The next day, I noticed the wing of the fly on my blinds. I picked it up, put it on my desk, and immediately looked up the meaning of flies, as well as the meaning of one wing. There was a powerful message there for me and, I believe, anyone else trying to 'go it alone' like I was. Here are some of the messages I discovered:[18]

- In Greek, the fly symbolizes Omnipresence and reminds us that a divine presence is always watching and buzzing with energy.
- In Native American tradition, the Navajo legend, Dontso, was called the "great fly" and was called during healing ceremonies to eat away dying flesh. The fly is considered a purifier and is asked to consume negative influences and fly away with them – leaving the afflicted free from malady.
- Throughout different parts of Asia, the fly symbolizes a wandering or aimless soul whose attention is in many

places. This signifies a need to evaluate the nuisances that are bugging you and the need to take stock of irritations that are being held onto.

- In Egypt, the fly symbolizes bravery, courage, tenacity and persistence in the face of opposition.
- Overall, the fly is a master consumer of waste and signifies the need to look at our 'poop' for the purpose of cleaning up what is no longer serving us.
- In terms of one wing, one of the things I learned was that the one-winged angel has the *semblance* of an angel, but does not have the ability to fly. This signifies the need for assistance from another.

The message from this was so clear to me. While I was created in the image and likeness of God, and have never left Home, I still need some assistance in remembering *Who* I really am and *Where* I really am because I've spent so much time *not* believing that. As the Course states (I'm paraphrasing), while we appear to be here (in the world), the Holy Spirit will send us various teachers through which It will remind us *Who* we really are, and *Where* we really are. It is difficult to do this on our own because we're so stuck in our illusions. We need the guidance of the Holy Spirit, who may at times speak to us through others.

In addition, I heard the message loud and clear that I'm not 'there' yet. During meditation the morning before I discovered the wing on my blinds, I kept hearing the word "surrender" over and over. I know that was the Spirit trying to tell me to get out of the driver's seat. In order to get where He is taking me, I need Him to be in control. While I have come a long way since the deep depression I experienced, I still have to take a look at any darkness that may still reside in me, and release it. That certainly is going to take some courage. I'm ready though, and I know that in order to help others I have to be sure I have fully taken care of myself. I have faith and know that the Spirit always knows best.

What about you? Is there any area in your life in which you've been avoiding asking for help when you know you could use it? The Holy Spirit was sent to help us along the way – to be that second wing – so that ultimately we may awaken and fly in our true Home, where we have been all along. Surrender with me.

> "Teach me to do your will,
> for you are my God;
> may your good Spirit
> lead me on level ground."
> ~Psalm 143:10

I come to you from our Father to offer you everything again. Do not refuse it in order to keep a dark cornerstone hidden, for its protection will not save you. I give you the lamp and I will go with you. You will not take this journey alone. I will lead you to your true Father, Who hath need of you, as I have. Will you not answer the call of love with joy?[19]
~A Course in Miracles

Chapter 10

Peace is on the Horizon

The Fastest Way to Peace – November 18, 2012

Yesterday, I was doing some reflecting on the path to peace. I pondered my path, and thought about some of my friends and family who are currently struggling to find peace in their respective situations. After morning meditation, I posted the following on the *Living in the Light* Facebook page:

> *The peace of God is not something we have to seek outside of ourselves to find. All that is required is surrendering to the Spirit and allowing for the release of any internal barriers in the way of our experience of the peace that is already ours.*

A few questions came my way afterwards, one of which I'd like to address here. The question was, "How do I release these 'internal barriers' faster so I can experience peace *now*?" This is an excellent question. The very fact that the question was asked shows a readiness and willingness to surrender and consider another way of looking at what is believed to be blocking the experience of peace in the present moment.

In my short experience with practicing this in my life, I have found that there are two things that *truly* accelerate the process of undoing all that we have placed in between ourselves and the peace that was granted us by God. Thanks to the Course, I have a daily reminder of the importance of these two things. The accelerated path to peace consists of:

1. Surrender

This step is all about releasing control of any given situation and making room for the Holy Spirit (or Jesus, angels, guides, ancestors – whatever works for you) to show you what you cannot see from your perspective. When we do this, we start to open up to the truth that there is more than one way of looking at things. We can either look with the Holy Spirit, or we can look with the ego. We know we are looking with the ego if we are *not* experiencing peace. That's where surrender comes in. Whenever we experience even the slightest sense of upset or frustration, *that* is the moment to surrender and ask the Spirit for assistance in viewing the situation (or person) in the Light of God.

2. Forgiveness

Frequently, what blocks us from experiencing peace is some form of grievance. Grievances can show up in a number of ways including, but not limited to: anger, resentment, fear, anxiety, hate, and jealousy. It's tempting to hold grievances and stay stuck in anger and resentment over what we perceive as another's wrong toward us. What we often don't remember in those moments of upset is that the only way to get to true peace of mind regarding that particular situation is through forgiveness of it. This is what the Holy Spirit will assist us with when we surrender. Forgiveness is such an important step that it warrants a little more explanation to ensure we are on the same page about what it means, as it is often misunderstood.

Forgiveness is not really about the other's actions – it's about recognizing our oneness (the Christ, the Higher Self, the Light – whatever you refer to it as) with each other. It is an understanding that beyond the veil of the body (and the veil of titles, states, countries, colors, political parties, economic classes, etc.), we are all one. Anything that *seems* to divide us is just another tool of the ego to keep us stuck in the belief that we are separate from each other. If we focus on seeing the Christ in each other – no matter what actions show – we will remember *Who* we really are.

I have to admit, I used to hear concepts like this and think to myself, *Yeah, but this person did something really crazy to me*; or, *Yeah, but what about murderers; Yeah, but...* Yes, we have to forgive even 'those people' if we want to be at peace. As I mentioned in the entry *The Power of Choice*, we all have two choices in every moment: to align ourselves with the ego or the Holy Spirit. Anyone who is acting out anything that is *not* love is aligned with the ego. At any point, they can choose otherwise. Why? Because that is not the Truth of *Who* they are. They are momentarily trapped in the lies of the ego. When you begin to recognize this, you start to have compassion for those who are caught up in this cycle. You look at them with love because you know *that* is really what they're crying out for. You become grateful for the situation arising, recognizing that the forgiveness of it was actually for you, as it inches you closer to eliminating your own belief in separation.

> *As* A Course in Miracles *explains, what the world judges as an attack is really an expression of fear, and fear is a call for the love that has been denied or rejected, and that underlies the fear. Thus, when I perceive you as attacking me and can remember what the Course calls the judgment of the Holy Spirit (that your attack is really a call for love), I recognize that it also mirrors my call for love. Both of us are now joined, in that we are yearning for the same love we believe we have thrown away. Our joining – and it does not have to be on a physical level; it certainly can occur in my own mind – is how I experience gratitude to you, because you are reminding me of the lesson I want to learn. In that experience of gratitude is where the memory of love is found.*[1]
> ~Ken Wapnick

If Jesus could forgive those who were attempting to crucify him, *surely* we can forgive the things that come up in our daily lives (Father, forgive them for they know not what they do. Luke

23:34). Jesus knew that they were caught up in the lies of the ego, and that they had no idea that they could not 'kill' him. Whenever we feel threatened or attacked (or tempted to attack another), an important thing to remember is that we *cannot* crucify each other. Attacking each other is pointless. We were created by, and are an extension of, an eternal Power that cannot *be* crucified. Jesus demonstrated that through the resurrection. That demonstration was not for us to view him as 'special,' but to prove the eternal and interconnected nature of us *all*. We, too, can demonstrate this in our daily lives.

Thankfully, we don't have to do such a dramatic demonstration as Master Teacher, Jesus. We can, however, prove this through the resurrection of our relationships with *all* life for as long as we appear to be in the classroom of the world. We can move from relationships filled with grievances to holy relationships filled with love, peace, and joy – where we only recognize the Truth in each other. Whenever we have grievances pop up, as they tend to from time to time, we can remember to surrender and forgive all over again. Eventually and ultimately, we remember there *is* nothing to forgive. *Nothing* can overcome what God creates.

> "Nothing real can be threatened,
> Nothing unreal exists,
> Herein lies the peace of God."
> ~A Course in Miracles

Living life this way cannot bring anything but peace, joy, kindness, love, compassion, and all of the fruits of the Spirit, because we are once again in harmony with our true nature. We see the Light in each other. We are *One* again. We are Home. Keep shining!

Don't Worry, Be Happy – November 20, 2012

This will be a short entry, but I HAD to share this funny story. On Monday morning, I was getting my boys ready for school when they started fighting over who would get to the sink first to brush their teeth. Normally I would have responded with a comment like, "No fighting, boys! Be nice to each other!" This day, without hesitation, I said, "Don't worry, be happy, boys!" and burst into singing the song by Bobby McFerrin.

I hadn't even heard or thought about that song in years, but it just rolled off my tongue with ease. The boys absolutely loved it and wanted to hear the real version of it. We had it on repeat during breakfast, and we couldn't help but smile. We were singing, dancing, and trying our best to do the whistling parts in the song. It was hilarious! This is now our new morning anthem.

In every life we have some trouble,
When you worry you make it double
Don't worry, be happy.
~Bobby McFerrin

Later that day, I was reading the daily digest from an e-group I'm a member of and one of the members wrote: *Reggae Jesus: Don't worry, be happy.* After I stopped laughing, I read it again. I was just reading parts of the "Sermon on the Mount," and was amazed by the similarity between the song and Jesus' message in the "do not worry" portion of this particular sermon. While I know the e-group member was joking, I loved the comment because that statement really does get right to the heart of Jesus' message.

It was a great reminder that, no matter what we're going through, worrying about it will *not* contribute to our peace of mind. All things will work together for good, as they always have, and for that reason we can smile – knowing that it's already done. Amen.

Therefore I tell you, do not worry about your life, what you will eat or drink; or about your body, what you will wear. Is not life more than food, and the body more than clothes? Look at the birds of the air; they do not sow or reap or store away in barns, and yet your heavenly Father feeds them. Are you not much more valuable than they? Can any one of you by worrying add a single hour to your life?

And why do you worry about clothes? See how the flowers of the field grow. They do not labor or spin... seek first his kingdom and his righteousness, and all these things will be given to you as well. Therefore do not worry about tomorrow, for tomorrow will worry about itself. Each day has enough trouble of its own.
~Matthew 5:25–34

I Want to Be More Loving in My Heart – November 27, 2012

While driving my 3 year old home from school he said, "Mommy, what do you want to be when you grow up?" I said, without pause, "I want to be more loving." He said, "That doesn't have a uniform!" He went on to tell me he was going to be a race car driver because he likes the outfit. Hilarious.

After I stopped laughing, I realized how profound what he said was. When asked a similar question, many respond with a type of job or some form of success. Many would think of things that have a 'uniform (professional dress code)' or things that would demonstrate their level of achievement. They would mention the material things they want to acquire, degrees they'd like to get, titles they want to add to their name, places they want to visit, etc.

What if we all responded, "I want to be more loving... I want to see beauty in all things... I want to see the light in all situations... I want to be more peaceful... I want to forgive more." Wouldn't that be something? These are all things that you don't have to apply for, get credentialed in, go to school for years to achieve, spend thousands of dollars on, get a loan for, etc. These are things you can start to practice *right now*.

Last week, I was guided to read some material by Howard Thurman. He was Martin Luther King, Jr.'s spiritual adviser and mentor. I had been reading much of Martin Luther King, Jr.'s old speeches and papers throughout the year and have been so inspired by them. We learn in school about the "I Have a Dream" speech, which is awesome in its own right, but he had *so* many other powerful writings. Many of King's writings were inspired by Howard Thurman. The common theme throughout their work can be summed up as, "We are all one in God."

I recently learned that Thurman used to say, "I am not Christian, I am a follower of Jesus." This was a bold and radical statement at the time, particularly coming from an African-American man (given the strong prevalence of Christianity throughout the community). I was so inspired by that because I have come to a similar place in my spiritual walk: Less dogma, more walking the talk. I sometimes feel like I am in a small minority who share this belief in my community, so it was inspiring to read work like this from someone who had such a significant influence on those who led the Civil Rights Movement. His book, *Jesus and the Disinherited*,[2] has brought me to new heights. Martin Luther King, Jr. thought it was so good that he carried it with him everywhere, and he would read it before he gave major speeches or went to important meetings. I can see why. I look forward to reading even more of his work.

While listening to a talk by Dr. Beckwith last week, he mentioned a poem by Thurman titled "More Loving in My Heart" from his book *The Inward Journey*.[3] It's such a powerful piece that I encourage you to read it in its entirety. I have included a brief excerpt below. I pray that it inspires you, as it has inspired me, to focus less on the 'uniform' and more on what's inside. May your daily interactions be flooded with love!

I want to be more loving in my heart. It is often easy to have the idea in mind, to plan to be more loving, to see it with the mind and give ascent to the thought of being loving. This is crystal clear. But I want to be more loving in my heart. I must feel like loving. I must ease the tension in my heart that ejects the sharp barb, the stinging word.

I want to be more loving in my heart, that with unconscious awareness and deliberate intent I shall be a kind, a gracious human being. Thus those who walk the path with me may find it easier to be loving, to be gracious because of the love of God which is increasingly expressed in my living. I want to be more loving in my heart.
~Howard Thurman

A Lesson from the Ancestors – December 2, 2012

Over the past couple weeks, I have felt overwhelmed by the Spirit of the ancestors. Almost daily, information has been rushing my way that led me to revisit some of the earlier historical appearances of the spiritual principles that have become so mainstream. The information that I was guided to review was primarily focused on Ancient Kemetic (Egyptian) Spirituality and African-American spirituality during slavery and the Civil Rights Movement. The central lesson that I was being reminded of became clearer as the weeks went on.

While soaking up Howard Thurman's work last week, I was also guided to reread the story of Ausar (Osiris), whose story, in part, shares striking similarities to the story of Jesus. That same day, I reread some of the book, *Ma'at: The 11 Laws of God*,[4] which is based on Ancient Kemetic (Egyptian) Spirituality. I first purchased this book in college, along with *Metu Neter: The Great Oracle of Tehuti and the Egyptian System of Spiritual Cultivation*,[5] *Of Water and the Spirit*[6] by Patrice Malidoma Somé, *African Spirituality: On Becoming Ancestors*,[7] by Anthony Ephirim-Donker, *Opening to Spirit: Contacting the Healing Power of the Chakras and Honouring African Spirituality*,[8] by Caroline Shola Arewa, and other books that I thought would help me understand the spiritual and cultural traditions of my ancestors. At that time, I couldn't fully understand everything I was reading, but I must have picked some of it up subconsciously because when I began reading it again last week it made perfect sense.

I noted how similar the language in *Ma'at: The 11 Laws of God* was to the language of the Course. The Course mentions that there are many paths to the Truth, and that it shows up in many forms, but the Truth itself does not change. *Ma'at: The 11 Laws of God* states that Truth is the Truth – it is not something to be believed in, but just *is*. So, what is the Truth? Both books sum it up in different ways, but the general idea is that we are *not* separate and our true state is the Love and Peace of God.

> *Your nature is an unconquerable peace, therefore nothing or no one in the world can be against you. All experiences come to you to promote your reclamation of peace, that you may, in turn, acquire wisdom and power.*
> ~*Ma'at: The 11 Laws of God (Law of Ausar)*

I have to admit, at the time of purchasing all those books on African Spirituality back in college, I was not coming from a place of love. I *certainly* wasn't in a place to receive the idea that we are *all* one in God. I was resentful over having to dig so deeply to uncover the spiritual and cultural traditions that were stripped of my ancestors. I was angry that the full history was not being shared in school, and that I had to piece it together on my own. I projected this anger into the world and it showed up as ill feelings toward certain groups of people, particularly those who I viewed as treating me differently because of the color of my skin and my desire to outwardly show my pride for 'my people.'

> *Man must have no preferences, and must be impartial and equal to all people and events. It must be realized that no one or no situation can be against one. This is the true meaning of Selflessness, and*

At-Onement, and establishes the foundation to spiritually share in
God's omniscience and omnipotence (to be able to spiritually affect
others. because we are a part of them and they us!).
~Ma'at: The 11 Laws of God

I did not make rude comments publicly, but internally I held onto
bitter feelings that I carried with me into the workplace and other
daily experiences. I viewed every negative interaction as an
example of the racism in the world, not realizing it was actually
coming from me. Since that time, I have forgiven (as discussed in
my *Forgiveness and Politics* entry), and am much further along in
viewing all people in the Light. I was able to revisit these books
and feel grateful for the Truth being expressed in such a way that
it reaches all people in the language they can best understand,
and from the Teacher they can best receive it from.

I have heard it said by many spiritual teachings that we are
not human beings having a spiritual experience but we are
spiritual beings having a human experience. Our identity is in
God and not the color of our skin, our brief history on Earth, our
religion, our worldly traditions, our political party, our economic
status, etc. As much as the atrocities committed throughout
history have pained me, I can now see the actions of the offenders
as the call for love that it was.

All actions are either an expression of the Love of God or a call for
the Love of God.
(Paraphrased from A Course in Miracles)

There is no room for hate to enter when we remember to only see
each other in Truth. We then move beyond borders and terri-
tories, mine versus yours, and we remember that we are all **one**.
God created us in His image and likeness. God did not create
separation – that is a concept of the ego. Slavery is an extreme
demonstration of what happens when people align themselves

with ego instead of the Spirit, or when people align themselves with their *human* identity instead of their *spiritual* Identity. No one who remembers their true Self – who is one with God – could bring harm to another because they know that what you do unto others is done to yourself. All beings are extensions of God – the One Life we all share.

Am I saying that we have to run up to those that have done wrong to us and give them hugs, hold hands, and sing *Kumbaya*? No, although we can if we're so inclined. We can answer their 'call for love' with compassion toward them for how strongly they are trapped in the games of the ego (competition, hate, fear, idolatry, anger, jealousy, etc.). From that perspective, we can move forward while not separating ourselves from people because of seeming differences – differences that do not even exist in the realm of Spirit. We cannot say we are all spiritual beings in one breath then condemn others, or think we are better than others, in the next. We have to choose which we believe is real (spiritual or human), and bring that perspective to our day-to-day interactions.

I have stated before that I believe we will not experience peace in the world, or the true experience of being 'in the world, but not of the world,' until we have peace in the mind. I have definitely seen it firsthand in my life. I didn't start seeing the Light in others until I began to remove the darkness from within myself. I didn't start finding peace in spirituality until I stopped viewing other paths as wrong (or stolen). This is why my No. 1 passion right now is freeing my mind from the mental slavery of the ego, and sharing my lessons along the way with anyone who has ears to hear.

I am grateful for the ancestors helping me purge any additional feelings of resentment regarding spiritual paths, or the origin of religion, that I may have been holding onto so that I can be "more loving in my heart." And, most importantly, so I can remember the Truth – we are One.

Part III

Revelation

Chapter 11

Revelation

> "There is no way to anticipate to whom God will come.
> You can attempt to describe who is most likely ready,
> willing, and able, but in the end, only God decides who
> and when and why."
> ~Carolyn Myss

December 11, 2012

At the beginning of December, I started feeling uncertain about what my next move should be. I wanted to know what I was supposed to do with this new level of understanding I had about God and life. I wanted to be absolutely sure that my actions were being led by the Spirit and not the ego. I wasn't sure if it was the Spirit or ego that was leading me to consider spiritual life coach training, which continued to cross my mind. I wrote about this in my journal multiple times, and ping-ponged back and forth about it. I also was struggling with what felt like an addiction to Facebook at that time. I began to care a lot about the number of people "talking about" my page and comparing it to other similar pages. It was clearly becoming a distraction. I needed help with releasing my attachment to success in the world, and was ready to receive my true life assignment – my purpose.

On December 9, my inner call was answered. I was guided to a new teacher: Mooji. *When the student is ready the teacher appears.* This has certainly been the case for me – at an accelerated rate this year. I understand now that the message is all really coming from one Teacher; I have been receiving that message through various expressions that would most resonate with me.

I was guided to listen to some of Mooji's talks after meditation/prayer time and reading my lesson for the day in the Course, which was "Let every voice but God's be still in me."[1] To say that Mooji was saying exactly what I needed to hear in order to advance to the next level of awareness would be an understatement. I felt that he held my hand and led me to the portal to *knowing* God, not just believing in God. He stirred something up in me (or out of me), and prepared me for what was about to take place. After listening to a few of his talks on YouTube,[2] I wrote down this message from the Spirit:

> *Don't be afraid to go against the grain. Everyone will awaken in their own time. Your time has already been determined – it is NOW!*

I knew this was in response to the yearning I had to help others find their true Self: realizing they *are* the Son of God. This statement from the Spirit reassured me that, "It's all good. Those who are meant to awaken through you will be sent to you. All others will awaken in their own time – no pressure." In one of the Mooji talks he stressed the importance of "being normal." He shared that even though you know you are not of this world, you can still navigate it normally while being aware of where you are. He also mentioned not trying to "be spiritual" and announce your transformation to the world, which admittedly made me think a little about the blog. I still believe I am on the right path with that since I was guided to start it to share my struggles and lessons learned along the spiritual path. I certainly did not start the blog for my glorification. If I had my way, I would have *never* shared the things I was most ashamed of (i.e. my promiscuity as a teen, the abortion, the affair, my fears, self-doubt, struggles with the ego, etc.) outside of my inner circle. I digress. Some of the most powerful words I heard from him that day were:

All things you see and the one seeing it is God.

What you are trying to find is the Truth, the way is not important. All paths lead to the Truth – maybe in another lifetime for some. Some ways are faster than others. What I am teaching you is available NOW.

The Truth, intact, perfect as it is, is here now but the person we have become may not be ready to embrace it.

Anyone who knows the Self knows it spontaneously. You don't have to navigate your path to enlightenment.

There must be the aspiration for freedom in order to leave the state of bondage to the body.

Enlightenment = realizing What you have always been, and that you don't have to become anything.

If Truth is what you're seeking, you don't even need to study – study leads to knowledge, but not necessarily to Truth. It may even lead to super-ego, or pride, not liberation.

Dropping the identity is less important than discovering the Truth.

You get the teacher who is meeting you at your level of readiness.

I kept reading through the statements slowly and, each time I did, I opened up more and more to the reality that I was standing at the doorway to awakening. I kept focusing on the statement, "Dropping the identity is less important than discovering the Truth." I felt this whole year had focused on releasing attachments, dropping my ego identity and releasing the belief in a small self that is separate from God. *Now he's saying that discovering the Truth is more important? Hadn't I discovered the Truth already?* Apparently not.

I woke up extremely emotional today for some reason. I dropped Kevin and the boys off at work and school respectively. As soon as I pulled off, streams of tears flowed down my face. I wasn't feeling particularly sad, so I wasn't sure why this was happening. I did feel like it was a shedding of the old, and like they were tears of purification. Soul tears. Tears of joy for the recognition of the Light within, the Christ within. I read my lesson from the Course for the day, "This day I choose to spend in perfect peace." I then listened to a meditation by Mooji and wrote in my journal that it "completely took me Home." The major questions that were burning on my mind were answered by Mooji's talks. I had no idea his words would be the primer for a much deeper realization of my true Self than I could have ever imagined. His words pierced through any remaining doubt about my true Identity and left me naked as I AM.

You don't have to try to be. You are.

Overcome the influence of the mind. Every thought is a tourist, just passing through.

Include everything, but tie yourself to nothing. (You don't have to be "anti-this or that.")

Your experience in the world becomes like looking at the moon during the day. It's there, but no one writes poetry to the moon when the sun is out. (Once you awaken.)

As long as there is a search, there is a sense that something is missing. There is nothing to strive or search for. You are already That.

Negative thoughts only have influence when you are disconnected from gratitude and the abundance that is.

After receiving all of that great wisdom from Mooji, I wrote this in my journal:

Share the unfoldment process. Don't worry about what others think about it. Just share openly and from the heart.

Then, after some more contemplation time, I wrote:

I am not a color
I am not my title
I am not my hair
I am not my economic status
I am not my sex
I am not my nationality
I am not my education
I am not a religion
I am not my style
I am not my popularity
I am all that God is
I AM THAT I AM

December 13, 2012

On Wednesday, December 12 ("12.12.12"), *it* happened. I woke up at 2:45 am with great anticipation. I felt like a kid on Christmas – I had no idea what my presents would be, but I just knew I was about to receive something. I got out of bed, gathered my journal, *A Course in Miracles* book, and my phone and went downstairs to my normal space of meditation and contemplation. After reading my lesson in the Course ("God is the only goal I have today"), I was guided to watch some more of Mooji's talks which, once again, were answering my remaining questions and ensuring me of the beauty of awakening to the Self. There are so many things he said that stood out, but what struck me most were the following:

You are not the doer… there is a Force behind the movement of all life.
The absence of ego is pure joy and liberation. Just express that joy and enjoy yourself.
Your attachments fall away, and all that will remain is your Essence. When you get there, you won't ask: "What to do?"

Can there be a greater purpose than a human being coming to the full realization of the Self?

Look after your body without too much devotion.

There was my answer about my purpose, about what to do next, about what happens after awakening – everything. After the talks, I went into a deep meditation. When I came out of the meditation, I had tears streaming down my face – they started pouring when I wrote the date in my journal: 12.12.12. I was in awe of the synchronicity of the date aligning like this at the very moment I felt whole and complete. I spent some time reflecting in my journal and wrote:

Yesterday, I felt a complete sense of peace. I was just expressing love and joy all day. Kevin was home sick and I made him a tray of food and cut out a heart with construction paper and wrote "I love you" on it and taped it to the tray. The night before, I got him a get-well card and just expressed my love for him. I was overwhelmed with compassion for him given he wasn't feeling well, and recently learned the news of his dad being diagnosed with cancer and given six months to live. Not that I didn't care before, but I just felt his pain inside – at least that's the best way I can describe it. It was like an increased intuitive awareness. Last night and the night before, I played music at dinner (like we used to in Spain) and it was incredibly peaceful. In fact, a jazz artist we have a mutual affinity for, Charles Mingus (who we went to see a tribute to on our first date), was the first to come on when I turned on the "Meditations" Pandora station. It was so peaceful that even Kevin commented on it. He mentioned he was looking forward to continuing the tradition.

I am awakening from the dream. I understood what the Course, my teachers, the great mystics, prophets, sages, saints, and others have said (or written) intellectually, but revelation has come. I **know** *God is. I know nothing in this world can give me the satisfaction, fulfillment, wholeness, completion, joy, peace, etc. that I am experi-*

encing right now. I feel no need to prove it, just feel it and express it. It's amazing. WAY better than what alcohol, drugs, sex, or anything else can bring. There is no match to God in this world. I'm ready to release my attachment to it. I can't help but cry in this moment. This is what I have been searching for all my life. I know that the right next step will be revealed to me – right now all I want to do is BE!

I sat there and felt the energy flowing through me. It was magical. The feeling I had inside was beyond words, and was something I had never felt before. After that moment of deep reflection and contemplation, I got up to do any work I needed to do for the day. I had an inner awareness that I was preparing for something, and that I needed to get my "work work" done early so that I would be ready. While in my office working, a spider appeared right in front of me. I didn't have time to look up the meaning right then, but I had a feeling it had some significance. After I finished working, I posted the following Mooji quote on the *Living in the Light* Facebook page, unconsciously announcing my newfound purpose:

If you talk about finding your true purpose, let it be this purpose: That you awaken fully to your true nature as the pure Self and thereafter live your life in and as Truth, Love, Joy, and Wisdom, the ever-free Self.

I was clear on my purpose, and ready to embody it fully. I noticed that ego was trying to take a hold on me while I was on Facebook (i.e. checking to see how many "likes" the photo had), but I was quickly able to disregard it. I was observing the thought, but I wasn't identified with it. That's when I really knew something was happening in me. *Is this what it feels like to have overcome the influence of the ego?* I couldn't believe it. I got in bed after that, and kept watching Mooji videos. In the middle of one of the talks, I had an overwhelming urge to lie down. Rather, it felt like an energetic force was pulling me down to the bed. That's when it happened.

I lay down, closed my eyes, and immediately began to see flashes of blue, indigo, magenta, and purple light streaming toward me. Then a bright, warm, white Light surrounded me and moved throughout my body. The Light formed what looked like a protective dome around me. I saw flashes of darkness flying swiftly toward the dome, but they were deflected. *No darkness could enter my field.* I could see it all happening – be an observer of it – but it was not possible for the darkness to touch me. Then I saw flashes of colors again, this time with celestial beings, angels, and other Light beings. They were coming close to me, and then fading out quickly. I intuitively knew they were welcoming me Home. The messages I felt coming through during that experience were, "You are not living IN the Light, you ARE the Light!" and "You are free."

I laid there for a while, enjoying the stillness and peace that came with that experience. There was a sense of calm permeating the air. There was a constant vibration of energy moving through my body, one that I still feel a day later as I type this experience. I didn't want it to end, and somehow I knew it wouldn't. I had *believed* Jesus when he said, "The Kingdom of God is within," and "The Kingdom is at hand," but I now *knew* it beyond a shadow of a doubt. I had seen *It* with my inner eye and could feel *Its* energy pulsating throughout my body. But that was only the beginning.

Something told me to log in to Facebook right away, and I didn't hesitate. My friend's status update was the very first thing I ran across, "Happy 12.12.12!" I hadn't really thought of the significance of the numbers beyond my quick interpretation of 'completion and wholeness' that I gave the date earlier that morning. I have never been into numerology – at least not in this lifetime – so I spent some time researching the symbolic meaning of this date. I could not believe my eyes. Everything I was reading confirmed what I had experienced.

I had no idea this was a date many spiritual seekers had been looking forward to. I knew it was the 'end' of the Mayan calendar, and that some people believed the world was going to end on that date, but I hadn't looked into the spiritual significance of the date. I was spontaneously drawn into this glimpse of Reality without formal preparation other than setting my daily intention on *Living in the Light*. One of the descriptions I ran across about the significance of this date was as follows:[3]

> *Through the power of the associated gateways held open by the Archangels on 11:11, a new force of the Christ Consciousness will be made available during the 12:12:12 Activation. The power of this awakening energy enables each person to have the experience of the Christ Light... Once experienced you will not fall back into old ways, as the Golden Christ Light literally expunges from your being frequencies that no longer serve you. Transformed by Light, the cells awaken to the coding embedded by your soul. This activation has been held in abeyance until the earth consciousness would support mass awakening. Awareness and preparation are key signatures for the transformation available through the Christ Light. That time is Now.*

> *The 12:12:12 represents an activation of Divine Love within, through and around you. When Divine Love activates the light-encoded filaments within your being, there is a communion of awakening. It moves the body into the 12-helix system and allows the connection of the DNA strands. This activates subtle energy that unites the new 12-chakra system. Light alone cannot create the connection, even though the Divine Intelligence is there within the Light Force. Divine Love is required to awaken the coding of your Soul's union with the completion inherent in the Twelve. This is the awakening of the Christ Consciousness.*

In terms of the number '12' itself, I learned:[4]

> *12 is a number of universal import and you see its repeating patterns in your culture; 12 hours of the day, 12 months of the year, 12 in a dozen, 12 zodiac signs, 12 apostles, and 12 days of Christmas, for example. These relationships are not a coincidence, nor are they about convenience. Within the 12 you find the number 3: the sacred trinity, third chakra, and number of creation. It is universal that when you put two things, ideas, or what have you, together, a third is naturally created.* **In these December dates, you have three threes. This equals 9. Thus the creational value is tripled and the result is the completion of a cycle,** *which is a meaning inherent in the number 9. From this we can plainly see the vibrations at play of creation and completion, in the cycle of development.*

> **These two dates, 12.12.12 and 12.21.12 are divinely linked. The 12.12.12 is the gateway to what will transpire on 12.21.12.** *Thus, the gateway that you align with on the first date will determine what world you see when the gate opens on the following date. Are we saying it is important what you are doing and being on these dates? Yes, and particularly where you are and what you are focused upon on 12.12.12 will be significant. Needless to say, what you will be focused on will likely be determined by all you have done in preparation during this year 2012 and leading up to it.*
> *Some of you will also note that 12.12.2012 = 11. This numerology also has a spiritual significance as to* **transcendence,** *and the doubled power of one, and its ability as an initiator and propulsion unit for the start of* **new growth and new evolutionary urges.** *No matter how you slice the numbers, there is potency inherent in these dates, and this is no mistake.*

Before this experience, I would have thought that was all "B.S." But, what I experienced on the morning of 12.12.12 was confirmation that there is absolutely a Greater Force at work around us and *within us*. After researching the numbers, I felt drawn to go to a park near my house and meditate there. I just *knew* something was going to take place there. I packed like I was going on a mini camping trip. I brought a towel, a blanket, water, my iPhone (for music), and some incense (which I rarely used at the time, but felt compelled to bring with me). I put on a warm sweat suit, a hat, and gloves because it was fairly cold outside.

As I walked to the park, I noticed my senses were heightened. My eyes were like magnifying glasses. I could see the finer points of everything and it was all beautiful. The colors were so vivid. I felt like I was walking through a dream. I was there, but I wasn't there. I felt energy, a presence, around me the whole time (which hadn't left since my morning meditation and "Light" experience). I was drawn to a particular part of the park to set up my blankets and sit – I had seen a vision of that spot in the park while at home preparing my things. I set up my incense, and planned to just sit in meditation until the incense burned fully. I had no idea what I was waiting for, but I wasn't at all afraid. I was like a puppet on the strings of the Infinite, going wherever I was guided to go and doing whatever I was guided to do. Everything was set up like a small ceremony, but for what?

I put on some light meditation music, and sank quickly into a sweet spot. I turned off the music after a short time because I had the feeling I needed to be present completely for what was about to happen. Then, the most amazing thing I have ever witnessed in this life happened. As I rested on my back and looked up at the sky, a swirling tunnel of light opened. Out of the tunnel came little beads of light that were gently raining on me. I could feel them as they landed on my body, sunk into my pores, and permeated every cell of my being. It was fantastic. It was not raining outside; there were only these little beads of light coming from the portion of the sky that was directly above me.

I felt pressure in my head for a little while; I was then able to see beyond the tunnel. I was in my body looking up at this tunnel, but I was also inside of it looking down at myself. I got a glimpse of the infinite realms beyond this world as I was suddenly projected into the Universe. As I looked back at Earth, it looked like a tiny speck compared to the many dimensions beyond. Then, I was fully back in my body; I started to see celestial beings again as I lay on my back and looked up at the sky. As they were coming forward and fading, I started instinctively calling out the names of ancestors, family members that had passed on, Masters, mystics, and more. "Grandma Hunter... Grandpa Hunter... Aunt Sil... Martin Luther King, Jr... Gandhi... Mother Teresa... Howard Thurman... Harriet Tubman... Jesus... Buddha... Rumi..." Then, spontaneously, I said, "I forgive the world, and I forgive myself." I kept lying there and taking in all of the Light that was pouring into me. It felt like the secrets of the Universe were being passed down to me.

When the tunnel disappeared, I could see little particles and microorganisms in the air. My eyes were like a microscope to the soul of the Universe. It was beyond words, but I'm trying my best to capture what I experienced. I *knew* I was awake in this dream we call life. My morning experience was not a fluke. I was really awakening to the Kingdom of God. I was *always* Home, in Heaven, as we all are, but I hadn't actually experienced it prior to this point. I am grateful to have awakened to *It*.

What do you do when you've arrived at a destination you have been longing to get to for so long? You settle in, unpack a bit, get accustomed to your new surroundings, begin exploring new territory, etc. That is what I feel like after this experience. I have just been lifted to a higher dimension, and am adjusting to it. Mooji's talks are helping me make sense of it. I know the right teachers will continue to come my way because I'm now vibrating at a level that matches that of a new set of teachers and teachings. I know that spiritual experiences like these have happened to many people, so there are many places I can turn to for a deeper understanding of it. For the past day I have felt that ego is in the background. It's like Mooji described: *When the sun is out, you can see the moon but you don't worship it. It's just there.* I love that. The ego is there, but I'm not focusing on it. What I saw yesterday was proof that this body and Earth are specks in the Universe. We are WAY more than our bodies.

Now that I have read a little more about 12.12.12, I am preparing for the next 'high energy' day: 12.21.12. I believe clarity and conviction are going to rise in me like never before. I have 'the fire' I was longing for. It's not just an intellectual under-standing – it's a deep inner knowing that I AM the Light – I AM one with all that is – God.

The next day, I was guided to listen to an audio program by Michael Bernard Beckwith titled *Your Soul's Evolution: Practices for Catalyzing Your Spiritual Awakening*, and it all came together. At the end of the talk, he described an enlightening experience he had, and parts of it sounded so much like what happened to me yesterday. I was able to make sense of what this is for – to reveal the Love of God *through* and *as* me. I know I will be guided as to what to do with this, and have already been guided to the exact things to read and do next.

Every question I have is being answered in unique ways that resonate with me. For example, this morning I was thinking about what to do next, in preparation for 12.21.12, and was immediately guided to pull out the Course and read part of the *Manual for Teachers*. The manual describes in great detail what a teacher of God is called to do. The first sentence I read said (and I'm paraphrasing) that pupils will be sent to me that are at a level of readiness to receive this form of the universal curriculum. Just reading that line sent chills down my spine. *Am I really being called to teach this?*

I am being guided by the Spirit to fast, study, and focus on embodying the 10 characteristics of a teacher of God, as outlined in the Course, for the next nine days. As the Course says, "To teach is to demonstrate."[5] To teach is not just about sharing these characteristics with others – it's about *living* them.

I have also been guided to make 12.21.12 a 'holy day,' and will plan to conduct a ceremony on that day. I will work through anything ego-driven that needs clearing as it arises. An assignment that just came to me as I was typing is to work with each of the 10 characteristics and write out how I will embody that quality. I will meditate first and see what flows through me each day relating to each of them. The 10 characteristics are: *Trust, Honesty, Tolerance, Gentleness, Joy, Defenselessness, Generosity, Patience, Faithfulness, and Open-Mindedness.* Since there are 10 characteristics, and this is a nine-day fast, I will work through two of the characteristics on one day. I know I will be guided as to which day would be the best one to do two characteristics.

I am in awe of all of this. While I believed "all things are possible," I had faith the size of a mustard seed that I would have a direct spiritual, or mystical, experience myself. Although I had the deep desire to awaken to the Truth, I used to think this lifetime was one of study that would accelerate my soul further, but not fully awaken me from the dream of separation from God. I feel very differently now. It's like I *have* this body, instead of I *am* this body. My body is a tool that I'm using to express the Divine in all that I do while occupying it. I have said that many times before (e.g. my *Soul Costumes* journal entry back in May), but now I really *know* it.

I finally looked up the meaning of the spider. There are many meanings, but the one that stuck with me is the symbolism as defined in India:[6]

> *In India, [the spider] is associated with 'Maya.' The term Maya comes from the Sanskrit root 'Ma' which means no form or limit. The term Maya describes the illusory nature of appearances. The spider's association with Maya brings about the understanding that not all things are as they appear to be.*

For me, this is more confirmation that I am transitioning to the next stage of the journey, and the illusion of the world (or, Maya) has even less influence on me.

After writing about the experience, something told me to listen to the song *I Had a Revelation*[7] by Georgia Anne Muldrow. I went to YouTube and found a clip of her singing it live at Agape. The lyrics moved me to tears. I played it at least three times, and allowed the tears to flow. I could not have been more grateful.

Living in the Spirit has set my soul free
I gave my whole life to God
And I began to see
I had a revelation
One day while I was in prayer
I had a revelation
I became so aware
My love for God was ever so true
I discovered God loves me and is me too
Now I know why I'm alive
God made me to reveal Its holy face
I am the hand of God
Everywhere I go
And Who I am matters to the Most High
I am the Life of God
That's why I am alive
I had a revelation
I am the face for God
I had a revelation
I am the arms of God
I had a revelation
I am fulfilling God's Will

I had a revelation
I am the Life of God

Nine Days and Nine Nights

I had no expectations for what would occur throughout the nine days and nine nights of fasting. I was focused on being present in each moment, without too much thought on what was to come. The only exception was preparing for the 12.21.12 ceremony, the plans for which unfolded as each day passed. What follows are my journal entries from the period of fasting. These have been only slightly edited for grammatical errors, flow, and illumination of some thoughts that were not fully fleshed out in the journal. This is my raw description of the insights I had during that period.

Day 1 | 12.13.12

I feel an energetic vibration infusing my body. I feel like my pores are open. There is an intense pressure in my chest and neck area. I need to look into what that means. I made it through the day without eating. I tried to switch from a juice-and-water-only fast to a raw food fast. I pulled out a banana, and was just about to bite down on it, but something in me let me know that was not what I was supposed to do. A Force took over and made me pull it out of my mouth and put it in the trash. I guess that was the Spirit's way of letting me know this is a liquid-only fast.

Today was a peaceful day. I felt connected, joyful and loving. When I went to the grocery store, there was a woman in line in front of me who forgot her debit card. She said she was going to come right back with her card, but I had a strong urge to pay for her food. I followed her outside and was going to give her the cash, but she had found her card in the car. She was grateful for the gesture. I was grateful for the shift in my level of generosity. In the past I may have just observed the situation without taking action, but that was not possible anymore.

I just remembered that the day before the revelation I felt very peaceful. I was at the car dealership in the waiting room and the news channel was blasting. I put on my headphones, turned on some calming meditation music, and read the Course in peace. I felt compassion for everyone who entered the room and looked stressed. I was smiling for no reason. I was joking with the mechanics and salesmen. My guard was down.

My 3-year-old son was much calmer that day. When he did get upset, I was quickly able to get him to settle down. I could also feel when his energy was negative. I actually *felt* the heat rise in him. I have an incredibly heightened intuitive awareness now.

I no longer have an addiction to Facebook and other social media outlets. When I logged in earlier today, it was to do a quick scan and post; afterwards I logged right off. I disregarded any negative posts and focused on the positive, spiritual quotes from the pages I had "liked." Later in the day I was guided to cut all social media out for the remainder of the fasting period.

Today's lesson in the Course was "Let me remember what my purpose is."[8] My purpose certainly revealed itself to me in the most powerful way yesterday. I know I am being prepared to walk boldly in the Light, and to shine brightly for all who are guided to me.

Today's characteristic of a teacher of God is Trust. One of the parts that struck me from the description of this characteristic was, "*When this power has once been experienced, it is impossible to trust one's own petty strength again. Who would attempt to fly with the tiny wings of a sparrow when the mighty power of an eagle has been given him? And who would place his faith in the shabby offerings of the ego when the gifts of God are laid before him?*"[9] Such a powerful passage. Now that I have experienced the Power of God, I can never go back to entirely believing in the small, ego-driven self.

I went on to read that all of the other nine traits rest on Trust. *Once that has been achieved, the others cannot fail to follow.* I can see that. It reminds me of other quotes I've seen within the Course, and other spiritual texts, that state doubt and trust cannot coexist. When you are living completely without doubt, you can't help but express more of the characteristics of the teacher of God.

Day 2 | 12.14.12

Today I woke up at 2:30 am. I am surprised I'm not feeling very hungry. I normally eat a healthy amount during the day. When I do fast, it's typically a raw food fast or juicing until dinner. Liquid only is something I have never done for an extended period. I feel like I'm being shown by the Holy Spirit that I am fully sustained by God – not the things of the world.

> "Man does not live on bread alone, but by every word that comes from the mouth of God."
> ~Matthew 4:4

I have read that this time (12/12/12–12/21/12 and the time period thereafter) is considered by some the "Second Coming of Christ." That prophecy didn't just mean Jesus, as an individual soul, would return. It meant that the Christ Consciousness within many individuals would be activated; or, that many would awaken to the Christ within them. I can certainly feel *something* activating in me. Whatever it is, I'm grateful for it. I believe we *all* have the ability to activate this Power within ourselves. This must be what Jesus meant when he said, "You can do all these things and more (John 14:12)." He meant that we all have the Power of God within us (Christ). There's nothing we cannot do once we activate that Power within, and collectively act from that Truth.

I have been tempted to use a pain reliever for the pain I am currently experiencing in my chest and throat but I am not giving in. I know it will pass. There's a quiet inner knowing that all things in this world come and go. I don't have to rush to move it away – it will go.

This whole process brings back memories of when I pledged a sorority. I had very little sleep and intensively studied the sorority's virtues. This time I am 'on line' with candidates for teachers of God, to reveal the Christ in all life while here on Earth. That is my sole purpose – revealing and expressing the Love of God.

I had to pause from writing for a few minutes. I just had a vision of myself at a retreat on the West Coast. It was such a powerful vision that something in me told me to change my travel plans for the New Year. I needed to get out West – soon.

Note: Up until that moment, I had been planning to go back to Yogaville, in Virginia, for a New Year's Eve retreat. Kevin and our youngest son were going to go to Phoenix to spend some time with my father-in-law. I was planning to have my parents watch my oldest son while I went on the retreat. After having that vision, I was led directly to Agape's Web site to register for the New Year Silent Meditation Retreat in southern California. I didn't know why I needed to go there, but I didn't question the Spirit's guidance.

I have such a strong pull to be outside in nature, so this retreat will be perfect. The weather will be much warmer than it is here, so I will have more of an opportunity to commune with nature and look up at the stars. It's calling me.

My lesson in the Course today is "Let me remember that my goal is God."[10] This is a powerful reminder that God is actually my *only* goal. It went on to say, "Our goal is but to follow in the way that leads to You. What could we want but to remember You? What could we seek but our Identity?" Indeed.

The characteristic of a teacher of God that I am contemplating today is Honesty. The *Manual for Teachers* describes "Honesty" as consistency. Honesty is when nothing that you say contradicts what you think or what you do. When there is no conflict, at any level within, it is impossible to be in conflict with another.

This was something I struggled with in the past, but I feel ready to embody this quality fully now. I am at a place in my life where I am acting according to my beliefs – not based on what I believe others want from me – and it has produced tremendous results. I cannot imagine going backwards on this one.

> "Happiness is when what you think, say, and do are in harmony."
> ~Buddha

I sat for about five minutes or so absorbing what I just read in the healing section of the Course. I completely believe what is written here, and I know that we all have the power to heal just like Jesus – I can feel it in me. I don't know who will be assigned to me, but I know that I am willing to be a vessel when I need to be used in that way. I don't want to do it for show – I just want to be used as He would have me be used. Then I read:

As the teacher of God advances in his training, he learns one lesson with increasing thoroughness. He does not make his own decisions. He asks his Teacher for His answer, and it is this he follows as his guide for actions.[11]

This is absolutely what is happening to me. I can feel the presence of the Holy Spirit, Jesus, and other guides with me right now. Anytime I have a decision to make, I want to take it to them. This level of communion is more fulfilling than I could have ever imagined. I am deeply grateful for it.

Day 3 | 12.15.12

I was dancing around with the boys at breakfast and was suddenly overcome with emotion. I had to leave the room, pause, and turn within for a moment. Something told me to count the number of months it had been since I started the *Living in the Light* blog – nine months! It has been nine months of sharing openly with the world, and I'm in the midst of a nine-day fast and purification process. The day of my "revelation" was on 12.12.12 which adds up to the number nine. Nine is considered the number of completion. Wow. I believe the blog was my first assignment this year. It was part of detaching from the ego, while teaching as I learned. It all led to this moment of revelation. I am in awe. *Is this really happening to me? This feels like a dream.*

I flashed back to the time when I was first introduced to the Course – six years ago. It was right after my affair, when I felt like a total failure and 'sinner.' The Course reshaped my definition of sin, and it gave me a step-by-step way to undo my false perception of myself and return to the Love and Peace of God within me. It planted a seed in me back then that has finally sprouted!

I feel like I'm in a fish bowl and can see out to the world, but I'm happily frolicking and wading in the water – completely unaffected by it. I want everyone to know the freedom that lies beyond the struggle they perceive as theirs. I now know that problems are our thermometers – taking our temperature on how closely we are aligned with our true Self and how closely we are aligned with God.

I am so emotional right now. I can actually see and feel every word of Truth I have read from every Master Teacher that has graced this planet. It is all being activated in me. I understand the passion they had for trying to reveal the Divinity that dwells within everyone.

I used to be tied to gaining more and more spiritual knowledge. I wanted to read book after book and demonstrate that I understood spiritual principle, world religions, the words of the great mystics, etc. I'm not discounting what I have taken away from this but now that I have returned to the Truth, I just want others to know how much beauty, peace, love, joy, and so much more lies beyond the words. When we strive to embody the qualities of God, instead of focusing on how many scriptures we can recite, the 'Kingdom of Heaven' is revealed to us – right here and right now.

I had it backwards before this revelation. The ego was activated and the Christ in me was deactivated. Now the Christ is activated and the ego is deactivated. Notice I said the ego is deactivated and not that it's gone completely. It's definitely still there, but I'm just not plugging into it.

Never in a million years would I have imagined that I would be sharing my 'crust' with the world. But you know what? What is crust or flakes on the skin? It is simply dead cells shedding so the new skin can reveal itself. That is what happened with me when I shared my story and stopped being ashamed and feeling guilty. The Christ in me has risen, and my innocence is shining through now. I'm not identified with the crust anymore. That layer is shed. I have been made new!

I used to ask, "How can anyone be happy and at peace with all the suffering in the world?" After 12.12.12, I can see that I had it flipped. The question should be, "How can you be upset with all the beauty of the Kingdom surrounding you?" What is real to you is what you will see. There is a quote I love that Dr. Beckwith shares frequently: "When you believe more in what you *don't* see than what you *do* see, then you *will* see what you don't see and you *won't* see what you do see." That is so true. When I focused intentionally on seeing the Divinity in all life, that's what I began to see. I saw the Light of the world shining through each and every one I encountered. In terms of the suffering of the world, I find that I have more compassion toward those who are experiencing the effects of those who do not share this same sense of

Reality (those who are extending violence, hatred, war, etc.).

Yes, Heaven is real; however, it's not some far-off place that you work all of your life trying to get to after your body is laid to rest. Heaven is here and now waiting for us to align ourselves with It again. We cannot experience Heaven with hate, anger, judgment, blame, fear, regret, doubt, shame, jealousy, and the like in our hearts; they don't live There. I had to ask myself, "Do you let just anyone come in and take up residence in your home that you didn't create or invite?" Neither does God. God is a protective field for Love and Light. No darkness can enter, or there would be no pure Home for us to return to. But, as I know all too well, when the ego is guiding one's life, it can *seem* as if Love isn't present and that darkness reigns supreme.

After I wrote the paragraph above, I was led to listen to a particular part of Dr. Beckwith's *Your Soul's Evolution*[12] audio program, in which he shared a Zen koan (like a parable or riddle) that was a beautiful illustration of the point I was making. He said, "Imagine a goose is in a bottle. There is only a small opening that the goose is unable to fit through. You can't break the bottle. How do you get the goose out of the bottle?" After pausing for a short time, while I'm sure the live audience was looking as stumped as I was, he said, "I said IMAGINE the goose was in the bottle. The goose was never even in the bottle. You just imagined it." That was just like me. I was imagining I was leading a life separate from God and that I had to work hard to make it into Heaven. In reality, I was living, moving, and having my being in Him all along. I was already free.

While walking through Target, I was no longer drawn to buy a bunch of material things. In the past, I couldn't get out of there without spending at least $100. This time, I got solely what I needed and headed for the checkout. I had a strange feeling as I was walking through the store. It was like I wasn't really there – like I was observing myself. I noticed the magazines and ads trying to convince people that happiness lies in beauty products, clothes, being up on the latest celebrity gossip, etc. My heart was crying out with compassion for those who were bound, as I once was, to those false perceptions. If everyone had even a small taste of true happiness and joy, then they could never believe in 'things' bringing them happiness. My only desire is to share this with whoever is sent to me so they, too, can awaken to the Truth that lies within them.

I noticed throughout the day that whenever I was trying to make a decision, what I needed to know was revealed right away. If not I felt a strong vibration in my body informing me to wait, and tune in, before jumping too quickly. I am actually being steered by the Spirit. I'm still feeling that prickly sensation in my face and neck. I can feel the energy of everything around me. I have never felt anything like this. Whenever I feel 'negative' energy around an individual, I am mentally sending Love and Light to them. Now that I am feeling the Divine connection I share with everyone and everything, I know that every time I send out Love it has a positive influence on all there is. I never want to forget that.

When I got home from the store, I was planning to stop in quickly and go for a walk, but I felt a spirit-like presence pull off my jacket and scarf. I was then guided to meditate. I am so glad I followed that guidance. I feel much more grounded. After meditation, I was inspired to look up information on pressure in the head and prickliness in the skin during a spiritual awakening, and found that these were all normal symptoms. I also ran across some great articles describing periods of spiritual growth which gave me some context for what is happening to me. I am so grateful right now! I just put on the song *Feels Good*[13] by Tony! Toni! Tone! so I could dance it out.

I received some messages from the Spirit about the ceremony

on 12.21.12. It would be indoors because of cold weather. I was to select a circle of Teachers that I wanted to be present at the ceremony, and I was to wear white. I thought for a moment about which Teachers I wanted to call on. Based on the little guidance I received so far, it felt like a rites of passage ceremony. I used to coordinate an African rites of passage program for youth when I was in college, so I spent a moment reflecting on the way we used to call on the ancestors and pour libation during our sessions. I'd like to incorporate that into this ceremony. I also need to look at a book I bought back in my college days, *Opening to Spirit: Contacting the Healing Power of the Chakras and Honouring African Spirituality* by Caroline Shola Arewa, which includes some guidelines for rites of passage ceremonies.

The 'high' feeling has tapered off a bit and reminds me of a flight after takeoff. I feel like I have reached my flying altitude. I am coasting now. It's like I have been swallowed up by the Spirit, and am resting in the belly of God.

I am in tears again as I watch a YouTube video dedicated to Mooji called *The Embrace*.[14] When I clicked on it, I thought the video was going to be a talk about the embrace of God; instead, it was a series of pictures of Mooji embracing his students and visitors from around the world. "Love is a universal language" came to my mind as I was watching it. I was reminded of a time when I heard Mooji mention a student who had come to visit him and didn't speak English. She completely received his message and was fully transformed by the experience. Powerful. No words are necessary when resting in the embrace of God.

I couldn't help but tear up as the Spirit showed me, as I was watching, that my own story will not only resonate in the US, but will resonate all over the world. I paused and said out loud, "Let me be a vessel. I am willing to be used as You see fit. I am ready to be a force for good. Overflowing with Love, Peace, Joy, Wisdom, and all else that You would have me be."

"We are the unicity of Being in its dance as existence. We are ever One, as Truth and Love."
~Mooji

While the global love fest in my mind was tapering off, I received another message. I received an assignment from Spirit to look into the PBS documentary, *This Far by Faith*.[15] After writing down the assignment, I immediately wrote, *I am an abolitionist. I release souls from bondage to the body.* I knew it did not come from me. It turns out the documentary was about African-American spiritual journeys from the Abolitionist and Civil Rights Movements. The description stated: *Ordinary men and women across the centuries have searched for their souls, day by day, to rise above the circumstances of their lives. These are their stories.* I suddenly started to understand why I had felt pulled toward conducting a rites of passage ceremony after completing the nine-day fast. While the message I have been called to share will resonate with a wide audience, my ancestors were calling me to not forget the people they had worked so hard to free. I was also being reminded to call on them for guidance and support along the journey.

I started doing some research on the documentary, and was in awe of the synchronicity. Just weeks prior, I had been guided to the book *Jesus and the Disinherited*, by Howard Thurman, and he was one of the spiritual leaders that was featured in the documentary. I was clearly on the right track. As I continued looking at the list of those featured in the documentary, there was one in particular who was calling out to me – Sojourner Truth. I had learned a little about her as a child. I knew she fought for the abolition of slavery and women's rights, but there must have been something more for me to learn. As soon as I read this paragraph I knew why I was guided to her:

> *The force that brought her from the soul murder of slavery into the authority of public advocacy was the power of the Holy Spirit. Her ability to call upon a supernatural power gave her a resource claimed by millions of black women and by disempowered people the world over. Without doubt it was Truth's religious faith that transformed her from Isabella, domestic servant, into Sojourner Truth, a hero for three centuries at least… In her old age, she had let go of Pentecostal judgment and embraced spiritualism. Her last words were: "Be a follower of the Lord Jesus."*[16]

That last line stuck with me because it was the same thing Howard Thurman stressed – being a follower of Jesus versus just believing in him. I went on to read that, throughout her work, she would go out into the woods and commune with the Holy Spirit and the ancestors. She even set up her own temple of worship there. One day she felt overcome by the Spirit, and from that day forward she felt the presence of an intercessor. She recognized this presence as Jesus. She felt herself being lifted "above the battlements of fear." I couldn't believe what I was reading! This is *exactly* how I feel right now. I can feel the presence of the Spirit in and around me. I hadn't realized that Sojourner Truth had shifted to a more spiritual perspective (versus religious) toward the end of her life. Now I had another kindred spirit to add to my circle of mentors on the 'other side,' right alongside Martin Luther King, Jr. and Howard Thurman.

After pausing to take in the magnitude of what I felt like I was being called to do, I was guided to read about Harriet Tubman. She was not featured in the documentary, so I did an online search to find out more about her history. I had also learned a lot about her during my childhood. She was certainly the most talked about abolitionist, and I was very inspired by her. I even had a chance to visit some of the locations where she freed slaves when I lived in Ohio. I was curious to see why I was being guided to learn more about her. It all became clear when I started reading more about her spiritual intuition. She began receiving visions from the Spirit about freeing slaves before she even believed it was a possibility. She followed *every* vision she received about where to go, who to talk to, what to avoid, and when to go. She did not compromise on what she knew she was called to do. I knew I had yet another mentor and spiritual guide to add to the circle.

This got me to thinking about the upcoming rites of passage ceremony. I wanted to make it special. Since these ceremonies typically include calling on the Spirit of the ancestors, I wanted to symbolically represent that in some way. Then I remembered what the Spirit guided me to do the day before – select a circle of Teachers. I decided I would print out pictures of the ancestors and Master Teachers that I feel most drawn to. I would put their pictures in a circle around me during the ceremony and I would call on them for the gifts I believe they could assist me with on the journey forward. Just the thought of feeling their presence in the room gave me goose bumps.

I started making my list right away, while the idea was fresh in my mind. It meant a lot to me because I viewed this list as those who I was calling on to come alive in me. I wanted to move from knowing about them to embodying their strengths. That day, the list included Jesus, Martin Luther King, Jr., Howard Thurman, Sojourner Truth, Harriet Tubman, Gandhi, Mother Teresa, Ma'at and Buddha. I knew the list wasn't complete, but it was a good start.

While I was still coasting on this spiritual high, a question arose in my mind about how to maintain this transcendent state of being. Within minutes, I was led to yet another talk by Mooji in which a woman asked almost the *exact* question. By this point, one would think I would have been used to these serendipitous moments. The feeling of awe and gratitude I felt overwhelmed me and I began to cry. I began pinching myself to be sure I was awake. Before my mind got too carried away with thoughts that this couldn't be real, I kept listening to the talk.

He began to describe how beautiful it is to die to one's attachments. He noted Jesus' comment about a seed dying to itself in order to become all that it was designed to be. He went on to say that we all are seeds – full of infinite potential. We cannot, however, feed anyone by remaining as a seed.

"Truly, truly, I say to you, unless a grain of wheat falls into the earth and dies, it remains alone; but if it dies, it bears much."
~John 12:24

He used a lovely metaphor to describe this process of dying to the self in order to become what God has designed. He described the self, the ego identity, as an ice cube dissolving into warm water. By dissolving what was not real, it was able to return to its Essence. The 'Essence' was always there, but just needed to return to its true state.

He went on to tell the woman who asked the question to *enjoy* the awakening process instead of analyzing it. He said:

Every cell in the body is rejoicing now! You're no longer interfering with the world... your body has a timelessness about it... a translucency... you were opaque when you were living in the ego... you were like an ostrich – also a bird, but can't fly. Now, you are like empty space. Just like the sun and the sunlight are not different, you are one with the One. It feels as though some Power is moving through you. There is an inner knowing that the world is not where you are residing. You can sit in any company and have no need to judge or feel separate. When people are with you, they will not feel separate. There is a type of water you drink and you'll never be thirsty again. You have had this water.[17]

I felt as if he was speaking directly to me. *How did I even find this video in the very moment I needed it?* I knew it was the Holy Spirit, guiding me to the right teacher for the moment. There was a part of me that didn't want this beautiful feeling to ever end. I remembered hearing from other teachers that I shouldn't be tied to anything staying the same in the world, and that the only thing constant is God. To me, that must have meant that I could not sustain this 'free' feeling in the world. I was conflicted about this, and was hoping Mooji's talk would address this.

A couple minutes later, he went on to say, "Whatever is subject to change, don't mind it. That's not your place. Don't be tied to the ecstatic state – *everything* comes and goes here. You are the witness of that which is happening... If the I AM is there, the witness of I AM is there. Rest in it... enjoy it. You are no longer a student. The more you contemplate, the deeper the joy. Life is not as important. What is needed for the moment is provided... all the forces come together to make it happen. When it's done, it goes right back into the emptiness. You're not carrying those actions with you into the future So, don't worry about 'and then'... don't say 'everything was going so beautiful and then.' None of the sages spoke like this... 'It was so good and then I lost it' (smile). If it comes and goes, watch it – that's ego. Only the ego has expectations. The Self is position-less. This is the peace that surpasses all understanding." I had been schooled. I sat there in stillness for longer than I can remember; in quiet contemplation of the manifestation of God within me.

∞

The characteristic of a teacher of God for the day was Tolerance. I think it's fitting that today's lesson is in tolerance when I have company coming over for dinner. It's a good challenge for me to stay in my natural state and not feed into the ego's need to talk about people, which tends to happen in group gatherings. The description of tolerance states, "God's teachers do not judge. To judge is to be dishonest, for to judge is to assume a position you do not have." I went on to read the portion of the *Manual for Teachers*, "How is Judgment Relinquished?", and received more guidance on how to master tolerance.

It is necessary for the teacher of God to realize not that he should not judge, but that he **cannot**... *In order to judge anything rightly, one would have to be fully aware of an inconceivably wide range of things; past, present and to come. One would have to recognize in advance all the effects of his judgments on everyone and everything involved in them in any way. And one would have to be certain there is no distortion in his perception, so that his judgment would be wholly fair to everyone on whom it rests now and in the future. Who is in a position to do this? Who except in grandiose fantasies would claim this for himself? Remember how many times you thought you knew all the 'facts' you needed for judgment, and how wrong you were! Is there anyone who has not had this experience?... Wisdom is not judgment; it is the relinquishment of judgment. Make then but one more judgment. It is this: There is Someone with you Whose judgment is perfect. He does know all the facts; past, present, and to come.*[18]

It went on to say, "It is not difficult to relinquish judgment. But it is difficult indeed to try to keep it. The teacher of God lays it down happily the instant he realizes its cost. All of the ugliness he sees about him is its outcome. All of the pain he looks upon is its result." All of these lines were incredibly moving to me, but the last one stirred something up in me. I wrote in my journal, *Is your judgment or God's more likely to be true?* I sat there for a minute and thought about all of the things in my life that I judged as 'issues' or 'challenges' and all of the people I judged as 'annoying' or 'arrogant.' I had so many judgments in the past, but I could feel them all falling away in this moment. I was closer to becoming judgment-free.

This shift in perspective was just in time because, while grocery shopping, I heard about a shooting at an elementary school in Connecticut that left 26 people dead. Many people were talking about how crazy the shooter must be. All I could feel was tremendous compassion for all involved in the situation, including the shooter. I also had a quiet knowing that all those who laid their bodies aside were resting peacefully in God, where they had always been. I quietly said a prayer, and did not let resentment take root in me.

After I said my prayer, I was led to read the section of the *Manual for Teachers* titled, "How many teachers of god are needed to save the world?"[19] In this section, the function of the body is discussed. The Course states, "The body's function is but to let God's Voice speak through it to human minds... What you use the body for, it will become to you. Use it for sin or for attack, which is the same as sin, and you will see it as sinful... use it to bring the Word of God to those who have it not, and the body becomes holy." What a potent passage. It made me think back to the shooting, as well as to the mistakes I made in my life. If everyone knew the true function of the body, we would have no more violent or hurtful acts against one another. If we all believed that we are all unique expressions of the One presence (God), we would remember that to attack another is to attack ourselves. The dream that Dr. Martin Luther King, Jr. eloquently spoke of would become manifest from this place of God-recognition in all life.

Day 4 | 12.16.12

I was guided to read Joel Goldsmith's book, *The Foundation of Mysticism: Spiritual Healing Principles of the Infinite Way*,[20] which is all about spiritual healing and communion with God. The Spirit hasn't guided me in the wrong direction yet, so I'm sure it will be exactly what I need to read. Joel Goldsmith (1892–1964) was a spiritual healer and mystic who started a healing ministry, The Infinite Way, based on the teachings of Jesus. Thousands visited his ministry location in Hawaii for healing when he was alive. He taught students and patients the way to direct communion with God. Many lives have been transformed via his most famous, and frequently referenced, book, *The Infinite Way*. Many of the popular spiritual teachers of today cite Goldsmith as one of their greatest inspirations.

I was also guided to open up the book *Interior Castle*[21] by St. Teresa of Avila, one of the most beloved Christian mystics. I opened directly to page 128 where she described her encounters with Jesus. She also offered advice to those who have mystical experiences on how to reintegrate to life afterwards. Once again, the Spirit guides are on point. I had been yearning to learn more about spiritual healing, and I was in serious need of support and guidance from someone who had been through several mystical experiences.

Note: For those unfamiliar with the term mysticism, let me take a moment to define it. I will be using this term throughout the remainder of the book and want to be sure we are on the same page. Wikipedia defines mysticism as "the pursuit of communion with, identity with, or conscious awareness of an ultimate reality, divinity, spiritual truth, or God through direct experience, intuition, instinct or insight." A mystic is defined as "a person who seeks, by contemplation and self-surrender, to obtain unity with or absorption into the Deity or the absolute, or who believes in the apprehension of truths that are beyond the intellect." Some examples of mystics include Martin Luther King, Jr., Gandhi, Howard Thurman, George Washington Carver, Paramahansa Yogananda, Kahlil Gibran, St. Teresa of Avila, St. Francis of Assisi, Rumi, Hafiz, Osho, and Thomas Merton. There are mystics that have emerged from all faiths and backgrounds.

Later in the day, I read "The Laws of Healing"[22] section of the Course. This paragraph stood out so much I had to write it down in my journal and read it a few times:

> *To use the power God has given you as He would have it used is natural. It is not arrogant to be as He created you, or to make use of what He gave to answer all His Sons' mistakes and set him free. But it is arrogant to lay aside the power He gave, and choose a little senseless wish instead of what He wills. The gift of God to you is limitless. There is no circumstance it cannot answer, and no problem which is not resolved in its gracious light.*

I needed to hear that. These words gave me a boost in confidence in the abilities God has placed in all of creation. It also released doubts and worries that had been on my mind about the abilities I may or may not see in myself. I now know that whatever abilities I am supposed to have for all that I am called to do have been, and will continue to be, given.

The Course describes Heaven as "the awareness of perfect oneness." The Course is directed toward the primary goal of the return to perfect oneness with God. Moving beyond the intellectual understanding, or *believing*, that all things created by God must have the same qualities, or be "created in His image and likeness," to *knowing* this is so. I believe I have reached the goal of the Course, but I don't want to 'call the win' too soon. I am still open to learning and growing more in order to reach my highest potential.

I spent a little time today continuing my studies on spiritual healing. I started with the healing section of the book *The Disappearance of the Universe*[23] by Gary Renard. I had read the book, and listened to the audio version, but I had a feeling I could use another refresher. Each time I listened to it, I had another insight. It helped tremendously in making the language of the Course simpler to comprehend.

While I had heard many times, and in many ways, the idea

that 'our thoughts create our experiences,' this time it clicked in a new way. The descriptions the book highlighted about healing being of the mind and not of the body resonated with me on a new level. The book mentioned that Mary Baker Eddy, a spiritual healer and the founder of Christian Science, often mentioned the following as her favorite quote from the Bible:

> *Does a spring pour forth from the same opening both sweet and bitter water?*
> *~James 3:11*

By referencing this quote, she was emphasizing that God does not create sickness. She was not the only one who felt this way. All of my readings on spiritual healing stressed this very point. They also stressed the power of the mind in healing. These were important points for me to let sink in. How many times had I heard someone say when a person was ill, "Well, I guess it was God's will." God wills only the very best for us, and created us in his image and likeness, so why would he will for us to 'die' of disease? He wouldn't. Why then do so many people get sick and how can sickness be healed? I desperately wanted the answer to this question, and spent hours reading through healing stories and books written by (and about) some of the greatest healers. I also reviewed my notes from an eight-week class I took earlier in the year which taught a healing prayer technique. It would take too long to write in my journal everything that I learned from all of this research, but this quote from Joel Goldsmith's *The Foundation of Mysticism* gets to the heart of it:

> *Every sin and every disease is ignorance of the truth that God consti-tutes individual being and that any and every phase of discord is the carnal mind [or, ego], the mortal mind... You are the temple of God. Your body is the temple of God, your mind is the temple of God, your being is the temple of God because God constitutes your being.*

This quote reminds readers that it is their faith in God that heals them. They are not the ego (or "carnal mind"), but they are the Son of God. Sickness falls away when one re-identifies with his or her true nature as Christ (the one child of God which is *all* of us). This really resonated with me, as I remembered how true this was in my own experience of healing from depression. The more I released the fears, doubts, and worries the ego had me believing in, and began to identify with the Christ within, the less depressed I felt.

While I was getting excited about what I was reading, and was feeling more and more equipped to share the 'good news,' there was still part of me that hadn't fully accepted the idea that: "There is no order of difficulty in miracles" (another one of my favorite quotes from the Course) when it came to disease. I was still holding onto a belief in differences between types of diseases and the ability for them to be healed. After meditating and praying for understanding, I was reminded that it is the mind that is being healed, not the body. In some people the shift in the mind translates to a physical healing, but in others it does not. Either way, the healing of the mind is carried forward to the soul's next stage of Eternal Life (whether in another body or not). This helped to ease my mind and allay my fears.

I am continuing to notice signs of a shift in consciousness in me. Yesterday, my 3 year old threw a race car at my head – HARD – and it hurt! He was angry because he couldn't have something he wanted. Then, he began kicking me, growling, biting, and pulling my hair. It was like he was possessed by an evil spirit. I couldn't believe my eyes. Instead of yelling or spanking him, I calmly grabbed his arms and drew him close to me in a tight bear hug so that he couldn't move his arms. I then began taking deep, slow breaths and saying, "Calm your body down" over and over. I'm eternally grateful to the woman who shared that technique with me. He eventually calmed down, and we had a more civilized talk about why he couldn't have whatever he was asking for at that time. This was extremely different from how the 'old me' would have handled this.

Last night we had friends over for dinner. Since I woke up at 2:15 am that day, by the time 8 pm approached, I was pooped! Earlier in the day, I was guided to purchase Doreen Virtue's book *Archangels and Ascended Masters: A Guide to Working and Healing with Divinities and Deities*.[24] In it, she provides a brief description of each angel, ascended master, and spirit guide that she has communicated with, and describes how to call on them. I read a little of the book in the evening, particularly paying attention to her words about how to invoke the presence of Jesus.

At about 8:15 pm, I went into meditation and sent out vibrations of love and gratitude to Jesus. I called to mind all of the wonderful things that had come my way through following his example, and sent him all the love and gratitude I had in me. I then explained the troubles on my mind, which included my low energy and my desire to remain in integrity with my practice of forgiveness and non-judgment. I asked that he be with me, and boost me with energy to make it through the night. I also asked for guidance in healing, which was still on my mind from the day before.

A short while later, I felt a warm presence saturating my body. The soothing presence was followed by intense, but painless, vibrations in my head and neck areas. The power of Love flowing through me was like warm water being injected into my veins. I just sat there in silent communion for a couple minutes – it was incredible. I mentioned how grateful I was for the Course and all the teachers that had been sent my way throughout the past year. I could feel the message was received and the love and gratitude was reciprocated.

When I got up, I felt renewed. I made it through the evening fine, and felt like I had gotten a full night's rest. Throughout the evening, there were numerous moments in which it was clear to me that I had entered another realm; another dimension of awareness. When the conversation was going somewhere that didn't align with me, I got a warm, tingly feeling in my body – it was like a warning not to engage in that type of discussion. I heard, "Just let it float by... you don't have to put your two cents in on everything... let the comments float by." I'm grateful for that reminder from the Spirit.

We had scheduled this gathering before I knew I was going to be fasting. We had decided on dessert and coffee/tea, and I didn't want to change it last minute. I was a major dessert fan, and thought it was going to be torture to sit there with everyone and not eat something. We had cupcakes, brownies, sweet and salty trail mix, fruit, and more. To my pleasant surprise, I didn't even want any of it. I am in awe of the way I am being supported by the Spirit in maintaining a laser-like focus on my goal. I am ready for all that is to come with this new level of being in the world. I know that all that I need will be provided as and when necessary (I have to keep affirming this for myself).

There is a line of the Course which states: "Infinite patience brings immediate results."[25] My "infinite patience" has come. I used to be so impatient, and was pushing so hard to make things happen. Now, I am just allowing myself to be guided in every step, knowing that all I need will arrive right on time or early. God is so good!

Reading about the many "mansions" of the soul's journey described in St. Teresa of Avila's book has been timely. I sat by a pond yesterday to soak in some information from her book *Interior Castle* in which she describes her mystical experiences in great detail and provides advice for each stage of spiritual development (or soul evolution). Some of the language in it is hard to decipher given the time period in which it was written. (It was written in 1577.) I also dusted off my copy of Carolyn Myss' book, *Entering the Castle: Finding the Inner Path to God and Your Soul's Purpose*, in which she breaks down St. Teresa of Avila's words in more modern language. I began reading, and the waterworks began.

You cannot experience cosmic sight and return to ordinary life. You cannot be lifted out of your body into timelessness and then reenter your physical form without changing your perceptions of reality.
~Carolyn Myss

God presses Himself so fully against the inside of the soul that when she returns to herself the soul has no doubt whatsoever that God was in her and she was in God. This truth remains with her forever. Even though years may go by without God granting this blessing again, the soul can never forget. She never doubts: God was in her; she was in God. This knowingness is all that matters.
~St. Teresa of Avila

I was so overwhelmed with emotion. The words of Carolyn Myss and St. Teresa of Avila were eloquently articulating what I was going through and how I had been transformed by it. They were also very candid about the challenges of having a mystical awareness while living in the world. The main one described as enduring the words and attitudes of those who do not believe in a Higher Power, let alone direct experiences of it. Or, those who do believe in God, but believe direct experiences were limited to the prophets of the past. I hadn't really thought much about that, but I knew the Spirit guided me here to prepare me for the pushback that was sure to come from those who don't believe, and/or may call my experiences blasphemous. I am so grateful for this guidance, and will remind myself of it whenever the road gets bumpy.

Let nothing disturb you.
Let nothing frighten you.
All things pass away.
God never changes.
Patience obtains all things.
He who has God lacks for nothing.
God alone suffices.
~St. Teresa of Avila

Today's characteristic of a teacher of God was Gentleness. This was an area that had been a struggle for me, particularly in parenting. My ears were wide open and ready to receive the guidance that was to come. When I read the passage from the teacher's manual, I had a major realization: God cannot work through you if you're holding onto anger, attack thoughts, resentment, etc. That is not the language He speaks. That seems like something that would have been very obvious to me after the transformation I have experienced since the breakdown in January, but it resonated in a new way this time. As I released ego-driven thought patterns and ways of being, God revealed Himself through my life in more ways than I can count. I know this is possible for everyone.

The might of God's teachers lies in their gentleness; for they have understood their evil thoughts come neither from God's Son nor his Creator. Thus, they join their thoughts with Him Who is their Source. And so their will, which always was His Own, is free to be itself.[26]
~A Course in Miracles

Gentleness has begun to come alive in me since the 12.12.12 revelation. I am no longer immediately responding with anger toward my sons when they throw tantrums. I am growing more patient, and have learned alternative, more gentle, ways to calm them down. What also helps me is the recognition I have that this world (the life I have here on Earth) is not all there is to the life of my soul. I am here to be a vessel through which God can flow, including in my home. If I can't love those closest to me, how will I love everyone else unconditionally as God does?

The word sage kept coming to mind throughout the day. I knew it must be a sign. I was guided to do some research on sage and was first led to this definition of the word: Having, showing, or indicating profound wisdom. That made me smile, as I paused and reflected on the Divine wisdom that was now flowing freely through me. That silent pat-on-the-back didn't last very long, as I received a message from the Spirit that made it clear I still had more to look up about sage. Apparently it wasn't about the wisdom that was starting to flow through me at all.

After spending some time online, it all became clear; I was supposed to use sage as a part of my rites of passage ceremony. I was guided to buy a white smudge stick in particular. The smoke of a burning sage bundle is said to be good for clearing negative energies that may have entered the energy field surrounding the body. Many Web sites recommended starting from the bottom of the body (the feet), and slowly and carefully moving up to the top of the crown. It was also recommended that the process begin with a prayer or stating an intention for the energy clearing, and then calling on spirit guides to assist in the clearing process. I thought this was a fabulous addition to the ceremony, and was grateful for the guidance.

Later in the day, I reopened Doreen Virtue's *Archangels and Ascended Masters* book. I have to admit, I used to have major doubts as to whether angels and other spirit guides were real. Whenever I went to purchase a self-help or spiritual book, I steered clear of the tarot cards, angel books, channeled material, and other New Age ideas. Now, ironically, here I was reading a book by one of the most popular New Age authors in the world about how to call on angels and other spirit guides.

The book had such clear definitions of the types of beings in the spirit realm that we can call on and what we can call on them for. The book was clear in its stance that none of them are considered to be 'God,' and that the book was in no way promoting polytheism, or the belief in multiple gods. This was important for me to read because I used to think that her books, and others like it, *were* promoting the worship of multiple 'gods.' What the book was intended to do was to help individuals access the power of the healers, masters, sages, saints, etc., that are available to assist us from the spirit realm. I was looking forward to trying it for myself to see if it worked.

*The deities in this book are aspects or creations of **the** God, with a capital G. The point that needs to be emphasized is that I'm not encouraging you to engage in the **worship** of divinities, but to **appreciate** them as gifts that our Creator has given us to help us love more, heal in all ways, and evolve on our spiritual path. When we accept their help, we're saying **thank you** to God.*
~Doreen Virtue, PhD

The following definitions that were outlined in the book helped to anchor me in this new realm I was about to tap into:

Ascended master: *A great healer, teacher or prophet who previously walked upon the earth, and who is now in the spirit world, helping us from beyond. Ascended masters come from all cultures, religions, and civilizations, both ancient and modern. They include legendary figures such as Jesus, Moses, and Buddha; saints; goddesses and gods; and bodhisattvas, devas, and deities.*

Archangel: *A powerful overseer of other angels, and a manager of specialized functions, such as clearing away fear, protecting humans, or healing. Different religions and spiritual groups talk about different numbers of archangels. Some groups claim there are only four, some say seven, and other groups say there are an infinite number.*

Avatar: *A living human being who is fully enlightened. Usually avatars are miracle workers and spiritual teachers.*

Deity: *A being who is revered for their spiritual contribution while on Earth, and for their help that continues from the vantage point of Heaven.*

God: *When the term appears with a lower-case 'g' (god), it means an aspect of the creator (God), which has a capital 'G.' This being has male energy or identity.*

Goddess: *An aspect of God the Creator that has female energy or identity.*

Lightworkers: *A living human who feels called to help Earth and her inhabitants in a way that uses spiritual energy. For instance, a lightworker might feel called upon to engage in healing, teaching, or artistic work to help make the planet a better place.*

These weren't all new terms for me, but my receptivity to them was much different after experiencing a taste of Reality. I started thinking about what I felt I was being called to do. I felt like I was on a scavenger hunt as part of some initiation process. Each day, I was finding something new that connected the dots that would lead to the reason for this happening to me, at this age (32 going on 33), and in this lifetime. *Am I a lightworker? Is this book, which has basically written itself through the documentation of my experi-*

ences over the last nine months, going to be something that helps lead others back to their true Identity? Is it possible I will become 'enlightened' in this lifetime? Is this really happening?

Everything started to feel so surreal. All I had just read reminded me of those old movies where teenagers find a Ouija board and start fooling with it, and spirits actually come out. They weren't totally sure it would work, but some part of them believed – and that was enough. I just *knew* my mustard seed of faith would be enough for me to access the spirit guides referenced in the book.

I was overwhelmed by a flood of visions that came to me shortly after reading through all of this information. I saw a vision that my book, the one about my spiritual journey that is being written right now, would be completed nine months from 12/21/12 (1+2+2+1+1+2 = 9). I started calling back to mind all of the references to the number nine lately. Then the birthing process came to mind. The book has been conceived, and it will be ready to be birthed (at least to the editor) in nine months. Once again, the tears flowed. I am so grateful to be used in this way. After all the self-doubt, fear, worry, shame, depression, anxiety, and guilt of the past, I was going to share my story of overcoming all of these in order to assist others in doing the same. What more could I ask for. I humbly accept this assignment.

After composing myself, I decided to get out of the house for a bit. I figured it was a perfect time to go pick up some of the essentials for the rites of passage ceremony. While at the store picking up my sage, some incense, candles, and some other items for the ceremony, I felt a strong energy pull toward a particular body scrub. I thought it would be great to exfoliate my skin while I was going through a period of fasting, so I took some time to smell the different scents. As I was looking at scrubs, I thought, *The Spirit knows me too well – I love a good pampering session!*

The scrub that was calling to me energetically was not my favorite of all the scents, so I ended up choosing another one.

When I went to check out, the store owner decided to throw in a small container of the scrub that was calling me. She said, "Since you bought so many items, let me give you this. You will LOVE it! It's called 'Oshun.'" I got a chill when she said that. I knew Oshun was a deity, or Orisha, in the Yoruba spiritual tradition, but I couldn't remember what she represented. Clearly I was supposed to find out, and the Spirit found a way to get the message to me even when I was being stubborn and trying to follow my own path (or nose).

When I got home, I immediately looked up the meaning of Oshun. The Orishas of the Yoruba tradition were not included in Doreen Virtue's book, so I had to look online for descriptions of her. I learned that, in the Yoruba spiritual tradition, she is the Orisha who reigns over love, intimacy, beauty, wealth, and diplomacy. She is also known as the "great mother" and river goddess. She represents the Yoruba understanding of the cosmological forces of water, moisture, and attraction. Her power and permeation is often likened to the Yoruba proverb "no one is enemy to water" (which reminds me of one of my favorite Fela Kuti songs that we play at bath time with the boys, *Water No Get Enemy*).[27] She is revered as Omnipresent and Omnipotent.

I liked the sound of all of this, but felt like there was something else I was supposed to know about her that hadn't been revealed yet. I wasn't fully 'getting it.' After spending some more time reading different sources, I also learned that she has influence over emotional healing. *Maybe she was with me to assist with anything I have left to be healed?* I knew that in the Yoruba tradition, everyone is said to have a spirit mother (or, Orisha). *Was she my spirit mother?* I had exhausted all of the possibilities I could think of, and finally decided that the reason for her being brought to my attention would reveal itself at a later time.

∞

I had never used card decks, angel/oracle cards, astrology, or numerology in the past. This was a lot to take in but, at the same time, it felt natural. That must be because the demonstration of their validity was made tangible to me right away.

Shortly after thumbing through the book and selecting some guides for the Friday ceremony, I began receiving more and more messages. When I was downloading or 'channeling' this information, there was an internal pressure in my eardrums. I could barely write fast enough to take down all that I was receiving in the moment.

I also have been slipping in and out of transcendental meditation without effort. Each time this occurs, there is pressure in my cheekbones and eardrums – I'm not sure what this means. Sometimes I feel like I'm missing messages that are trying to be communicated to me because I don't fully understand what I'm doing. I was just kind of drawn into all of this.

After writing down those thoughts, I just got the sweetest embrace from God. I absolutely can tell the difference if it's a communication from God, or if it's an angel or spirit guide. That's one thing that's absolutely clear. All I could do is just sit and take it in. It felt like confirmation that I am on the right path. My chest and head started to get warm. During the encounter, I saw purple images for a while, and then a bright white light embracing me. Like an electric shock, I could feel *Its* warm vibration pulsating through my body.

After that encounter, I had a vision of the rites of passage ceremony. I saw myself receiving wisdom from each teacher for the next stage of my spiritual journey. The wisdom was transferred to me via light to my head. It was incredibly beautiful, and motivated me to narrow down my choices for my 'circle of teachers.'

Later in the day, I was guided to open the *Archangels & Ascended Masters* book again while the boys were at the table eating a snack. It opened right up to the Laughing Buddha,

Maitreya, who is known as "The loving one." He helps with joy, laughter, sense of humor, lovingness, and peace (global and personal). He encourages the retention of your childlike qualities, and centering the mind on the intention of enjoying yourself and being present in each moment.

It is no accident that I was led to open the book right on this page. I opened up to it about an hour or so after I was playing with the boys and noticed my mind drift to the things I wanted to read later in the day. The message I received was, "Don't take yourself so seriously!" One of the messages from him that I underlined in the book was, "Laughter truly is the best medicine of all – you take yourselves far too seriously, and in so doing, you edge out the secret of harmony on your planet: living in joy. Today, seek out 10 people who are not smiling, and go out of your way to put a smile on their face. In that way, you will have lit 10 candles of light amid darkness." The reference to "light" made me smile. After reading some more about him, I decided to look for a small laughing Buddha statue to have at the ceremony.

Day 5 | 12.17.12

I had some powerful dreams and visions last night. I woke up so sure that this is my time to wake up and be a benefit to humanity; it's what I am here to do (it's what I believe we are *all* here to do). I am ready to be all that God created me to be. With assistance from my guides, I am ready for all of my gifts to be fully activated and used in the world.

I just called on Mother Mary for assistance in motherhood, and felt her join with me. There was warmth in my chest, arms, and head during the experience. The message was about compassion for my 3 year old, and drawing out his gifts. I felt her expressing, *He is very gifted. Spend time with him. What is he drawn to? Nurture his curiosity.* I needed to hear that. For the longest, I was exasperated by my efforts to get him under control. This week, I've been receiving all the guidance I need to stay encouraged in mothering him. I realize that I set the tone for the relationship, and I have to do more than discipline. Between Laughing Buddha and Mother Mary, I felt loved and supported on the path to sustained peace in raising my sons.

A short while later, I received a message from Osiris, who I learned was an Ascended Master that was great to call on for spiritual ascension (or 'enlightenment'), clear communication with God, and creative projects. The message I felt coming through was, *You are doing well – keep up the discipline. Remain focused on the intention to ascend. Don't get pulled into worldly affairs. This is a time of focus and deep contemplation. I've already seen the finish line and you are victorious. Remember to breathe. Create your silent space. You will only feel the fear when you are disconnected from the Voice.* What a fabulous message of encouragement. I went back and read the message from him that was shared in Doreen Virtue's book and, to my amazement, it was remarkably similar! This was confirmation to me that the messages I was hearing were not hallucinations.

I just received a clear message emphasizing that I need to heal my view of what Christianity did to Jesus' message. I have a block there that needs to be released before I ascend. Tolerance will not have been mastered without letting this go. It is amazing to me that there are really beings that can hear my every thought and feel everything in me that needs to be released. In the past, I hoped there was someone listening, but now I know for sure that there is. Nothing is sliding by. There will be no 'fast ones' pulled on my spirit guides.

I thought I had forgiven Christianity for the way I felt Jesus' message – and living example of the Power that resides *within us all* – was a rare topic of discussion in many of the churches I had attended. I had been made to feel like a sinner instead of being made aware of my wholeness, and being shown how to embody the Christ within. I began to feel bitter when I found that there are many teachers outside of traditional Christianity (as I had experienced it) that I believed were more clearly sharing the teachings of Jesus and, most importantly, how to embody them.

What I have experienced directly through following and *living* the teachings of Jesus has been so profound and has removed the static from the hotline to the Divine that I now know was always within me. I started to wonder why this wasn't being taught to everyone. Why is it that I sat in churches almost every week, and didn't feel any closer to God, but the year that I spent the least amount of time sitting in a pew, I have a powerful awakening? In my opinion, it was because I wasn't being taught how to directly commune with God. Instead, I was coming back week after week to get my two hour 'fix' and then went back to living life in the same old way (judging, complaining, worrying, doubting, etc.). Not because I *wanted* to live life that way, but I had no idea how to move from theory to practical application.

I don't think there's anything wrong with going to church, but I now know that the cultivation of a personal daily spiritual practice is essential. It is in our *inner* temples that we can dissolve the perceived separation between the physical world and the spiritual realm. I now release the blame for my lack of individual spiritual practice on the church, or Christianity as a whole. I forgive and let go.

*Note: I have since found Christian churches that do indeed actively teach about the Divinity of all life – that we are **all** the 'Son of God;' Churches that focus on sharing spiritual practices (such as meditation, contemplation, and affirmative prayer) that facilitate the activation of the Christ within. Unity Churches are one example of this, but there are others I have since come across.*

As I was writing that last paragraph, I felt tremendous compassion for those who made the decision about what should and shouldn't remain in the Bible about what Jesus represents

(Council of Nicaea).[28] Part of me believed that, because they may not have had a direct experience with the Divine themselves, they may not have fully understood the words Jesus shared. They interpreted statements like "I and the Father are one" to mean he was the *only* Son of God versus him being in a state of mystical awareness of his oneness with God. They interpreted "only begotten son" to mean that Jesus alone was the only begotten son versus him representing the oneness in which we were created – the Christ presence that permeates all of creation.

Another part of me believed that they knew full well what he meant, which is why certain books were left out. *The Gospel of Thomas, The Gospel of Mary,* and other ancient manuscripts that were left out of the Bible (e.g. *The Nag Hammadi Scriptures*),[29] were filled with sayings by Jesus that referenced more clearly the idea that we are *all* the Son of God, and that the Kingdom is within. Regardless of what happened in those discussions, what is done is done. I forgive them, and I forgive myself for the resentment I was holding onto. I release my attachment to my way being the right way to view Jesus. I allow everyone to come to their understanding. What a weight off my back! Now, I can share the message as I am guided without having any attachment to the interpretation of others.

Today's characteristic of a teacher of God was Defenselessness. I found this fitting for the lesson I am learning in not feeling the need to defend my beliefs or put another down for theirs.

God's teachers have learned how to be simple... Their joy comes from their understanding of Who created them. And does what God created need defense?... It is not danger that comes when defenses are laid down. It is safety. It is peace. It is joy. And it is God.[30]
~A Course in Miracles

∞

I'm feeling exhausted right now. I feel like I'm getting a tiny taste of what Jesus' 40 days and 40 nights may have been like: Bumping up against temptation but persevering, knowing that God cannot be overcome (and I am one with God). I know God has my back but, man, I am tired and hungry. I just got a message as I was writing this: *We see you're working hard. You are persistent when you want something. Remember to rest. You will begin to embody more of your true Inner Self instead of acting from ego. Your inner gifts are being activated.* I needed that. I had been getting up by about 3 am each day to study while the house was quiet.

The fast has reached a sluggish point. However, whenever I have a task that I have to get done, I get what feels like a 'turbo boost' of energy from the Spirit. It feels like a lot of changes are happening fast. I even notice changes in my face. There is a more peaceful and serene look, and my skin is glowing. I can't complain about any of it. This is the experience of a lifetime.

I was reading an article about Mother Teresa in which she discusses how her passion for helping others arose. She said it bubbled up when she discovered she had a "Hitler inside" of her. I can completely relate to this. After uncovering and releasing the ugly thoughts which were contributing to my negative life experiences, I wanted nothing more than to help others release their own.

I have been reflecting on all of the lessons that were presented to me throughout the year, and the teachers that were assigned to me. I am now seeing life as a classroom. I am also seeing very clearly that I was causing positive or negative experiences based on my thoughts and perceptions, which then informed my actions. In each moment, I now know I have two choices: love or fear. Whichever one I choose to respond with will create my experience in the world. How many times have I heard "What you put out comes back to you?" More than I can count. Now I really get it, and I don't wish to put anything out into the world that I don't wish to have in return.

Since 12.12.12, I have felt like I am lucid dreaming (dreaming while awake or fully conscious). I have read enough of the mystics and ancient spiritual teachings to be familiar with the idea that the world is an illusion. To me, that used to be a helpful idea to help me distinguish between the spiritual realm and physical realm. I would affirm things like, "I am not my body" and other affirmations of a spiritual identity versus a human one, but that was not actually my day-to-day experience. There was still a disconnect. My human existence, and daily affairs, felt excruciatingly real, and I found myself unable to fully control my response to life's occurrences. Now, I am aware of the choice I have in each moment. I am consciously taking each action, while maintaining the awareness that this is not Reality. I feel like I am finally gaining control of my reactions, after many years of feeling as if my actions were determined by external conditions. I am so grateful!

I am on the train heading to an important meeting for work, and I feel no fear. I was waiting for that 'butterflies' feeling I normally get when I have a 'big' meeting, but I don't have that. I have been given a glimpse of why I am here and how the next stage of my life on Earth is going to unfold for me. Right now I feel like nothing can bring me down from this high.

I can feel the spirit of my grandmother with me as I ride the train. She used to ride the train often. My grandfather used to work for the railroad, so she received free tickets. A calming, joyful feeling comes over me whenever I feel her presence.

"It is done to you as you believe (Matthew 9:29)" has become one of my favorite scriptures. It keeps popping up to me in visions. While on the train, these affirmations came to me:

I believe in the Power within me
I believe there is nothing I cannot do
I believe I will be a guide to awakening to Self for multitudes
I believe there is no order of difficulty in miracles
I believe nothing is impossible in God
I believe I was made in the image and likeness of God
I believe I am called to heal minds

Two lessons were sent my way while I was at the train station back in DC. I didn't realize until almost 6 am (my train was at 7:15 am) that my return train was booked accidentally for the next day instead of for this afternoon. I didn't panic like I normally would have. I just got ready, ordered a taxi, and calmly made my way to the station. On the way, I was feeling such joy (Ironically, this is the other characteristic of a teacher of God that I was to practice today.)! No caffeine needed, I had joy for no reason. I happily went to the counter and took care of my business, and remained calm throughout the entire ordeal. The woman was incredibly helpful, and I was grateful and at peace. Not only did I select a wrong date for the return, but I did it for a different station in that city which was located about 35 minutes from the meeting location. I forgave myself, paid the change fee, and moved on.

When I got out of the cab, I realized I didn't have enough cash for a tip. I forgave myself and an inspired idea popped into my mind. I remembered the driver's name. I will send him a holiday card with a larger tip than I would have normally given. I am not attached to whether he knows it was me, but I do want him to have his tip.

Then I went to buy a smoothie and got yet another lesson. I ordered a 'green smoothie' and asked them to add protein powder, as I was thinking it would give me some stamina for the day. I sat down to drink it but couldn't. I felt the Power in me rise up, and that's when I knew I had made the wrong choice. The word "Trust" popped in my head. I went back and kindly asked if they could make it without the protein powder. They did so without hesitation. That one went down just fine. I can see clearly that I am being guided to stick to the fast strictly, and trust in the Power within to guide me every step of the way. I hear you, God. I hear you.

I just had some random thoughts about how I was trying to make the book happen earlier this year, and how it wasn't flowing. The blog entries were the only things that were coming effortlessly. I would sit down at the computer, and write them in an hour or less. I didn't think about them in advance or schedule them, they just flowed through me. I am now seeing that I needed to go through this experience first in order to get ego out of the way and be guided solely by the Spirit.

> "My life is not my own,
> To You I belong,
> I give myself,
> I give myself to You."
> ~William McDowell

I am clear that this book idea did not come from me, it came *through* me. I am incredibly grateful to be a vessel. Now that ego is out of the forefront, I can't even write fast enough! Divinely inspired ideas and visions are flowing left and right. I was like a clogged drain; God could not flow through with all of my fear, doubt, worry, guilt, shame, resentment, etc. The song *I Give Myself Away*,[31] by William McDowell, came to mind after writing that last line. I used to listen to that song over and over on the way to work when I was deeply depressed. At the time, I wasn't ready to give myself away, but I am ready now. I am completely releasing my attachment to my ego identity, and fully turning my life over to God. I am 100 percent available for God to have His way, and do His Will through me. It's all I desire.

I looked up the symptoms of spiritual awakening earlier this year and something told me to look them up again. At the time, there were still a few I was struggling with. I knew I was being guided to do a 'gut check' to see how I was measuring up today.

12 Symptoms of Spiritual Awakening (Source: Unknown)

1. *An increased tendency to let things happen rather than make them happen.*
2. *Frequent attacks of smiling.*
3. *Feelings of being connected with others and nature.*
4. *Frequent overwhelming episodes of appreciation.*
5. *A tendency to think and act spontaneously rather than from fears based on past experience.*
6. *An unmistakable ability to enjoy each moment.*
7. *A loss of ability to worry.*
8. *A loss of interest in conflict.*
9. *A loss of interest in interpreting the actions of others.*
10. *A loss of interest in judging others.*
11. *A loss of interest in judging self.*
12. *Gaining the ability to love without expecting anything in return.*

What a perfect description of what I am experiencing right now. And what a drastic shift from where I was just one year ago!

I just randomly thought about how it was in 2007 when I first started the daily lessons of the Course, and $2+0+0+7 = 9$. Yet another nine!

I am being guided to include Alice Coltrane in the rites of passage circle on Friday. I have been listening to a lot of her music, and I have the feeling her spirit will guide me in a music project that has been on my mind. That makes me smile. I have been excited to bring back other styles of meditation music that have sat dormant, at least in the mainstream eye, for many years.

There is more variety in meditation music than many are aware of. I'd love to share the wonderful music from the 'Free Jazz' movement, and profiles of the artists whose spiritual journeys, and mystical awareness, deeply influenced their music.

I just slipped into a deep meditation on the train, and got this message:

Nothing in the world can give you power. All of your Power comes from God. Do not worry about others' judgments of you. Just continue to allow the gifts and guidance from God to flow through you.

My pores feel like they're opening and New Life is pouring through them. My face and neck are still tingling, and my eardrums have pressure in them. I prepared myself to receive the message that the Spirit was trying to communicate to me. I was reminded of my assignment to print the photos of the circle of teachers and to print the manuscript (I was guided on what order to print my blog entries, and other stories from my journals that would be included in the book).

While that Divine energy was flowing through me, Marianne Williamson's "Our deepest fear" quote came to mind. It had been one of my favorite quotes for a while, but now I felt like I was being guided to view it from the perspective of where I am now.

Our deepest fear is not that we are inadequate. Our deepest fear is that we are powerful beyond measure. It is our light, not our darkness, that most frightens us. Your playing small does not serve the world. There is nothing enlightened about shrinking so that other people won't feel insecure around you. We are all meant to shine as children do. It's not just in some of us; it is in everyone. And as we let our own lights shine, we unconsciously give other people permission to do the same. As we are liberated from our own fear, our presence automatically liberates others.[32]
~Marianne Williamson

As many times as I have read this quote, at no other moment did it touch me as deeply as it did this time. It felt like the Spirit was showing me what my greatest fear was so that I could release it, and fully let my Light shine. Although I had been sharing more of myself via the blog, when it came to talking about my 'new' way of thinking around friends and family, I held back. I didn't fully allow my Light to shine because I wasn't sure how it would be received. I wasn't sure how they would react to the spiritual experiences I was having. It was difficult for me to stay silent, though, because I truly believe we *all* can experience this level of communion with God (and more) as we commit to *Living in the Light* and release our ego-driven thoughts and ways of being. I am ready to release that fear. And, I know I *have* to release it in order to genuinely be of service to others.

My meeting for work went well. I could feel the presence of my guides the entire time. I felt less nervous than normal. I noticed a little apprehension rise up as I was talking about my professional background, but that is all. I think it was because I really am not tied to that identity anymore, so I felt like I wasn't in harmony with the Truth of who I am. I don't respond to the "What do you do?" question in the same way I would have even just one year ago. In the past, I would jump immediately to my professional credentials, but now I could see myself saying, "Serve God." That is what I do now.

I feel like I'm straddling two worlds – physical and spiritual. I notice I am increasingly detached from the physical world and am less affected by the things that used to bother me like people talking loud on the train, people with attitudes, people looking at me funny or staring, etc. Everything, including my toddler hitting me in the head with a race car, has been just rolling off of my back. It has never been this way for me, at least not in all areas of my life. I can feel myself being pulled further and further across the bridge from the physical world to the spiritual realm where I know so much more than I can imagine awaits.

The bridge that He would carry you across lifts you from time into eternity. Waken from time, and answer fearlessly the Call of Him Who gave eternity to you in your creation. On this side of the bridge to timelessness you understand nothing. But as you step lightly across it, upheld by timelessness, you are directed straight to the Heart of God. At its center, and only there, you are safe forever, because you are complete forever. There is no veil the Love of God in us together cannot lift. The way to truth is open. Follow it with me.[33]
~A Course in Miracles

A question just came to me: *What does the new world you want to live in look like?* I imagine the 10 characteristics of a teacher of God, as outlined in the Course, being fully embodied in me. I can also see myself completely at peace, full of joy, living in Truth, and sharing my gifts as guided by the Spirit.

After writing that, this line from the Course came to me: *Teach not that I died in vain. Teach rather that I did not die by demonstrating that I live in you.*[34] Such a powerful message from the Guide who I know has been with me every step of the journey: Jesus. What a wonderful way to sum up the way I would like to live, and the way I would like to support others in living.

Day 6 | 12.18.12

Today's characteristic of a teacher of God was Generosity. As I sit and reflect on my day, there were so many little moments of expressing generosity that I hadn't even thought twice about. I asked the deliveryman if he wanted to come inside out of the cold. I sent a friend a quick note just to see how she was doing. I invited a friend to join me on a consulting project that matched with his strengths. Looking back on them, I thought about what a big deal I have made generosity to be. I tend to want to give money, start a nonprofit organization, or organize a benefit. I'm always thinking big. Reflecting on the little moments of generosity reminded me of Mother Teresa's "one, one, one" strategy. It's the little things, truly.

I was guided to go to the park again today. I had a feeling there would be some signs shown to me, but I didn't want to get my expectations up too high. After settling on my blanket, I slipped into a deep meditation. When I came out of the meditation, the entire park was in black and white, but everything I focused my eyes on was yellow. It felt like a visual symbol of the power of perception; I have the ability to perceive everyone and everything in the Light (regardless of appearances).

Shortly after, two eagles began circling around the treetops above my head and then flew off together. I looked up the meaning of the eagle, and there were two definitions that stood out to me:[35]

Aztec and Mayan meaning of eagle (I looked up this meaning given 12/21/12 was the end of the Mayan calendar):
The eagle carries the veil of night and dark over our existence and awareness. It's affiliated with the dawning sun, and is a magnificent celestial power, able to shine light into our world.

Christian eagle meaning:
Associated with Christ. Because the eagle seems to easily ascend the skies, looking into the sun with unblinking focus, we relate symbolism of Christ's unblinking faith in the Way, the Truth, and the Light. We also see themes of renewal (baptism) as the eagle plunges the soul of man into the sea, and lifts them out renewed and cleansed.

It is also said that the eagle is symbolic of expanded perception, or "Not allowing the illusion of limitation to ground us in our flight." The fact that there were two of them flying together made me think of my guides, or the Holy Spirit, being with me every step of the way. I am not alone in this journey that I have been called to embark on.

I began calling on my guides and ancestors for guidance. Immediately upon doing so, the wind picked up around me. It was unseasonably warm that day (61 degrees in mid-December), but the breeze was so strong it sent a chill through my body. My heart began to flutter at a pace I have never felt. I wasn't sure what was happening and, this time, I was a little bit scared. Part of me knows that I have nothing to be afraid of, and another part of me is afraid of some spirit guide popping up in front of my face and catching me off guard. I feel silly even writing that down, but it's the truth. The veil between the physical and spiritual realm is getting thinner and thinner right before my eyes. I have not yet fully released my attachment to the physical world, so I know I am only being shown what I can handle. Right now, this seems to mostly include symbols ('signs'), visions and inner guidance.

The heart palpitations threw me off guard, so my request to my guides and ancestors was cut short. Even still, I had a strong feeling I was going to receive a response. I sat for a while, waiting for a sign or an inspirational thought to come from them. Moments later, a 'wish flower (dandelion)' flew by. This was strange because there were no others around, and all of the grass and trees were brown and without leaves. The flower was white, full, fluffy, and whole. I later read that the meaning of the dandelion in medieval Christian times was the dissemination of the teachings of Christ. This was even more confirmation on the purpose that has been revealed to me.

I thought I had gotten what I came for, so I moved from my blanket to a table to write for a little while before heading back to the house. As I was walking, a sun shower started right where I was standing. Everything else was dry except for the area in which I was standing. I stood there and raised my hands, palms faced up, and allowed the rain to wash over me. The intensity of the moment brought tears to my eyes. It was healing for my soul. I couldn't wait to look up the symbolism of sun showers.

I found out later that sun showers are symbolic of healing, protection, luck, and good fortune. I gratefully accept all of those! After the water stopped, I walked over to the table and began to write notes in my journal about what had just happened. As I was writing a V-shaped twig landed on my journal. I didn't think much of it, but then I saw another one on the table. I thought it was 'overkill' with the symbols and that I must have been looking for meaning that wasn't there, so I dismissed it and kept writing.

When I got home from the park, I got back to work and forgot about the 'V.' I went to the bathroom and noticed there was a V-shaped twig in my hair. Third time was a charm – I had to know what this could mean. In researching the meaning of the letter 'V,' I discovered that it stands for victory, freedom, and peace. I gratefully receive that additional confirmation that I am heading in the right direction. I am so glad I followed my intuition and went for a walk in the park. Beautiful day, indeed.

My stamina seems to be increasing, which is surprising given I have not eaten anything in six days. The smell of food at Union Station yesterday was certainly tempting. I have decided I am not going to cook for the remainder of this week. I would rather order or pick up food for the boys and Kevin so that I am less tempted to 'taste' along the way. I have lost a lot of weight. I really don't want to keep it off as I am way too skinny right now. Thankfully, it shouldn't be too hard to put it back on since I'm spending Christmas with my parents who always prepare a wonderful dinner.

Today was very productive. I put all of my blogs and some of my journal entries together in a Word document, in the order that I was guided to, and am amazed at how the story unfolded. This is clearly Divinely ordered. All of this happened just after my 70th blog post and reaching 7,000 followers. Then add to this the nine-month process of writing and the nine-day culmination of this chapter of my life. The numbers seven and nine can both symbolize completion.

I am so grateful to have been given this assignment. It is what I always was longing for (making a difference in the world), but in a way that I would have never imagined. I trust you, God. I trust you.

After writing that last line down, I was swept into an amazing state of mystical union with God. Like a warm embrace; a sweet kiss of unconditional love. I sat still and allowed the tender vibration to move through my body until it faded. It was a moment of pure bliss and complete peace that I will never forget.

I started thinking about how wonderful God is, and wrote this:

God is so generous, he gave us all everything. All we have to do is recognize it, accept it, and use it. We have all the Power we need to do all that God would have us do. We are powerful. We are the Son of God.

There is so much happening every day, and I haven't been able to catch Kevin up on it all. I told him about what happened on 12.12.12, but haven't been able to discuss any of the signs and mystical moments that have transpired since then. Sometimes I feel inhibited in my communication with him, or anyone else for that matter. I fear that what I am experiencing will be viewed as crazy or made-up. I'm so glad he at least believed what I have shared thus far. I need to keep that in mind and allow myself to open up so that he can better support me on this journey.

Day 7 | 12.19.12

I was guided to look up "Mysticism and mental illness." I read a couple articles, and found them even more intriguing than I thought I would. I had mentioned the idea of the lines being blurred between mysticism and mental illness to Kevin a few weeks ago, after discovering that Ken Wapnick's dissertation[36] was on mysticism and schizophrenia. Kevin has a passion for developing treatments for mental illness. As a neuroscientist, he spends the majority of his time focusing on the known, and what can be researched and/or proven. I spend the majority of my time focused on the invisible realm that cannot always be proven by science (although this is shifting). That is not to say that he does not believe there could be 'something' else out there, but he is not interested in spending the majority of his time studying and analyzing what cannot be seen with the physical eye. Needless to say, I was not excited about bringing up this subject with him again. I did have a feeling that we would do something with our joint knowledge on the topics of spirituality, mental health and the brain, despite our unique perspectives.

The articles I read seemed to show that the experiences described by many mental illness patients, schizophrenia in particular, mimicked that of a mystical experience. I hypothesized that the difference in how a person responds to it could have something to do with their spiritual knowledge and preparedness. For example, if I had described my 12.12.12 experience to a mental health professional, I would have likely been diagnosed with something or told I was hallucinating. Had I not been practicing spirituality, studying the great mystics of the past, and becoming familiar with the idea that there is more to life than what the eye can see, I might have allowed myself to be given medicine to stop me from hearing voices and seeing things that 'aren't there.' Or, I may have even been taken to a mental hospital. I would not have contested because I would not have had any reference point for these same types of experiences happening to many mystics, prophets, spiritual teachers, saints, sages, etc.

Everything I read over the past year prepared me for what I am experiencing now – union with the Divine. This has sparked an interest in working with patients in mental hospitals, although I am not sure in what capacity. There may be an alternative lens through which practitioners can view the experiences patients describe. More importantly, there may be a way to support the patient in understanding what could be occurring (e.g. glimpses of other realms) other than labeling them with a mental health disorder. I know Kevin would say I'm oversimplifying this, and there is much more I need to learn about the varying symptoms patients experience, but I enjoy thinking about alternative ways to look at mental health challenges.

Today's characteristic is Patience. The Course states, "Patience is natural to those who trust... Those who are certain of the outcome can afford to wait, and wait without anxiety." Patience used to be something that would not be at the top of the list of characteristics others would attribute to me. Now I feel like I am living more fully in the present, waiting to be guided by the Spirit regarding what to do next. I am resting with certainty that the outcome will be greater than I can imagine, so I have no need to rush the process.

I started getting really hungry this morning and thought to myself, "It has been seven days. Isn't seven the number of completion? I could stop here, right?" Then another Voice said, "Read about Jesus' 40 days and 40 nights." I started to read the book of Matthew and had to take a pause to write when I read verse four: "It is written: 'Man does not live on bread alone, but on every word that comes from the mouth of God.'" I guess that was my answer, especially since for the entire day the phrase "The Love of God sustains me" kept popping up in my head.

I kept reading and noted that it was after the final test in the desert that he began preaching the good news of the Kingdom and healing every type of disease and sickness among the people (Matthew 4:23). As many times as I have heard that verse in church, it never meant as much to me as it did in that moment. I realized that *all* of the tests I was being given, and all of the trials I went through, were only to support my journey to awakening in Christ and assisting others in doing the same. Or, as the old saying goes, "There can be no testimony without a *test*."

After that, I read the entire Sermon on the Mount. Three verses stood out to me, and I knew it was because they had a message I was supposed to let sink in. I wrote them down and read them over and over until I received it.

You are the light of the world.
~Matthew 5:14–16

Do not worry about tomorrow, for tomorrow will worry about itself. Each day has enough trouble of its own.
~Matthew 6:34

Do not worry about what to say or how to say it. At that time you will be given what to say, for it will not be you speaking, but the Spirit of your Father speaking through you.
~Matthew 10:19–20

I had been worrying a little about what I was being called to do, and if I was ready to take it on. Reading these words helped me get more centered in the present moment. They also reminded me that I am never alone. As I was sitting there contemplating my life's purpose, I fixed my eyes on a quote that was in the margin of my Bible. It was a quote from Harriet Tubman (I was reading from *Aspire: The New Women of Color Study Bible*[37] which features inspirational quotes throughout) that read, "The Lord who told me to take care of my people meant me to do it just as long as I live, and so I do what he told me." Wow. If Harriet Tubman could rise to the challenge of freeing as many slaves as possible in her lifetime, how can I *not* rise to the challenge of freeing as many minds as possible in my lifetime?

Every time I looked at the sky today, the sun peeked through a small opening in the clouds, making expansive rays that stretched from the clouds to the earth. It reminded me that, no matter what is going on around me, I can be the light that shines through.

While walking down the hallway at my son's school, I saw little raindrop-sized lights all around. I had seen them earlier in the day as well when I went to lunch with Kevin – they were all around him as we were talking. I didn't spend much time thinking about the deeper meaning; I believed it was just me adjusting to the new 'frequency' I was experiencing.

I spent a good amount of time outside during the day, and had the opportunity to watch the sun set. Every time I looked at the sun it looked like it was twirling in a circle and radiating little beads of light (there go those little light beads again).

I walked into my son's classroom and he was having a *fit*. They gave him candy, and he was completely out of control. I almost spanked him, but I remembered my fast. I did, however, have to be stern with him in order to get him to the car. I also had to take him to the bathroom at the school to try to calm him down as he kicked, screamed, pulled my hair, scratched, flailed his arms, laughed, took his shoes off, and spit (yes, all of that). When we got to the car, which seemed like it took forever, I remembered my lesson for the day: Patience. All I could do was smile.

Day 8 | 12.20.12

Wow, it is day eight of the fast already! It didn't seem to fly by while everything was happening, but now it seems like a whirlwind. Last night I was so exhausted – the lack of sleep is catching up with me. I hadn't been able to keep myself from staying up late and getting up early to absorb more and more Truth. I was determined to finish reading the text of the Course as soon as possible. Now, even after a full night's sleep (8 pm–3:45 am), I look and feel tired.

All thoughts of how tired I am quickly dissolve, though, when I reflect on all of the lessons and insights that are coming my way. I am being purified and, at the same time, upgraded so that I can bring Love and Light into the world through me.

I'm so grateful for the lunch date with Kevin yesterday. We had the opportunity to chat in more detail about what's happening and he is so supportive and happy for me. His encouragement was timely because I was still feeling distant from those close to me. I realize this perceived distance is of my own creation, though. I am the one who chose to keep the experiences to myself for fear of the opinions of those who wouldn't understand (there goes ego again – popping up for a visit). Sharing with him helped me to stand up tall again, walking more confidently in, and as, my true Self.

Christmas is coming, and we're going to the Philly area to be with my family. After 12.12.12, I sent my sister a text saying, "I HAVE to talk to you today. Had an amazing experience yesterday. Amazing!" When I was unable to call her, I sent another text that said, "Sorry I didn't call. I will tell you the full story over Christmas break. It's a long one, and is still unfolding. In short, we are absolutely NOT our bodies. The world we see is NOT the Real World. Can't wait to share." How's that for a cliff-hanger?

She has an interest in spirituality, and we've discussed our evolving beliefs on numerous occasions, so it wasn't a strange statement for me to make. I chose the language I did because of her familiarity with the Course. I ultimately decided not to tell her over the phone because I finally had a chance to sit down and type up the experience. The first draft of the 12.12.12 experience alone was eight pages long, and that wasn't even the full story. It was certainly a much 'juicier' story to share in person than over the phone. Her response was, "Wow. Cool. Can't wait to hear it!!"

She's excited to hear the story, but now I'm wondering whether to share it with just her or the whole family. I know my parents would be open to it, given their friend's recent near-death experience. I do wonder if they would give me a hard time about not eating for nine days. I'm not sure they would understand that part.

On second thought, they would absolutely be able to tell. All of my clothes are too big now. I have lost at least 10 pounds. My face is very thin, and my stomach fat is almost all gone. Before you start thinking, "Hmm, maybe I should try that," let me say that I would not advise this to anyone without consulting your health and wellness practitioner. I also would not do this with an intention of losing weight. For me, this fast was 100 percent about being vigilant about my spiritual practice. I plan to go right back to eating on December 22, and am sure I will gain the weight back soon. I was not overweight before this, but now I am under-weight. My ribs are showing – not healthy looking at all for me. OK, I am off my soapbox.

Now back to my perceived dilemma. As I write this out, I'm thinking I may have to tell my parents. My mom, especially, will wonder if I am sick because I have never been this skinny in my entire life. I'm not sure which parts of the story I will tell, but I am sure I will be guided regarding what to say and do. I will leave this in the Spirit's hands.

The following prayer came to me after I wrote that last line. I am grateful for the teachers who were sent my way throughout the year who strengthened my prayer practice. These words realigned me with the Power of God that resides within.

Morning Prayer
I am so grateful for the Love of God. Ever-present. Operating in, through, and as all life.

I am living, moving, and having my being in God, and so is everyone else. All the qualities of God are ours, always.

All the Love, Joy, Wisdom, Creativity, Peace, Abundance, Prosperity, Compassion, and Kindness of God is our Divine birthright. It's what we were created to express!

So, I release any thought of lack, limitation, scarcity, unworthiness, guilt, shame, unforgiveness, anger, resentment, hate, or attack, and know that all that God is, I am. All that God is, We are.

So grateful to remember the Truth about myself, and all life, and to be reconnected to Who and what we really are. We were made in the image and likeness of God and there is nothing we cannot do!

I release this Word, knowing that all things are working together for the good of those who Love Him. Everything is going to be alright! And so it is. Amen.

While driving home from running errands, I felt drawn to the sun and sky. I couldn't take my eyes off the sun whenever I had a moment to stop. Once again, I felt like a puppet on strings. Then, I thought, *I'd rather be a puppet on the strings of the Infinite than a puppet on the strings of the world.* The thought made me laugh out loud. If I could give myself a high five, I would. That is the truth right there.

Today, I am reminding myself that I can move through the world as normal, but be guided as to what to say and do. My steps are Divinely ordered. My life is not at all my own. It's a partnership, a union with the Most High. My purpose here on Earth is not to acquire things and make myself important and successful in the eyes of others (which I so desperately cared about in the past – particularly at the time the depression and anxiety set in). My purpose is to extend the Love of God in which I was created – to *be* the Christ within. What an awesome task!

I slipped into a deep meditation while sitting at the park and taking in the sun. It felt as refreshing as a cool glass of water on a warm, sunny day. It has become as necessary as water for me to remember my true Source of infinite supply which, like the sun, never ceases to give.

My mind trailed to my last blog post which was about how to spend your day. What I wrote there was remarkably similar to what is in the "How should a teacher of God spend their day?"[38] section of the Course's *Manual for Teachers*. I only read this section in detail after writing that post. I know that synchronicity happened for a reason. It was a good reminder of the importance of daily practice. Being completely at peace doesn't just magically happen one day. It takes intentional focus to undo the thinking of the world and come back to your true Self. I pray that by sharing my journey, it can be less of a struggle for others to return Home.

This evening, I felt guided to watch the online archive of Dr. Beckwith's talk from Agape last night. I skipped ahead trying to get right to his talk and instead landed at a part where he was doing the reading for the day. He was reading a quote from Harriet Tubman – the *exact* quote I wrote in my journal yesterday! Then, I listened further and he referenced one of the Bible verses I read yesterday. I hadn't written it down in my journal, but it was one that resonated with me deeply. It was like a gentle reminder from the Spirit that I cannot bring any of my old baggage with me. I need to be fully reborn. I believe tomorrow's ceremony will be symbolic of that rebirth.

And no one pours new wine into old wineskins. Otherwise, the wine will burst the skins, and both the wine and the wineskins will be ruined. No, they pour new wine into new wineskins.
~Mark 2:22

As I lay in bed on day eight of this fast, I am feeling grateful. I am deeply grateful that this is my appointed time to wake up. I am grateful to know how it feels to be at one with God. Whether this 'high' stays, I now have no doubt that there is much more to me than this body. I am infinite. I am free!

Today's characteristic of a teacher of God is Faithfulness. As I read the following line, I reflected on the need to retain the memory of this feeling of union with God in order to ensure that my trust is fully on Him and not on the things of the world:

Faithfulness is the teacher of God's trust in the Word of God to set all things right; not some, but all.[39]
~A Course in Miracles

As I think about tomorrow's Rites of Passage, I am scanning my mind for any negative thoughts that still remain in me. I want to remember them so I can ask for Guidance in releasing them during the ceremony. I am ready to die to my *self* so I can live as my *Self*.

Day 9 | 12.21.12

I was guided to listen to another Mooji talk this morning. This one was titled "My life is so different."[40] This was sent my way in perfect timing. There was a question from a young woman that came up during the talk about 'getting' the Truth at a fairly young age, and not fitting in with friends anymore. She mentioned how isolated she felt. I can really relate to that. While I have Kevin to talk to about all that is shifting and transforming in me, he can't relate fully to how I'm feeling.

There's so much that I've read, listened to, and experienced in this year that is really hard for me to sum up when in a quick conversation. Most times, I don't try. Writing the blog has been therapeutic in that it allowed me to share my insights as they came throughout the year. It has been like an online journal. Most of my friends and family didn't read every post, but they did catch some, and at least have a small glimpse of what has occurred.

I still find it challenging to converse about worldly issues that I am not at all worried about (e.g. the financial market). I used to be into debating political issues, but now I don't see the need to defend my beliefs. That doesn't mean I'm apathetic; I no longer have the desire to debate about these things. I now can see beyond the veil of the world and into the Light that is forever shining. I know there is no turning back now. I have been changed. That reminds me of the gospel song that my grandmother used to sing while playing the piano at the house: *I Know I've Been Changed*[41] by LaShun Pace.

I know I've been changed
I know I've been changed
I know I've been changed
Angels in Heaven done signed my name

I was reading the lesson in the Course titled "There is nothing to fear,"[42] and had to pause to write down this Guidance from the Spirit: *To know fear, you must be looking from this body… Spirit knows no fear.* This is exactly what I need to remember. I need to post this somewhere. Since 12.12.12, a fear of being different has crept into my mind and made a home. Specifically, I have been feeling afraid of speaking Truth in a world that very much believes in illusion. All of my feelings of self-doubt, unworthiness, and shame from the past started coming back full force. This quote shifted something in me. It reminded me that I am so much more than "Kandace Jones" – I am Spirit. When I stop identifying myself with the body, the fear subsides so quickly. This needs to become a part of my daily practice.

While I was in reflection mode, I spent some time making a list of my tendencies. I was reminded of a comment made by my spiritual boot camp coach, the Rev. Jennifer Hadley: *We need to look at our tendencies in order to heal them.* I was ready to be honest with myself about what was still residing in me so that I could ask the Spirit to assist me with healing and releasing it during my rites of passage ceremony. The list included the following: the need to be right, the need to be liked, separation (the idea of an individual self separate from God), judgment (good/bad, better than/less than, etc.), unworthiness, guilt, lack of confidence, fear, and annoyance/frustration with my children's tantrums.

Today's characteristic was Open-Mindedness. When I first wrote the characteristic in my journal, I thought, *I'm very open-minded.* Then I read the first line and quickly regained my humility. It stated that open-mindedness is one of the *last* attributes that is acquired by a teacher of God, and that it is directly linked to forgiveness. "How do the open-minded forgive? They have let go of all things that would prevent forgiveness… no clouds remain to hide the face of Christ… it is given to the teachers of God to bring glad tidings of complete forgiveness to the world."[43] Given my tendencies that were still creeping into my mind, I could see that I still had some growing to do in this area.

As I sat quietly, and allowed that lesson to sink in, the following came to mind about the upcoming holiday season:

As we light our trees and candles this holiday season, let us not forget the Light in our hearts, the Christ within.

Heaven is not something we only get to experience when we leave this body. Heaven can be experienced NOW. When we release anything coming from the ego, all that remains is the Love of God that is our True Nature, our natural inheritance.

I felt drawn to the park this morning, and I'm so glad I came. It's so peaceful here. Being here brought me back to center after dropping the boys off at school and running some errands. I'm so grateful for this beautiful 'breathing space' being right down the street from my house. This space will certainly be a regular place of respite for me, and holds a special place in my heart after 12.12.12.

> "The real cancer is the belief that I am this body...
> The greatest healing is to know Who you are."
> ~Mooji

I have some calming meditation music playing in my headphones as I sit and take in the surroundings. Although the leaves are almost all gone, I still find the trees incredibly beautiful. As I sit here, I can feel the Spirit moving through me. Today is another 'high vibration' day, as was 12.12.12, and I can certainly feel it.

There is an unwavering peace that has come over me or, rather, revealed Itself through me. I surrender and allow It to take the lead in my life. Only the Spirit knows how my life here can best be used, and I want it to be for the highest good of all people. I know I could not do this on my own. Only the Spirit knows all things past, present, and future. There is nothing for me to figure out. It is in His hands. All I can do is say "thank you" and celebrate this next phase of my life.

When I got back to the house, something told me to look up at the sky. The first thing I saw was a cloud shaped perfectly like an angel. I mean, it looked like someone painted an angel in the sky. I stared in awe for a minute or so then rushed inside to grab my camera. By the time I got it out, the cloud had changed form. It was so beautiful though, and reminded me that the angels, ancestors, and guides are always with me. The visual is one that will remain etched on my mind.

I went inside, and began preparing for the rites of passage ceremony. Thanks to Caroline Arewa's book *Opening to Spirit*, and faint memories from the youth rites of passage program I used to coordinate back in college, I had developed an outline for the flow of the program.

Order of Program:
Invocation
Libation/Elements
Purification
Call to Ancestors and Guides
I AM THAT I AM
Blessing of Divine Endeavors
Wisdom Sharing
Prayer/Meditation
Ase!

Materials:
Candles
2 stones
Grandma's crystal glass w/water
2 bowls
Incense

Straw mat
Sage
Lighter
Ashtray

Set up:
Materials (candles, stones, Native American eagle symbol, etc.) at the front of the room near the fireplace. Photos of guides, ancestors, enlightened beings, etc. that I was calling on for support in this transition to the next stage of my journey placed around the room in a circle.

Circle of Wisdom:
Jesus, Buddha, Paramahansa Yogananda, Martin Luther King, Jr., Gandhi, Howard Thurman, Harriet Tubman, Sojourner Truth, Alice Coltrane, St. Teresa of Avila, Ma'at, Mother Mary, Osiris/Ausar, Archangel Michael, Archangel Gabriel

Time:
12:12–1:12 pm

The ceremony was more beautiful than I could have imagined. I am so grateful for feeling guided to do this. I didn't script it; I just allowed the words to flow naturally and genuinely from the heart. I prayed the most powerful prayers I have ever prayed, and was amazed at how effortlessly it flowed from my lips. I wish I could remember what I said.

I poured libation and, in doing so, honored my grandmother, grandfather, and aunt who made their transitions. I also paid homage to ancestors I am unaware of who have been guiding me and supporting me along the journey. After that, I used sage to cleanse negative energy from me and while I ran it up and down my body, I named each tendency I was releasing. I included ones I had experienced recently, as well as those that were more present during some of the more challenging times in my life (like the "bad habits" I wrote in my journal on the way to my personal retreat back in January). I said them slowly, and really allowed myself to feel that energy moving out of my body.

Doubt... dishonesty... judgment... aggression... sadness... attack... selfishness... impatience... lack of faith... closed-mindedness... the need to be right... separation... attention-seeking... unworthiness... guilt... lack of confidence.

I had to collect myself before beginning the next portion. My face was drenched with tears. I moved on to the qualities I wished to embody, and asked my ancestors and guides specifically for guidance related to the area they embodied most strongly during their time on Earth. I, then, went into meditation to prepare myself to receive whatever they would like to share with me. The meditation was deep. I saw many flashes of light pouring into my head and directly into my spiritual eye. I felt so much Love energy radiating through every part of me. It was purifying. It was illuminating. It was elevating. I just sat there for a while, taking it all in. When I 'came to,' I thanked each of them for their presence.

I ended the ceremony with the following closing prayer from the book *Opening to Spirit*:

Great guardians of all directions
Spirit-keepers of all elements
All those who walked before me
I thank you for your guidance and presence here today.
I carry your love within me as we part in peace.

A grasshopper appeared out of thin air just as I finished the closing prayer. It literally appeared right in the middle of the room; it couldn't have hopped across the room to arrive at that point because I would have seen it. I took out my phone and looked up the meaning of grasshoppers.[44] Of course it was perfectly fitting for the moment.

*The grasshopper moves to its own rhythm and tune, indicating this creature is an **advocate of intuition** and listening to our inner voices. The grasshopper encourages us to listen to our own stirrings – those beautiful chirping lullabies that sing in our hearts are indications of our inner beauty and creativity. The grasshopper totem reminds us these inner musings must never be silenced – rather, they should be nurtured, and always remain as the background music to the performance of our lives.*

*The grasshopper chooses those of us who are **innovators**, forward-thinkers, and those who progress in life by unorthodox methods. This is because grasshopper symbolism recognizes **tremendous leaps of faith, impressive jumps in progress and consistent forward momentum**. Those with this totem are likely to aim high, and achieve amazing feats – they take great leaps where others fear to tread (or jump, in this case).*

*Another special feature of the grasshopper totem is that it calls to those who have natural clairvoyant abilities. Just as the grasshopper uses thousands of tiny eyes to formulate the 'big picture' so too do those [to] whom the grasshopper is called. In other words, **those with this totem are visionaries**. They see things intuitively, seeing beyond what the concrete world holds, and they use this special vision to see the world with a childlike wonder.*

This whole process has been simply phenomenal! And that little grasshopper just put icing on the cake. This was certainly one of the most powerful ceremonies I have ever participated in, and I am clear that it was *not* coordinated by me. I am taking this process very seriously, and feel like this was the perfect culmination, or transcendence, event (although I am clear there are higher dimensions to reach – I have only just begun exploring the Kingdom).

Reflecting back on the ceremony, I remember hearing, *You have all you need* and *Relax into the Presence that you are* while in deep meditation. Those were the only words that came to mind to describe the flow of Love and Light that was being transmitted to me from the Spirit. I am certain that any other wisdom that was transferred to me during that time will make itself known in time and as necessary.

I was not sure what to expect when I entered into this nine-day process. It has completely exceeded my expectations. I have not missed being on Facebook and have come through fine without food. God is absolutely my all in all. I am entering back into my routine in a new awareness, and with immense compassion for those who are walking the road Home, who have not yet seen the shortcut that is right within them. I pray I can guide those who cross my path and have "ears to hear and eyes to see."

That evening, Kevin and I went to a ceremony at Unity Church in DC titled "Awakening to a New Level of Evolution for a Global Shift in Consciousness." This ceremony was the perfect completion to this week of revelation. The Rev. Sylvia Sumter gave a beautiful overview of the Christ Consciousness that was indeed pouring forth at this time to all who are available to receive it. There was indeed a global awakening happening, and it was time for me to actively play my part in it.

After meditation, there was a symbolic crossing of the bridge into an awakened consciousness. Each person was given a candle, and came to the front to walk across a bridge and state the gift they were bringing to the world with their new level of awareness. When it was my turn I said, "The gift I bring is healing." Kevin was up next, and my eyes welled up when he said, "The gift I bring is forgiveness."

During the ceremony, The Great Invocation was read, and it felt like the appropriate closing prayer for the week:

The Great Invocation[45]

From the Point of Light
within the Mind of God
Let Light stream forth into our Minds
Let Light descend on Earth
From the Point of Love
within the Heart of God
Let Love stream forth into our Hearts
May Love increase on Earth
From the Center
where the Will of God is known
Let Purpose guide our Wills
The Purpose which the Masters Know and Serve
From the Center
which we all call Humanity
Let the Plan of Love and Light work out
And may it seal the Door where evil dwells
Let Light and Love and Power
Restore the Plan on Earth
Let Light and Love and Power
Restore the Plan on Earth
Let Light and Love and Power
Restore the Plan on Earth

I'm feeling like an incubation period would be helpful after all that has transpired, so I'm glad I'm going to the Agape silent meditation retreat. It will be my first official silent meditation retreat (although you could say I got a glimpse of what it might be like while at Yogaville). Just like a newborn needs time to adjust to the world, so do I. I have been reborn. Gone are my attachments to the old ways of being that were not serving me or humanity – they don't live here anymore (at least I don't think they do).

∞

December 22, 2012

I watched a couple more videos this morning about symptoms of spiritual awakening or ascension, and found them very helpful. I am experiencing all of the symptoms, and know I need to surrender and allow the process to unfold. As I release my old ways of being, some old habits are resurfacing (like concern about what others think), and I'm learning that this is normal. This is the time to heal these things so that the new can be born in me, so that the characteristics of a teacher of God can become my natural mode of operation in the world.

Every step I take shows me a sign almost immediately that it was either the right decision or that I need to "choose once again,"[46] as the Course says. I'm feeling torn about whether to get more involved in a local spiritual community. Part of me thinks it's good to connect with other like-minded individuals, but another part of me wants to continue to focus on going within. I want to be sure I am not going to church to get something from someone else, believing that I can't provide it for myself from the Christ within. I want to go because I want to fellowship with others, share, grow, and offer assistance to those that have not yet found their inner Light. I can do this in a church or on my own. I'll take this to my Guides and I know I will receive an answer in time. This inner struggle I was having was one I knew stemmed from my dependence on church to fill me up in the past.

I took the boys out to eat at a place with an indoor playground so they could burn off some energy. They had a ball, but it was challenging to get them out of there. My oldest ran off right when we got outside. It's moments like that when I really feel myself losing my temper. I don't want to; I want to be peaceful in each moment. I don't have a handle on my son's behavior, and now 'Terrible twos' has turned in to 'Tumultuous threes.' I could really use some assistance with this one. I am writing this in the car, and he is in the back screaming because I wouldn't let him run across the parking lot. Just writing it out in my journal is already helping me to feel better.

I am grateful that I have found other ways to deal with the behavior than spanking, but I still find it incredibly challenging. I find myself wishing the situation would be different at times, but then I am always reminded by the Spirit that there is indeed a way to be at peace no matter the circumstances. When I come from that place of peace and unconditional love, our interactions are always much smoother.

After we got home and settled, and the boys were playing with my husband, I went to meditate in the bathroom (my secret quiet space while the boys are running around because it has a lock on it). It was a deep meditation that called up some emotions I had relating to supporting others in their healing process. I had some fear about it, but in this meditation I was reminded that I am always either choosing between my own strength and the strength of Christ in me. There goes that quote I love so much from the Course again – *The presence of fear is a sure sign that you are trusting in your own strength.* I have to remember where my Power lies. It's not me doing the work, it's the Spirit working through me. I am a vessel. After receiving that reminder, I felt guided to read Joel Goldsmith's book *The Foundation of Mysticism* and listen to the audio of *The Infinite Way*, both of which I had purchased weeks ago, but hadn't done much with.

December 23, 2012

All I want to do is sit in quiet and feel my oneness with God. It feels so good. Meditation and prayer time has been more fruitful than ever before, so I would expect that I would be happy about that. Instead, there is an unrest that has formed. All I want is for everyone else to know how beautiful it is to know their true nature. Knowing one's true nature beats everything in this world; there is nothing in this world that can take it away.

I logged into Facebook this morning and did not feel a need to stay on too long. What I was most interested in were quotes posted by the pages I "liked" that keep me focused on the Truth. I no longer feel the need to post on my personal page throughout the day. Even though the fast was over, I still didn't post anything yesterday. Actually, I didn't even log in to my computer. I can feel the difference in myself as I begin to navigate the world with this new level of awareness. I now need to shift my perspective about 'others' so I can remain as I am. I am not this ego identity, so why am I concerned about fitting in? Of course I fit in – we are all One!

If only everyone could feel one minute of what I felt since the day I received that kiss from Heaven. Love would replace fear. Joy would replace sadness. Peace would replace unrest. Faith would replace doubt. While I appear to walk this Earth, the best thing I can do for myself and others is to forgive and love unconditionally.

I downloaded four podcasts by Mooji to listen to on the way to and from my parents' house, which is three hours away. I started listening to one of them and got my answer to the dilemma I raised earlier this morning. In it he said, "Life is not meant to be lived at this level... there will always be struggles here." It was a good reminder to remain in the space beyond the world – that space in which I witness all that happens as it comes and goes without being attached to it; knowing that all things in the world have a beginning and end. I'm so grateful for the Spirit's answers – always guiding me to exactly what I need to hear when I need to hear it.

I was reminded of the idea of projection, an idea that many spiritual teachers and psychologists discuss. All that we see and experience is a result of what we are projecting outward based on the thoughts within our own minds. When we remember this, we would not get as upset with whomever or whatever seems to be frustrating us; we would recognize the point of focus lies within. When we shift our thoughts, our experiences will shift. Even in the situation with my oldest son. When I am upset with my son for flailing his arms and having a tantrum, I can remember that the source of my upset is not really the tantrum; it's the projection of my inner anger onto him. If I remember that it is my projection, and remember to see the Light in him, I will be less bothered by these incidents.

> "Our life's experience is the out-picturing of our own state of consciousness."
> ~Joel S. Goldsmith

I can also remember that all actions are either expressing Love or are a call for Love, as the Course states. So, when he is acting out, he is really just calling for Love. Surely, I can respond with Love. If I don't spend time with him, show him that he matters to me then he will keep doing these things to grab my attention. I really need to take that in. He needs my love and affection – that is all that's going on here. He needs me to *be present*. I have found it tough to do all the time, but I can certainly make more of an effort. I hear my guides confirming as I write this that this is the right course of action. The only way to reverse attack is with Love. Love is always the answer. I need to control my inner response, take a deep breath, step away if I need to, and then return to the situation calmly and with Love.

As I write this out, I am surprisingly grateful for my son

giving me this opportunity to practice forgiveness and unconditional love real-time. This also gives me the opportunity to practice being at peace regardless of the circumstances. I have to admit that yesterday I was wishing the situation would go away. Now, I *want* to be triggered so that I can clear away the root cause of my anger and return to the peace from which I came. This is the peace that surpasses all understanding; the peace of God. Today's lesson in the Course was perfect, "My heart is beating in the peace of God."[47] Yes, it is.

December 24, 2012

On my way to the grocery store near my parents' house, following the Spirit's guidance, I turned on *The Infinite Way* audiobook. The quality of the reading and the content were on point. It reminded me of the book *Think and Grow Rich* by Napoleon Hill that Kevin and I had gotten into years ago, but more spiritual. It broke down universal truths that go well beyond having success in the world, although living in accordance with them could surely bring about material success (but that is not the goal). It is one that I could see myself listening to over and over in order to keep myself focused on what is Real. It's all a mind game until I get to the point where I am completely at peace, regardless of the circumstances.

The audiobook actually repeats a lot of the same principles found in the Course – and other spiritual teachings I have read. The audiobook summed up the messages in the way that I needed to hear at this time. It focused on the mystical aspects of Christianity, which was fitting for Christmas Eve. I would love to share it with some family and friends, but I have a feeling that is not wise to do at this time. I will share when and if I am guided to in the future.

I was thinking earlier about the way I am teaching myself or, rather, teaching is happening through me. I have become my own minister (in partnership with the Spirit), turning within for guidance instead of feeling powerless and looking for something outside of me. I am always being pointed to the perfect next thing to read or listen to. The Holy Spirit is a fabulous Master Teacher.

> "There is nothing separating anyone from this inner communion with God except the turmoil of the mind."
> ~Joel S. Goldsmith

December 25, 2012

It's Christmas!! Today, I am reflecting on the Christ within, as well as appreciating the masterful example that Jesus provided us all in embodying all that we were created to be. I was thinking about how God created nothing impermanent. For so long, I was living in a trance and believing that all that was 'real' was what my eyes could see. Now I know that when we live in alignment with Truth, the veil is removed and, ultimately, we see that Heaven was here all along; we see what Jesus saw.

Now that I have seen what is Real, I am forever changed. I can't just go back to my old ways of holding onto grievances, being sucked into the media's interpretation of events that occur, and more. I turn within for the clearest Guidance there is.

I used to feel biblically inept. I envied those who could quote scripture at the drop of a dime, and could pray with 'fire' while quoting it off the top of their heads. Now, I look right past that to how they are living their life. I do not do this to judge, but merely to notice the alignment of word and action. There are so many who are saying the words, but not living them. I used to be one of them. I used to say, "All things are possible in God" in one breath and then say, "This is the worst thing in the world. It's never going to get better" in the next. As Jesus said in the Gospel of Thomas, "A person cannot mount two horses." Or, as was recorded in the Bible, "No one can serve two masters" (Matthew 6:24). *Which do I believe? What God created or what was created by the ego? The Kingdom of Heaven or the world?*

As I close out this incredible year, I set the following intention for the year to come: To release all attachment to the world and live fully, and freely, in the Spirit in each moment.

Chapter 12

Into the Silence

December 29, 2012

I have arrived in Joshua Tree, California, for the Agape New Year Silent Meditation Retreat. I am so grateful for the time and space to detach from daily life and remember the Truth. I have come to realize that there is nothing more important than remembering the Truth about ourselves and living accordingly. It can be so easy to get sucked into worry, doubt, fear, anxiety, depression, and more, when focusing on the perspectives of the world. Meditation frees me from all of that noise.

Whenever I pause to listen to the 'still small Voice' within, all becomes clear. In these moments, there is no question in my mind that I am right where I am supposed to be. I know I have all that I need to go where God would have me go and do all that He would have me do; there is no thought that fears something may *not* work out for my good. *I know that I know that I know that I am that I am that I AM!*

"Meditation is about removing the layers of distance we perceive exist between ourselves and God."
~Michael Bernard Beckwith

It's somewhere around 8:15 pm Pacific Standard Time, but it feels like 11:15 pm to me because of the time difference. We are taking a short break before going back into the next meditation sitting. I'm fighting sleep as I try to stay in a meditative state. I should be adjusted to the time by tomorrow, after a good night's rest. Last night I didn't go to bed until 3 am and was right back up at 7:30

am. I know all this talk going on in my head (and now on the pages of my journal) about being too tired to concentrate is the ego's way of pushing me out of this state of awareness and keeping me bound to my bodily existence. I will not fall for it. *Focus, focus, focus.*

Now it's 10:30 pm. I made it through the meditation sitting without completely falling asleep, but there were a few head nods that startled me awake. I'm looking forward to getting some good rest tonight, but now I'm waiting on the bathroom. Since I signed up for the retreat late, there were no more double rooms available. I'm sharing a room with three other women *and* we share a bathroom with another room. At this moment, I'm wishing there was at least a sink in the room so that I could brush my teeth, wash my face, and worry about taking a shower in the morning before 6 am meditation.

A woman from the room next door just came over with a note asking if she could "get in the rotation," so I let her go ahead of me. She is taking longer than I had hoped though. Now that I got this all out of my head and onto the paper, I am already feeling better. I am reminding myself that all is well because this human existence is not all that I am. My Identity, and Home, is in God, where I am eternally clean and good. I am so grateful to have remembered this Truth in this moment of falling into the complaining tendency of the ego. The meditations will get easier, and I'll get used to the bathroom situation. Besides, these are all small things compared to all that I know God has for me. I'm taking a deep breath, and feeling immense gratitude for what I feel is going to occur on this retreat. I can feel the releasing happening already. This was the right decision.

December 30, 2012

Today's lesson in the Course is, "The stillness of the peace of God is mine." What a fitting lesson for my first full day of silence at the retreat (with the exception of calling the boys this morning – they sounded so happy!).

I placed a question in the box for Dr. Beckwith in the back of the room about the transition from *believing* in God to *knowing* God, or revelation. I specifically mentioned that there are some around me who have not yet made this transition. I have compassion for their struggles but also find myself longing for them to realize the Truth about themselves. I do respond to their perceived struggles with a positive word of encouragement, or try to share another way to look at the situation, but many times they think that's not the 'right' way to look at it. They seem to have a strong belief, as I did not too long ago, that they *have* to respond in a certain way to situations (e.g. retaliation, griev-ances), and don't realize they can *choose* to respond in Love regardless. I wanted to hear how he has responded to that in the past, as I didn't feel like I quite had it down. Or, at least, I didn't feel like others understood where I was coming from.

Morning meditation began promptly at 6:00. The ceremony opened with ancient wisdom from the Andes, and a Peruvian couple – with their daughter – shared music from their country. The music took me into a deep peace, and pure stillness. When they finished they said, "Music is the language of the soul." I had to smile as I had said something similar about music being the language of my soul in the past.

After meditation, I decided to check out one of the yoga classes. There were two types to choose from, and I felt guided to take the Naam Yoga class. It was the most unique and fun yoga experience I've ever had! I feel reinvigorated – like I was just cleansed by healing waters. I feel as if the past is washing off of me bit by bit. This cleansing is coming as tears, pain in certain parts of the body, and in other ways I have yet to tune into. I am just letting it go. When the tears come, I let them be. I'm not trying to hide my emotions to look good for others. I am just allowing my true Self to reveal itself in all its purity.

Now that I have the recognition and the awareness that "I AM," I need to shed anything that can't live at that level. I am in awe of what is being revealed to me in the still moments. I need to remember to maintain the habit of sitting in pure stillness, until it becomes a way of being 24/7. No music. No mantras. No guided meditation. Just me, reconnecting to my Higher Self – the Christ in me.

> "To the individual who can most perfectly practice inaction all things are possible."
> ~Plotinus

One of the things Dr. Beckwith reminded us of throughout the day is to return to the beginner's mind; to "become like a child." I needed that reminder because I was starting to feel like I had 'arrived,' and that there was not much more spiritual progress for me to make. While it is true that I have awakened to the Light in me, I have only just begun. Once attachment to the ego is released, Life is just beginning. I have so much more of the Kingdom to explore. As Jesus said, "In my Father's house there are many mansions."

The more we sat in meditation, the less my mind wandered. I had never meditated for hours and hours straight and, in the beginning, I wasn't sure how I was going to make it. I loved that Dr. Beckwith addressed this head-on during the sittings. He encouraged us to notice when we lose our awareness, but not let it distract us. The distractions will always be there, but we can choose to remain in the stillness. I thought, *Just like the world. The distractions will always be there, but we can choose to extend Love despite them.*

It's 10:50 pm, and I made it through the evening meditation OK. I am still so tired. Tomorrow night we're going until midnight so I'll need to get some good rest, and may even need to have a Chai tea (even though I haven't been drinking caffeine).

I felt some serious resistance this evening. I guess the ego is fighting hard against the peace I'm so rapidly accelerating back to. I know that the outcome is already guaranteed by God, but sometimes I wish I could press fast forward through this shedding period. I'm ready to be totally free. I know if I'm really ready for it, I need to be fully present during the session tomorrow. It's the final day of 2012; an opportunity for me to make tremendous strides toward dropping my attachment to the ego, my sub-personalities, the pretense, the catering to the desires of the world... all of my inauthenticity.

I thought I had already shed a lot, but I keep noticing more of my old tendencies popping up such as worrying about what others think, worrying about what to wear, being concerned about my stomach poking out – silly stuff. Here I am at a silent meditation retreat where everyone is relaxed and has their guard down, and the ego still has to 'show out.' I don't want my money and time spent here to keep me stuck in my old ways. I'm ready to ascend and step fully into a higher dimension of living. I'm ready to rest in God in each moment. I'm ready to feel and express joy and loving kindness every day – not just when I feel like it, or when I'm putting on a front for the benefit of others. I'm jumping in, and I know the Spirit will catch me. Here goes nothing!

December 31, 2012

A lot came up for me during this morning's meditation. I actually saw a vision for the book coming to life, and it was so beautiful.

I couldn't stop the tears from flowing down my face. I know this is about to happen. I'm about to step into my role as a teacher of God, and not because of my pushing and manipulating, but because of my surrendering and allowing the highest vision for my life to flow through me from the Divine. It is very fitting that I sit here at a retreat hosted by Dr. Beckwith, the teacher that was sent to me at the time when I was ready to birth what I came here to do in this lifetime. I recalled his lesson from the March workshop on the stages of the spiritual journey, and noted my transition to stage 3 (with glimpses of stage 4). I now feel ready to learn practices that will help me make the final transition to stage 4.

I'm so glad I skipped yoga this morning. Something told me to get out the manuscript and start editing (I was guided to bring it with me), and I did just that. Ideas were flowing faster than they ever had before. The joy I was feeling after 12.12.12 began rushing back to me. This is what I was supposed to do in this lifetime. I can feel it. I am on the path to completing one of my assignments, and I won't even try to speculate what the next one might be. What an incredible feeling. All those years of searching for something to complete me or make me successful in the eyes of others, when my true gifts were right inside of me; waiting for me to allow them to come to fruition. It's harvest time!

It is now break time after the second meditation sitting. The ego has just lost its battle. The tears are flowing with each meditation. I'm not sad at all so I know they are tears of release, tears of joy, tears of love, and tears of gratitude. I am really looking forward to sharing my testimony with Dr. Beckwith and his wife, Rickie. They have been a tremendous part of my healing journey, each contributing to my transformation through their words and music.

During meditation, the song *From Within*[1] by Rickie Byars

Beckwith came to mind as one of the songs that takes me 'there;' it ended up being one of the songs she did right after we came out of meditation. I *thought* the tears were flowing earlier, but once she started playing that song, they really started streaming. I couldn't catch them fast enough with my tissue. I let them flow, soak my scarf, drip on my pants, make lines on my face, and swell my eyes. *Who cares? I'm free!* I thought.

Now I know what all of my life experiences were for. I believe I chose them before I came into this body to prepare me to be a Light for anyone who feels disconnected from the Peace that lies within. I am here, and am available to support all who feel guided to me. While Dr. Beckwith was praying, a gospel song came to mind. The chorus of the song kept playing over and over in my mind: *Lord, I'm available to you. My storage is empty, and I am available to you.* That's what my soul is singing right now.

Available to You[2]
By the Rev. Milton Brunson
Lord, I'm available to You. My will I give to You.
I'll do what You say do. Use me Lord
To show someone the way, and enable me to say
My storage is empty, and I am available to You
Now I'm giving back to You, all the tools You gave to me.
My hands, my ears, my voice, my life; so You can use them as You
*   please.*
I have emptied out my cup, So that You can fill me up
Now I'm free and I just want to be available to You.
Use me Lord to show someone the way and enable me to say
My storage is empty and I am available to You.

We just wrapped up another meditation sitting. This time we focused on a quality that appears less frequently in our lives (or, at least it is appearing that way). I focused on joy. I want to express more joy in my day-to-day living, especially at home with the family. That reminds me of the quote by Maya Angelou that speaks about giving your smile to your family if you only have one left in you. I love that. I used another old gospel song that popped in my head as a mantra to focus on during the session. "Joy, Joy... down in my soul... sweet, beautiful, soul saving joy... joy, joy in my soul." It is interesting to me that these songs are coming to mind. *Is this the ancestors reminding me of something or trying to take me back to my roots in the Baptist church?* I did call on Harriet Tubman and Sojourner Truth during my rites of passage ceremony, and asked them to guide me on the journey to fulfilling my destiny – was it them? I could feel the Spirit reminding me, once again, to embrace it. All paths lead to the Truth. I thought I had already forgiven that, but the fact that it came up during meditation lets me know there was still healing to do. I am grateful for yet another reminder.

> "If you only have one smile in you, give it to the people you love. Don't be surly at home, then go out on the street and start grinning 'Good Morning' at total strangers."
> ~Maya Angelou

It's officially 2013 now! Tonight's ceremony was so magnificent. It was a traditional Peruvian ceremony, complete with a drum healing circle and a bonfire. Every detail of the evening's program was carefully crafted to guide us to a higher level of awareness, as well as to shed old ways of being. It was truly a sacred ceremony in which healing took place for many people, including myself.

The night ended with dancing and a traditional meal of collard greens, black-eyed peas, and cornbread. What a fabulous way to bring in the New Year! My heart is so full right now. I am overjoyed.

January 1, 2013

This morning's meditation was transformational. I found myself praying deeply after it was over. I had to write down the words that were flowing to me.

I recognize the Power within and allow it to flow through me effortlessly. Any remaining doubt is shut down before the Force of Love, grace, and healing moving through my being. I am that I am!

I release any blocks in the way of the fullness of the expression of the Love of God operating through and as me. I am one with the One and, in that Place, there is nothing that can stand a chance. Sickness cannot live in the presence of God, guilt cannot live in the presence of God, resentment cannot live in the presence of God, anger cannot live in the presence of God, unforgiveness cannot live in the presence of God... There is NO power that can overcome God and His immortal Creation. I was made in the image and likeness of God, and remain as God created me.

In this moment, I pause and feel the presence of God surrounding me, the Love of God enfolding me, and the Peace of God permeating every fiber of my being. It's Who I Am! I am so grateful to remember the Truth about myself, and everyone else.

I release this Word knowing it is bond because it is the Word of God. I feel it. I know it. I receive it. And so it is! Amen!

What a moving prayer! Just reading back over it shifted something within me. As I was sitting in the stillness, taking in the words that had just come through me, the Peruvian family began to sing a lovely song invoking the ancestors. During the song the following came to me:

> Don't fly so high that you can't see those who need your assistance rising up.

I had received my answer to the question I put in the box on the first day of the retreat. Dr. Beckwith was unable to get to all of the questions, but the ancestors made sure I did not leave the retreat without closure on this. It was a reminder to be compassionate, and to be on the lookout for those who are *ready* to receive guidance. I had my marching orders. And I was ready to step into fulfilling my destiny.

Epilogue

A s I write this, it is almost nine months since the culmination of the nine-day fasting period – exactly as the vision I received then showed me. At that time, I couldn't see why it would take me another nine months to finish it, but it is quite clear now.

It took me some time to acclimate to this new level of awareness, and to reenter life. I returned from the retreat on a high, yet desired to remain somewhat reclusive. I was not yet ready to return to a frequent level of activity with anyone other than my immediate family. I felt I needed some time and space to sustain the awareness of my identity in Spirit, and detach from my identification with the personality I had developed over the years. Although I had been warned by my teachers not to be too attached to the high feeling – as everything changes in the physical world – I secretly craved to retain the blissful state I was in.

Although I continued to feel the presence of the Spirit within and around me, I began to feel lonely. It seemed like everyone around me was living in a different world than I was. I didn't feel comfortable sharing all that happened with my friends and family, so I mostly kept it to myself. I avoided getting into long discussions with anyone, so they wouldn't question what was different about me.

After about a month of vacillating between owning my identification as a child of God and falling back into my ego identity, I was intuitively guided to a spiritual counselor to seek assistance with adjusting to life after mystical experiences. I have no idea how I landed on her Web site, but she was exactly who I needed. Navasha Daya[1] is the lead singer on the song that inspired the title for the blog, *Live in the Light* by Fertile Ground. I had no idea that, in addition to launching her solo career, she was an ordained interfaith minister and spiritual counselor, so I would not have been inclined to go to her Web site to seek counsel. This was yet another indication of a Greater Hand guiding my life. I knew the symptoms of depression all too well, and could feel them trying to creep in again – I was not having it.

With her guidance, and my continued daily spiritual practice, I was able to shake off the spiritual depression I experienced in less than two months. I wrote about the experience in greater detail in an entry dated February 24, 2013.

Sweet Surrender | February 24, 2013

Just when I thought I was close to releasing my attachment to the ego, it came back for a riveting encore performance. After months of blissful peace and awe-inspiring mystical experiences, I found myself getting agitated by things that hadn't bothered me in quite some time. I felt fatigued, even though I was getting plenty of rest. I didn't feel like talking with people, mainly because I felt like no one would understand what I was going through. I felt incredibly lonely.

These emotions were all too familiar. The feeling was highly reminiscent of the depression I went through over a year ago. *How could I be depressed again after all of this spiritual work?* I thought. I wasn't buying it. In fact, I tried to ignore it because I didn't want to give it power over me. I started saying things like, "This too shall pass" and "Joy will come in the morning," but they didn't have much of an effect.

I pulled the book *Dark Night of the Soul*[2] by St. John of the Cross off my shelf. The book explains what the *Dark Night of the Soul*, or spiritual depression, is but I couldn't bring myself to read it. I really thought I could skip this step. I thought I would go on living in the bliss of the peace of God without interruption for the remainder of this lifetime. I was wrong. The *Dark Night* happens to many spiritual seekers. Most of the famous mystics, saints, and sages wrote about this period with eloquence, illuminating the experience and paving the way for seekers to come.

The *Dark Night* is a stage of feeling detached from God, and detached from the world; a spiritual limbo. This stage comes after one has made significant spiritual progress, and has enjoyed a period of peaceful union with God. In this stage, you understand intellectually that you are one with God and, in fact, have experienced that Truth directly via mystical experiences, but you cannot *feel* the connection at the moment. Mother Teresa, one of the many mystics I admire, spent the last 50 years of her life in the *Dark Night* (yes, 50 *years*). I remember sharing this with Kevin last week when I was trying to describe what I was going through, and he said, "So, what did she do to get by?" He asked it in a way that showed tremendous empathy for what I was going through. He didn't want me to go through depression again. I was grateful for his concern, but had a sense this was something I *had* to go through.

The descriptions I read of other people's journeys through the *Dark Night* highlighted different means for getting through it. There really was no one-size-fits-all solution. Instead of trying to follow a cookie-cutter plan, I decided to surrender and rely fully on the Holy Spirit to guide me each step of the way. As soon as I did, I could barely keep up with the solutions that came my way. Every day I was guided to the right book, audio, or teacher to connect with; each with the exact words I needed to hear. I also remained steady in my prayer and meditation practice, regardless of its fruits.

It all came to a crossroads yesterday, after listening to the *Autobiography of a Yogi*[3] audiobook by Paramahansa Yogananda and almost finishing the book *Before I Am*[4] by Mooji. I was so grateful to my spiritual counselor for recommending Yogananda's autobiography. The audiobook led me on his spiritual journey, which highlighted mystical experiences not dissimilar from my own. It also gave me a preview of what can come when one is fully surrendered to the presence of God working through them. He, and his teachers, had spiritual experiences that were beyond anything I could have imagined for myself.

Mooji's book put me in touch with the choice I needed to make once and for all – ego or Spirit; body or soul. Prior to that time, I was alternating between them. Some days I was fully flowing in the recognition that "I am as God created me" (Lesson 162 from *A Course in Miracles*), and so is everyone else; other days I found myself slipping into some of my old ego-driven tendencies. I was sitting on the couch, and the following prayer poured through me as the tears flowed:

Lord, show me where there is still an attachment to ego in me
I want to be fully aligned with and immersed in You
You are all I need
Reveal my hidden thoughts
Reveal my unconscious guilt
Guide me to the right Teacher, human or in Spirit, who can help me
Uncover and remove any traces of darkness in the crevices of my
*   mind*
My deepest desire is to consistently experience the wholeness in
*   which I was created*
I surrender all
I am not in control, You are
I humbly allow Your Will to be done through me

After putting my pen down and setting my journal aside, I entered into a deep meditation. It was healing to my soul. I could feel the power of the Love of God flowing through and embracing me. My body had that now-familiar warm and tingly vibration, and a complete peace washed over me. I knew the desires of my heart had been heard. I was like a child again. I no longer was plotting or planning the next move; I was making myself available for God to work through me and unfold the plan for this body. The desire to control things to my liking was slipping away. With ego aside, the vessel (this body) is unclogged so God can pour through without interruption. This must be what my teachers have referred to as "beginner's mind" or "becoming like a child."

I now focus on living my life in a state of surrender. I have released the attachment to the feeling of ecstasy that comes from spiritual experiences, and I am making myself fully available to be led by the Spirit moment to moment. Every day is a blank slate upon which my sole intention is to allow the Spirit to use me to bring Light to the world. This journey of surrender has given shape to concrete ways for me to assist others in returning to inner peace – the answer to the deep longing I experienced from the time I began sharing my story publicly. And I know this is only the beginning.

I could not be more grateful for this dramatic shift from controlling and manipulating to allowing; the shift from suppressing and holding onto destructive emotions to allowing them to be felt and releasing them. The fruits of letting go have been far more abundant than I could have imagined. I look forward to continuing to share in the harvest with all who cross my path. This is the life we were created for – a life of total surrender to the Grace of God.

Pour Your Spirit into my thoughts, words, and actions,
So they may extend only Your Love –
Today and always.
Amen.

Acknowledgements

There are so many that supported me on the path to completion of *From Stress to Peace: An Intimate Journal on the Journey from Living in Darkness to Living in the Light*. Abundant gratitude to God, the Holy Spirit and all of the angels and guides who were with me from the time I received the inner nudge to share my story publicly through writing the last word of the memoir, and beyond. With each passing day, may I surrender deeper and allow more of Your Light to shine through me. Yeshua (Jesus), I cannot thank you enough for *A Course in Miracles* – your words spoke to me in the language that most resonated with me and returned me to Peace. I know that you are with me always and for that, and much more, I am eternally grateful.

To my incredible husband, Kevin, I love you more than words could ever express. Thank you for teaching me the meaning of forgiveness and unconditional love. The kindness and love you display on a daily basis inspires me to step further into my true Self.

To my sons: You are two of my greatest teachers. Thank you for the opportunities you provide daily for me to practice extending only Love. I am grateful that you chose me to support the evolution of your soul. I love you dearly.

Thank you to my immediate and extended family who encouraged and supported me throughout the process of beginning the *Living in the Light* blog and through the process of completing the book: Clarice Taylor, Michael Taylor, Kaitlyn Taylor, Dora Newsome, Penny Newsome Gallagher, Herb Hunter, E. Lavonne Lewis, Marianne Lewis, Carl Barclay, Venetta Jarvis, Brenda Daniels, George Jones, Bernadine Jones, Dietra Hughes, Kevin Hughes, Audra Jones, Autumn Mays, Vertrell Jones, Tashia Tucker, Sandra Weatherly, Kristin Weatherly.

Thank you to all those who commented on drafts of the manuscript: Talitha Anyabwelè, Kimberlie Bryson, Melissa Howell, Kevin Jones, Rasheedra Nelson, Valerie Newsome, Aseelah Shareef, Danisha Thomas, and Elizabeth Stephens Wilson. Your feedback was invaluable in ensuring this book blossomed in to all it was intended to be.

To all of the teachers and counselors sent to me at just the right moments along the journey, I give thanks for you. Your words of inspiration kept me focused on the path to peace.

To DeAnna L. Carpenter, you are such a blessing. I am truly grateful for the time you dedicated to this project and the encouragement you provided along the way. Keep building!

To the entire publishing team at O Books, I am truly grateful for all that you did to bring this book to fruition, and get it out to the world. You rock!

To the Marketing and PR team and everyone else who supported getting the word out about this book, thank you for all that you have done, and continue to do, to share this message with the world.

To the N.O.L.E. crew, I treasure our connection and know that we were brought together for a Divine purpose. Thank you for the laughs and the safe space to shed tears. *Saps qui som?*

To all of my friends, blog readers, clients, and supporters, thank you for your encouraging words. You inspire me to continue on this journey of being authentic and supporting others on the path to Peace. Much Love and Light! Keep shining!

~Kandace

About the Author

Kandace Jones is the founder of Living in the Light, where she supports others in releasing stress and returning to the peace that lies within. Her messages of inspiration reach tens of thousands across over 40 countries daily via her Living in the Light blog and Facebook page.

In 2012, after battling depression and anxiety, Kandace had a profound spiritual awakening which inspired her to write *From Stress to Peace: An Intimate Journal on the Journey from Living in Darkness to Living in the Light*. As a Certified Spiritual Life Coach, teacher of *A Course in Miracles*, Reiki practitioner, and lover of spiritual wisdom, her passion for assisting others on the spiritual journey is palpable. Through the *From Stress to Peace 21-Day Challenge*, *From Stress to Peace Retreats*, *Living in the Light Community*, audio programs, workshops, and other supports, she shares step-by-step tips and daily practices for others to follow to facilitate their journey to unshakable peace.

As a former saleswoman and marketer, she has a knack for sharing messages in a way that inspires action. Her professional career began in marketing with Procter & Gamble, Time Warner, and Forbes Magazine.

Kandace has a tremendous passion for youth development,

which led her to transition her career from business to education. She has a certification in youth development, and has overseen the operations of after-school programs in over 200 schools. She also co-founded a non-profit supporting the expansion of youth social entrepreneurship, study-abroad, and cross-cultural exchange throughout the African Diaspora. She was later appointed to a position in the Obama Administration where she supported reform efforts aimed at dramatically improving the nation's lowest-performing schools.

Despite this career success, Kandace had an inner struggle that ultimately drove her to hit rock bottom. Now on the other side of the pain, she is grateful for the experience being used not only to move her *From Stress to Peace*, but to inspire the same shift in thousands of others.

Kandace lives in Washington, DC with her husband and two young sons. She loves to travel, and has visited over 25 countries. Visit her popular blog at

www.livinginthelight.com.

Book Discussion Guide

Would you like to share the *From Stress to Peace* journey with friends, family, your spiritual community, and more? This discussion guide is designed to support small group discussion of themes touched upon throughout the book to support your journey *From Stress to Peace*. The discussion guide includes reflection questions for each chapter of the book as well as brief summaries of key themes. I pray you find this useful for the journey!

To download your free discussion guide, visit

www.kandacejones.com/discussionguide

See below for a sampling of the questions included in the guide.

1. What were the signs that Kandace began to notice just before her breakdown? Are you currently experiencing or have you ever experienced any of these? After reading chapters 1–3, what steps might you consider taking to bring yourself back into harmony?

2. At the beginning of Chapter 2, Kandace shares descriptions for the thought patterns that were most prevalent for her. Do you find yourself subscribing to any of these? If so, what can you affirm in place of those thoughts? Write down the thoughts you have been having and create affirmations to refute each of them. (Need ideas for affirmations? Visit the *Living in the Light* Facebook page at www.facebook.com/livinginthelight or Twitter page @coachkandace.)

3. There are a number of quotes shared throughout the book. Which one resonated most with you? How might it apply to your life?

4. In Chapter 2, Kandace shares a story about forgiving her dad. Is there anyone in your life toward whom you have been holding onto resentment? After reading this, and the other examples of forgiveness throughout the book, what steps might you take to transform the thoughts you have about this person?

5. The following quote from *A Course in Miracles* is shared early in the book: "Creation is eternal and unalterable. Your sinlessness is guaranteed by God." As you read this statement, what thoughts, if any, arise that say this is *not* true? What daily practices might you consider to remember the Truth about you (your wholeness and completion)?

6. In Chapter 3, Kandace makes a list of the things that she is attached to that keep her mind off of the reality of God. What do you find yourself attached to? How might these attachments be leading you to behave in the world? (Review Kandace's list of "attachments and bad habits" in Chapter 3 for ideas.)

From Stress to Peace 21-Day Challenge

A re you ready to experience peace, regardless of the circumstances you are facing? Then you don't want to miss the *From Stress to Peace 21-Day Challenge*! The 21-day challenge includes, but is not limited to, the following:

- A *Spiritual Life Assessment* to determine which areas in your life you would most like to focus on bringing harmony to and which spiritual qualities you would most like to cultivate (e.g. Patience, Joy, Peace, Unconditional Love)
- Templates for designing a consistent daily spiritual practice that fits with your lifestyle and schedule (e.g. Scheduling prayer and meditation time into your day)
- A tracking tool to support developing and sustaining your daily spiritual practice
- Four prerecorded training sessions, including, but not limited to, the following topics: Meditation 101, Power of the Mind, The Root of Stress, Releasing Fear, Prayers to Re-Align with God, Healing the Past, How to Forgive Anyone and Anything, Power Affirmations, and Daily Spiritual Practices for Busy Lives.
- Guided meditations and resources to support deepening your inner peace
- Coaching on applying spiritual principles to day-to-day life situations and challenges
- Coaching on releasing resentment, fear, doubt, worry, and other negative thought patterns
- Insight into the profound spiritual wisdom of *A Course in Miracles*, a self-study spiritual guide to inner peace
- Introduction to practices to support your journey beyond the 21-day program

The series consists of four prerecorded calls, a 50-page workbook which includes daily inspirational messages, journal/reflection questions, insight into the first 21 lessons of *A Course in Miracles*, as well as Q&A in-between sessions via e-mail and the private *From Stress to Peace* Facebook page.

To learn more about the *From Stress to Peace 21-Day Challenge*, read testimonials from past participants, or to register, go to:

www.kandacejones.com/classes.

I look forward to supporting you on the journey to unshakable peace!

Living in the Light Community

Are you committed to personal and spiritual growth, but find it challenging to stay focused on the path?

Are you ready to make a bold commitment for this to be the year that you return to peace?

Would you love to be connected to a loving, supportive community of individuals who are also committed to the same goal?

If you answered "yes" to any of these, continue reading to learn more about the *Living in the Light Community*! Membership in the *Living in the Light Community* includes the following:

- 2 one hour recorded live sessions per month including 30 minutes of spiritual teaching and 30 minutes of Q&A, live coaching, and discussion facilitated by Kandace Jones
- Access to resources and tools to deepen your spiritual practice
- Introduction to meditation, prayer and breathing techniques aimed at returning to the Peace of God
- Deeper insight into the powerful principles for returning to peace shared in *A Course in Miracles,* and other profound spiritual texts, to support and accelerate your self-study
- In-class exercises to facilitate the release of past hurts, fears, pain, etc.
- Audios and videos to provide encouragement and support

your daily practice
- Ongoing Q&A and authentic sharing/discussion via the private Facebook page
- New connections with like-minded individuals committed to *Living in the Light*
- Ongoing, real-time coaching and support as challenges arise on the path to consistently *Living in the Light*
- 10% off future *Living in the Light* offerings (classes, retreats, seminars, etc.)

See below for a sampling of the topics discussed on our bi-monthly calls.

- Practicing Self-Love
- The Secret to Unshakable Peace
- Building Your Forgiveness Muscle
- Daily Practices to Accelerate the Dissolution of Ego
- Creating Your Experience
- Releasing Guilt
- Powerful Self-Inquiry Questions for Personal Growth

To learn more about the *Living in the Light Community,* visit

www.kandacejones.com/livinginthelight.

We look forward to having you!

Notes

Chapter 2

1. Jongsma, Arthur E. *Adult Psychotherapy Homework Planner.* Hoboken, NJ: Wiley, 2006. Print.
2. Pfeiffer, Richard H. *The Real Solution Assertiveness Workbook.* New York: Growth Pub., 1998. Print.
3. Franklin, Kirk. *He'll Take the Pain Away.* 1997. *God's Property.* Kirk Franklin's Nu Nation. Gospocentric. Verity Records/ Legacy.
4. Huber, Cheri. *The Depression Book: Depression as an Opportunity for Spiritual Growth.* Murphys, CA: Keep It Simple, 1999. Print.
5. Smith, Huston, and Huston Smith. *The World's Religions: Our Great Wisdom Traditions.* San Francisco, CA: HarperSan Francisco, 1991. Print.
6. Landmark Education. *The Landmark Forum.* http://www.landmarkworldwide.com/the-landmark-forum
7. Landmark Education. *Self-Expression and Leadership Program.* http://www.landmarkworldwide.com/after-the-landmark-forum/advanced-programs/self-expression-and-leadership-program
8. *A Course in Miracles: Combined Volume.* Second ed. Mill Valley, CA: Foundation for Inner Peace, 1992. Print. http://www.acim.org
9. Williamson, Marianne. *A Return to Love.* New York, NY: Harper Collins, 1992. Print.
10. Williamson, Marianne. *Enchanted Love: The Mystical Power of Intimate Relationships.* New York: Simon & Schuster, 1999. Print.
11. Yancey, Philip. *What's So Amazing About Grace?* Visual Edition. Grand Rapids, MI: Zondervan, 2003. Print.
12. Tolle, Eckhart. *A New Earth: Awakening to Your Life's Purpose.* New York: Plume, 2006. Print.

13. The Art of Living:
    http://www.artofliving.org/us-en/art-living-course-part-1

Chapter 3

1. Yogaville Satchidananda Ashram:
    http://www.yogaville.org
2. Yoga Journal. January 2012.
    http://www.yogajournal.com/livemag/18
3. Platt, David. *Radical: Taking Back Your Faith from the American Dream*. Colorado Springs, CO: Multnomah, 2010. Print.
4. Hesse, Hermann. *Siddhartha*. New York, NY: New Directions, 1951. Print.
5. Light of Truth Universal Shrine (LOTUS):
    http://www.lotus.org
6. Satchidananda, and Patanjali. *The Yoga Sutras of Patanjali*. Yogaville, VA: Integral Yoga Publications, 1990. Print.
7. Rozman, Deborah. *Meditation for Children: Pathways to Happiness, Harmony, Creativity, and Fun for the Family*. Yogaville, VA: Integral Yoga Publications, 2009. Print.

Chapter 4

1. "Lesson 48." *A Course in Miracles: Combined Volume*. Second ed. Mill Valley, CA: Foundation for Inner Peace, 1992. 77. Print.
2. "Lesson 71." *A Course in Miracles: Combined Volume*. Second ed. Mill Valley, CA: Foundation for Inner Peace, 1992. 121. Print.
3. Beckwith, Michael Bernard. *Life Visioning: A Transformative Process for Activating Your Unique Gifts and Highest Potential*. Boulder, CO: Sounds True, 2013. Print.
4. Rev. Jennifer Hadley:
    http://www.jenniferhadley.com
5. Centers for Spiritual Living:
    http://www.csl.org/about-us.html

6. Fertile Ground. *Live in the Light*. *Black Is...* Blackout Studios, 2004. CD.
7. Living in the Light blog: http://www.kandacejones.com

Chapter 5

1. *The Best of Miles Davis & John Coltrane*. *Straight, No Chaser*. Columbia/Legacy, 2001. CD.
2. Unity Church of Washington, DC: http://www.unitywdc.org
3. "Season 1: Episode 3: Maya Angelou." *Oprah Presents Master Class*. OWN. Chicago, IL, 16 January 2011. Television.
4. From Stress to Peace 21-Day Challenge: http://www.kandacejones.com/classes
5. King, Martin Luther, Jr. *Strength to Love*. New York: Harper & Row, 1963. Print.

Chapter 6

1. Butterworth, Eric. *Discover the Power Within You: A Guide to the Unexplored Depths Within*. 40th Anniversary ed. New York: Harper & Row, 2008. Print.
2. Black Sheep. *Wolf in Sheep's Clothing*. Fontana Island, 1994. CD.
3. Kelly Price. *This Is Who I Am*. Zomba Gospel LLC, 2006. CD.
4. "Episode 4: The Power of Forgiveness." *Oprah's Lifeclass*. OWN. Chicago, IL, April 2012.
5. "Lesson 46." *A Course in Miracles: Combined Volume*. Second ed. Mill Valley, CA: Foundation for Inner Peace, 1992. 73. Print.
6. Houston, Whitney. *Greatest Love of All*. *Whitney Houston*. Arista, 1985. CD.
7. Chopra, Deepak. *The Seven Spiritual Laws of Success: A Practical Guide to the Fulfilment of Your Dreams*. London: Bantam, 1996. Print.
8. Prabhupada, A. C. Bhaktivedanta Swami. *Bhagavad-Gita As*

It Is. Complete ed. Los Angeles: Bhaktivedanta Book Trust, 1983. Print.

9. King, Martin Luther, Jr. (1957, December). *Loving Your Enemies*. Dexter Avenue Baptist Church, Montgomery, Alabama.

Chapter 7

1. Renard, Gary. *Fearless Love*. Abridged ed. Sounds True, 2008. CD.

2. Bee symbolism: http://www.whats-your-sign.com/bee-meaning.html; http://en.wikipedia.org/wiki/Bee_(mythology)

3. Holmes, Ernest. *The Science of Mind: The Complete Edition*. New York: Jeremy P. Tarcher, 2010. Print.

4. Sorensen, Christian. *Foundations of the Science of Mind*. United Centers for Spiritual Living, Department of Education. 2007. 72–73. Print.

5. Ibid.

6. Holmes, Ernest, and George P. Bendall. *The Holmes Papers: The Anatomy of Healing Prayer*. Marina del Rey, CA: DeVorss & Co., 1991. Print.

7. Chopra, Deepak, Debbie Ford, and Marianne Williamson. *The Shadow Effect: Illuminating the Hidden Power of Your True Self*. New York: HarperOne, 2010. Print.

8. "Ian Patrick: Life, Death & the Illusion." *Living A Course in Miracles*. Jennifer Hadley. May 2012. http://www.livingacourseinmiracles.com

9. Lawrence, Donald. *Spiritual*. Donald Lawrence & Company. Verity Records, 2011. CD.

Chapter 8

1. "Lesson 69." *A Course in Miracles: Combined Volume*. Second ed. Mill Valley, CA: Foundation for Inner Peace, 1992. 117. Print.

2. Sullivan, Jazmine. *Home*. East Hill Video, 1999. Hill

Elementary; Philadelphia, PA.
http://youtu.be/ARg9F76caoM

3. Ladybug symbolism:
http://www.symbolic-meanings.com/2007/11/13/brief-symbolic-meaning-of-the-ladybug/,
http://www.experienceproject.com/stories/Love-Ladybugs/141399

4. Jazzanova. *Let It Go.* Funkhaus Studio Sessions. Sonar Kollektiv, 2012.
http://youtu.be/c2AeFOOdML0

5. Moorjani, Anita. *Dying to Be Me: My Journey from Cancer, to Near Death, to True Healing.* Carlsbad, CA: Hay House, 2012. Print.

6. Holmes, Ernest. *This Thing Called You.* New York: Tarcher, 2007. Print.

7. Living in the Light Facebook page:
www.facebook.com/livinginthelight

8. O'Quinn, Greg. *I Told the Storm.* Greg O'Quinn 'N' Joyful Noyze. Word Entertainment, 1998.
http://youtu.be/XZFtc5-4_Nc

9. "What is Forgiveness?" *A Course in Miracles: Combined Volume.* Second ed. Mill Valley, CA: Foundation for Inner Peace, 1992. *Workbook* Part II, 401. Print.

10. Renard, Gary R. *Secrets of the Immortal: Advanced Teachings from A Course in Miracles.* Sounds True, 2006. CD.

11. "Choose Once Again." *A Course in Miracles: Combined Volume.* Second ed. Mill Valley, CA: Foundation for Inner Peace, 1992. Chapter 31, 666. Print.

12. *Mother Teresa at 100: The Life and Works of a Modern Saint.* TIME. August 2010.

13. Mother Teresa; Edward Le Joly, and Jaya Chaliha. *Mother Teresa's Reaching Out in Love: Stories Told by Mother Teresa.* New York: Barnes & Noble, 2002. Print.

14. "The Way to Remember God." *A Course in Miracles: Combined*

Volume. Second ed. Mill Valley, CA: Foundation for Inner Peace, 1992. Chapter 12, Part II; 218. Print.

Chapter 9

1. Hay, Louise L., and Cheryl Richardson. *You Can Create an Exceptional Life.* Carlsbad, CA: Hay House, 2011. Print.
2. Vanzant, Iyanla. *Call in the Queen.* http://youtu.be/QE9rhC-h9s4
3. "The Decision for God." *A Course in Miracles: Combined Volume.* Second ed. Mill Valley, CA: Foundation for Inner Peace, 1992. Chapter 5, Part VII; 90. Print.
4. LaBelle, Patti. *New Attitude.* MCA, 1984. http://youtu.be/QWfZ5SZZ4xE
5. "Finding the Present." *A Course in Miracles: Combined Volume.* Second ed. Mill Valley, CA: Foundation for Inner Peace, 1992. Chapter 13, Part VI, 1.7, 2.1–5; 250–251. Print.
6. "Finding the Present." *A Course in Miracles: Combined Volume.* Second ed. Mill Valley, CA: Foundation for Inner Peace, 1992. Chapter 13, Part VI, 5.1–4; 251. Print.
7. "Finding the Present." *A Course in Miracles: Combined Volume.* Second ed. Mill Valley, CA: Foundation for Inner Peace, 1992. Chapter 13, Part VI, 7.1–3, 10.1–4; 252. Print.
8. Lehodey, Vitalis, and a Monk of Mount Melleray. *The Ways of Mental Prayer.* Dublin: M. H. Gill & Son, 1955. Print.
9. "The Holy Encounter." *A Course in Miracles: Combined Volume.* Second ed. Mill Valley, CA: Foundation for Inner Peace, 1992. Chapter 8, Part III, 4.1–6; 142. Print.
10. Arie, India, and Idan Raichel. *The Gift of Acceptance.* http://www.soulbird.com/media/videos/24091/33691
11. http://www.lotus.org/docs/paths_are_many.htm
12. "The Call for Faith." *A Course in Miracles: Combined Volume.* Second ed. Mill Valley, CA: Foundation for Inner Peace, 1992. Chapter 17, Part VII, 2.1; 368. Print.
13. "How Stress Affects the Body." *HeartMath*, 2010.

http://www.heartmath.com/infographics/how-stress-effects-the-body.html

14. Myss, Caroline M. *Entering the Castle: Finding the Inner Path to God and Your Soul's Purpose*. New York: Free, 2008. Print.

15. *Foundation for A Course in Miracles* Outreach. Question & Answer #313 (November, 2003): http://www.facimoutreach.org/qa/questions/questions58.htm

16. Renard, Gary R. *Secrets of the Immortal: Advanced Teachings from a Course in Miracles*. Sounds True, 2006. CD.

17. *Prayer of St. Francis*: http://en.wikipedia.org/wiki/Prayer_of_Saint_Francis

18. Fly symbolism: Venefica, Avia. *The Buzz About Fly Symbolism*. Token Rock. Glendale, AZ. April 27, 2010.

19. "God or the Ego." *A Course in Miracles: Combined Volume*. Second ed. Mill Valley, CA: Foundation for Inner Peace, 1992. Chapter 11, Intro., 4.3–7; 194. Print.

Chapter 10

1. "Our Gratitude to God." Excerpts from the workshop held at Foundation for A Course in Miracles, Temecula, CA: http://www.facim.org/online-learning-aids/excerpt-series/our-gratitude-to-god/part-x.aspx

2. Thurman, Howard. *Jesus and the Disinherited*. Reprint ed. Boston: Beacon, 1996. Print.

3. Thurman, Howard. *The Inward Journey*. New York: Harper, 1961. Print.

4. Ra, Un Nefer Amen. *Ma'at: The 11 Laws of God*. Brooklyn, NY: Khamit Media Trans Visions, 2003. Print.

5. Ra, Un Nefer Amen. *Metu Neter*. Brooklyn, NY: Khamit, 1990. Print.

6. Some, Malidoma Patrice. *Of Water and the Spirit: Ritual, Magic, and Initiation in the Life of an African Shaman*. New York: Putnam, 1994. Print.

7. Ephirim-Donkor, Anthony. *African Spirituality: On Becoming Ancestors*. Trenton, NJ: Africa World, 1997. Print.

8. Arewa, Caroline Shola. *Opening to Spirit: Contacting the Healing Power of the Chakras & Honouring African Spirituality*. London: Thorsons, 1998. Print.

Chapter 11

1. "Lesson 254." *A Course in Miracles: Combined Volume*. Second ed. Mill Valley, CA: Foundation for Inner Peace, 1992. 421. Print.

2. Mooji on YouTube:
   http://www.youtube.com/channel/UCpw2gh99XM6Mwsbk sv0feEg,
   http://www.youtube.com/channel/UCp6EwdDH1IsR7Qh 2pEuUvCg

3. 12.12.12. Christ Consciousness:
   http://www.thegabrielmessages.com/the-121212-activation/

4. 12.12.12. Numerology:
   http://www.simion7d.com/December2012.html

5. "To teach is to demonstrate." *A Course in Miracles: Combined Volume*. Second ed. Mill Valley, CA: Foundation for Inner Peace, 1992. *Manual for Teachers*, Introduction, 1. Print.

6. Spider symbolism:
   http://www.whats-your-sign.com/spider-symbol-meaning.html

7. Muldrow, Georgia Anne. *I Had a Revelation*. Agape International Spiritual Center, Culver City, CA, 2009.
   http://youtu.be/i-T5o9ctDUc

8. "Lesson 257." *A Course in Miracles: Combined Volume*. Second ed. Mill Valley, CA: Foundation for Inner Peace, 1992. 423. Print.

9. "What are the characteristics of God's teachers?" *A Course in Miracles: Combined Volume*. Second ed. Mill Valley, CA: Foundation for Inner Peace, 1992. *Manual for Teachers*, Part 4, 9. Print.

10. "Lesson 258." *A Course in Miracles: Combined Volume.* Second ed. Mill Valley, CA: Foundation for Inner Peace, 1992. 423. Print.

11. "Are changes required in the life situation of God's teachers?" *A Course in Miracles: Combined Volume.* Second ed. Mill Valley, CA: Foundation for Inner Peace, 1992. *Manual for Teachers,* Part 9, 26. Print.

12. Beckwith, Michael. *Your Soul's Evolution: Practices for Catalyzing Your Spiritual Awakening.* Sounds True, 2009. CD.

13. Tony! Toni! Tone! *Feels Good.* Motown Records, 1990. http://youtu.be/Jfoxsfhi-kk

14. Mooji. *The Embrace.* http://www.youtube.com/watch?v=MJYvErgXDww

15. Williams, Juan, and Quinton Hosford Dixie. *This Far by Faith: Stories from the African-American Religious Experience.* New York: William Morrow, 2003. Print.

16. Sojourner Truth: http://www.pbs.org/thisfarbyfaith/people/sojourner_truth.html

17. Mooji. *Awakening Bridge.* http://www.youtube.com/user/AwakeningBridge/videos

18. "How is judgment relinquished?" *A Course in Miracles: Combined Volume.* Second ed. Mill Valley, CA: Foundation for Inner Peace, 1992. *Manual for Teachers,* Part 10, 27. Print.

19. "How many teachers of God are needed to save the world?" *A Course in Miracles: Combined Volume.* Second ed. Mill Valley, CA: Foundation for Inner Peace, 1992. *Manual for Teachers,* Part 12, 31. Print.

20. Goldsmith, Joel S. *The Foundation of Mysticism: Spiritual Healing Principles of the Infinite Way.* Lakewood, CO: I-Level, 1998. Print.

21. Teresa of Avila, and Dennis Joseph Billy. *Interior Castle: The Classic Text.* Notre Dame, IN: Christian Classics, 2007. Print.

22. "The Laws of Healing." *A Course in Miracles: Combined*

Volume. Second ed. Mill Valley, CA: Foundation for Inner Peace, 1992. Chapter 26, Part VII, 553–558. Print.

23. Renard, Gary R. *The Disappearance of the Universe: Straight Talk about Illusions, Past Lives, Religion, Sex, Politics, and the Miracles of Forgiveness.* Carlsbad, CA: Hay House, 2004. Print.

24. Virtue, Doreen. *Archangels & Ascended Masters: A Guide to Working and Healing with Divinities and Deities.* Carlsbad, CA: Hay House, 2003. Print.

25. "Time and Eternity." *A Course in Miracles: Combined Volume.* Second ed. Mill Valley, CA: Foundation for Inner Peace, 1992. Chapter 5, Part VI, 88. Print.

26. "What are the characteristics of God's teachers?" *A Course in Miracles: Combined Volume.* Second ed. Mill Valley, CA: Foundation for Inner Peace, 1992. *Manual*, Part 4. IV, 12. Print.

27. Kuti, Fela. *Water No Get Enemy.* Fela Anikulapo Kuti & Africa 70. Kalakuta, 1975.
http://www.allmusic.com/album/expensive-shit-mw0000958870

28. Council of Nicaea:
http://en.wikipedia.org/wiki/First_Council_of_Nicaea

29. Meyer, Marvin W. *The Nag Hammadi Scriptures: The International Edition.* New York, NY: HarperOne, 2008. Print.

30. "What are the characteristics of God's teachers?" *A Course in Miracles: Combined Volume.* Second ed. Mill Valley, CA: Foundation for Inner Peace, 1992. *Manual*, Part 4. VI, 14. Print.

31. McDowell, William. *I Give Myself Away. As We Worship Live.* E1 Entertainment, 2009. CD.
http://youtu.be/O7ofQmeao9I

32. Williamson, Marianne. *A Return to Love: Reflections on the Principles of "A Course in Miracles."* New York, NY: HarperCollins, 1992. Print.

33. "The Illusion and the Reality of Love." *A Course in Miracles:*

Combined Volume. Second ed. Mill Valley, CA: Foundation for Inner Peace, 1992. Chapter 16, Part IV, 340. Print.

34. "Teach not that I died in vain..." *A Course in Miracles: Combined Volume.* Second ed. Mill Valley, CA: Foundation for Inner Peace, 1992. Chapter 11, Part VI, 7.3–4, 209. Print.

35. Eagle symbolism:
http://www.whats-your-sign.com/symbolic-eagle-meaning.html

36. Wapnick, Ken. "Mysticism and Schizophrenia." *Understanding Mysticism.* Image Books: Garden City. 1980. Synopsis: http://sandra.stahlman.com/wapnick.html

37. *Aspire: The New Women of Color Study Bible.* Grand Rapids, MI: Zondervan, 2006. Print.

38. "How should a teacher of God spend their day?" *A Course in Miracles: Combined Volume.* Second ed. Mill Valley, CA: Foundation for Inner Peace, 1992. *Manual,* Part 16, 40. Print.

39. "What are the characteristics of God's teachers?" *A Course in Miracles: Combined Volume.* Second ed. Mill Valley, CA: Foundation for Inner Peace, 1992. *Manual,* Part 4. IX, 15. Print.

40. Mooji. *My Life is So Different.*
http://www.youtube.com/watch?v=KWQmlBmoJac

41. Pace, LaShun. *I Know I've Been Changed.* 601 Records, 2005. CD.
http://youtu.be/k9gbJM0x7qA

42. "Lesson 48." *A Course in Miracles: Combined Volume.* Second ed. Mill Valley, CA: Foundation for Inner Peace, 1992. 77. Print.

43. "What are the characteristics of God's teachers?" *A Course in Miracles: Combined Volume.* Second ed. Mill Valley, CA: Foundation for Inner Peace, 1992. *Manual,* Part 4. X, 16. Print.

44. Grasshopper symbolism:
http://www.whats-your-sign.com/grasshopper-totem-and-symbolism.html

45. The Great Invocation:
    http://www.beliefnet.com/Prayers/Protestant/Violence-Disasters/The-Great-Invocation.aspx
46. "Choose Once Again." *A Course in Miracles: Combined Volume.* Second ed. Mill Valley, CA: Foundation for Inner Peace, 1992. Chapter 31, Part VIII, 666. Print.
47. "Lesson 267." *A Course in Miracles: Combined Volume.* Second ed. Mill Valley, CA: Foundation for Inner Peace, 1992. 429. Print.

Chapter 12

1. Beckwith, Rickie Byars. *From Within. From Within.* Eternal Dance, 2003. CD.
   http://www.youtube.com/watch?v=IaJBl1IJIM0
2. Brunson, Milton. *Available to You.* Rev. Milton Brunson and the Thompson Community Singers. Word, Inc., 1988.
   http://www.youtube.com/watch?v=eopVmm_uvHQ

Epilogue

1. Navasha Daya:
   http://navashadaya.com/
2. St. John of the Cross, and E. Allison Peers. *Dark Night of the Soul.* Garden City, NY: Image, 1959. Print.
3. Yogananda. *Autobiography of a Yogi.* Los Angeles, CA: Self-Realization Fellowship, 1981.
4. Mooji. *Before I Am: The Direct Recognition of Truth.* Mooji Media, Expanded ed., 2012. Print.

BOOKS

O is a symbol of the world, of oneness and unity. In different cultures it also means the "eye," symbolizing knowledge and insight. We aim to publish books that are accessible, constructive and that challenge accepted opinion, both that of academia and the "moral majority."

Our books are available in all good English language bookstores worldwide. If you don't see the book on the shelves ask the bookstore to order it for you, quoting the ISBN number and title. Alternatively you can order online (all major online retail sites carry our titles) or contact the distributor in the relevant country, listed on the copyright page.

See our website **www.o-books.net** for a full list of over 500 titles, growing by 100 a year.

And tune in to myspiritradio.com for our book review radio show, hosted by June-Elleni Laine, where you can listen to the authors discussing their books.

mySpiritRadio